Cultural Thematics

CULTURAL THEMATICS

The Formation of the Faustian Ethos

T. K. Seung

New Haven and London, Yale University Press, 1976

Library of Congress catalog card number: 75–43335
International standard book number: 0–300–01918–1

Designed by John O. C. McCrillis
and set in Baskerville type.
Printed in the United States of America by
The Murray Printing Co., Westford, Massachusetts.

Published in Great Britain, Europe, Africa, and
Asia (except Japan) by Yale University Press, Ltd., London.
Distributed in Latin America by Kaiman & Polon,
Inc., New York City; in Australia and New Zealand by Book & Film
Services, Artamon, N.S.W., Australia;
in Japan by John Weatherhill, Inc., Tokyo.

To
John Robert Silber,
astute and loyal custodian
of our prodigious Faustian legacy

Contents

Preface

This is an inquiry into the transformation of the medieval ethos into the modern ethos. It covers roughly the three centuries from the twelfth to the fourteenth, the formative period of what Spengler has called the Faustian culture. In this inquiry, I have used the transition from allegorical to literal sensibility as my guide to the cultural transformation in question. I have drawn my materials primarily from literature and secondarily from theology and philosophy. I should have covered the other dimensions of culture, if this investigation were to be comprehensive. But I have limited myself to this selective approach in order to conduct this investigation as a simplified experiment for a full-fledged project in the future.

The nature of allegory is by no means an obscure topic among scholars. As a radically different mode of speaking and writing from our literal mode, allegory in general and medieval allegory in particular have been the objects of many technical treatises. In contrast to this, because of its familiarity to us, literalism has seldom become the target of scholarly scrutiny. In either case, the mode of speaking and writing has usually been taken as no more than a linguistic convention. In this volume, however, I have paid special attention to linguistic convention by taking it as the expression or embodiment of a form of sensibility, that is, the mode of perceiving and responding to one's world and oneself. As such an expression or embodiment, linguistic convention is not simply one convention alongside others but the fundamental matrix that animates the entire cultural system.

The role of language in any given culture is like that of the central nervous system in an organism. It is through the power of language that the various conventions of a cultural system are held together in a meaningful whole. It is this conception of language as the meaning-generating matrix that Wittgenstein appears to intimate in his notion of language games. In *Philosophical Investigations*, he makes the pregnant statement that "to imagine a language means to imagine a form of life (*Lebensform*)." As the matrix of meaning, language comes to embody the form of life or the form of sensibility.

Recently Marshall McLuhan and Norman O. Brown have called our attention to the crucial role that is played by the form of sensibility in shaping the overall pattern of a cultural tradition. In *The Gutenberg Galaxy*, McLuhan has tried to reveal "linear sensorium" as the cultural foundation of the modern West. In *Love's Body*, Brown has maintained that the Protestant literal sensibility has been the guiding spirit of modern scientific mentality. But neither McLuhan nor Brown has yet inquired into the genesis of linear sensorium or Protestant literal sensibility. To perform this inquiry is the aim of this book.

In this study, allegorical sensibility is taken to be the expression of transcendent theocentricism, and literal sensibility to be that of immanent anthropocentricism. Hence the transition from allegorical to literal sensibility is assumed to reflect the transformation of the theocentric medieval ethos into the anthropocentric modern one. In the process of delineating this transformation, I have devised cultural thematics. By 'cultural thematics' I mean the investigation of the thematic pattern of a given culture. In this thematic approach, a cultural tradition is conceived of as a constant interplay of existential themes or motifs, in analogy to a dramatic production or a musical composition. The thematic dimension in a work of art is chiefly due to its function of reflecting the nature of our life or existence. A work of art turns out to be an attempt to work out a cluster of thematic problems precisely because it reflects our way of being human, which consists in a series of existential projects for resolving its thematic conflicts. Hence the analogy in question is anchored in a justifiable circular chain.

This thematic inquiry is very much like what Heidegger has attempted in his *Being and Time*, and cultural thematics may very well be called existential thematics. He has tried to disclose our ways of being ourselves, being together with others, and being in the world; my thematic approach is to reconceive these existential modes in a thematic framework on the cultural level. Laboring under the influence of the Cartesian egocentricism, Heidegger has amply expressed his contempt for the cultural or communal dimension of human existence by consigning it to the domain of inauthentic existence. But human existence is always inextricably culture-bound; even the Heideggerian existential solipsism is only a cultural product of our age. All along in his existential analysis, in fact, Heidegger has implicitly relied on the cultural framework. My cultural approach in this volume is designed to render this implicit reliance explicit.

To recognize the culture-boundness of human existence is to admit its historicity. In *Being and Time,* Heidegger has assumed that his existential structure is timeless and true of all ages and all cultures. He thus operated with the naïve conviction that the timeless structure of human existence can be disclosed in an ahistoricistic approach. The irony of this naïveté has been manifestly shown in his presentation of the provincial structure of twentieth-century European existence as the universal existential structure. My project in cultural thematics is to remedy this ahistoricistic limitation in the Heideggerian enterprise.

Contrary to Heideggerian ahistoricism, my approach in cultural thematics openly stands on the historicist premise that every culture is the embodiment of an existential structure unique to itself. In Heideggerian language, the thematic nexus of every culture is an "existential project" on the communal level, that is, the stance one takes on being oneself, being with others, and being in the world. As soon as we admit the historicity of our existential structure, we shall realize the need to provide a historical or cultural context for the Heideggerian existential analysis. It is to fulfill this need that we are about to undertake this inquiry into the formation of the Faustian tradition. Since we are still living in the waning days of the Faustian culture, the investigation of its formative period is intended to sketch the essential outline of the contextual framework for our own existence. Hence this essay in cultural thematics is meant to round out the historical and cultural perimeters of Heidegger's existential phenomenology.

The transition from allegorical to literal sensibility is a radical change in what Wittgenstein would have called a "language game." For Wittgenstein, who views language as the embodiment of a form of life, the language game constitutes the form of culture because the form of culture is what he calls the form of life. He makes this point in his "Lectures on Aesthetics," when he says, "What belongs to a language game is a whole culture." Because of this intimate connection between language and culture, linguistic and cultural analyses are really two sides of one and the same existential analysis. As a matter of fact, Heidegger has made extensive use of language in his existential analysis.

But linguistic analysis is subject to the same errors of ahistoricism and contextual naïveté that have been committed in existential analysis. Furthermore, most of the "grammatical analyses" as conducted in contemporary linguistic philosophy are not concerned at all with the problem of understanding the overall form of a given language or its analysis as a game. Most analytical philosophers are too firmly ensnared by a few conspicuous trees of philosophically privileged words to command an overview of the entire linguistic forest. In contrast to this contemporary trend, to inquire into the transition from allegorical to literal language is to investigate a structural change in the overall pattern of a language game. I have employed this structural transformation as my guide in this inquiry to test the fruitfulness of Wittgenstein's pregnant statement.

Thus this pilot project is an endeavor to extend Heidegger's existential analysis and to apply Wittgenstein's linguistic approach to the cultural matrix of our own existence.

T.K.S.

Austin, Texas
April 1975

Acknowledgments

Among a few other things, this book advocates cultural contextualism as a cardinal principle of hermeneutics; that is to say, to provide an adequate cultural or historical context is an essential prerequisite for understanding any human endeavor, whether it be a work of art or a social custom. This contextual, or historicistic, approach goes against the spirit of formalism that has dominated various contemporary schools of interpretation such as the New Criticism, structuralism, and phenomenology. With their acontextual or ahistoricistic approach, these formalistic schools have advocated direct-confrontation between the interpreter and the object of interpretation. But this formalistic approach only betrays contextual naïvété, because contextual reference is never dispensable for any act of interpretation.

The indispensability of contextual reference is dictated by the finitude of a cultural object. If a cultural object were in and by itself a complete system of signs or meanings, it could be understood in direct confrontation. But since no cultural object is such a complete whole, the alternative in its interpretation lies, not between having and not having contextual reference, but between having it implicitly and explicitly. Even practitioners of the formalistic approach usually make implicit use of some contextual framework in their allegedly direct confrontation with the objects of their interpretation, and their implicit framework inevitably turns out to be none other than their own cultural context, which can be held in abeyance only through an act of self-critical reflection and restraint.

The unconscious use of one's own context in the formalistic approach leads to the unfortunate consequence of displacing the object of interpretation from its own cultural context to that of the interpreter. This contextual displacement produces a systematic distortion in the contextual understanding of any historical object. The distortion may not be serious when there is no grave discrepancy between the context of the interpreter and that of the object, insofar as the accidental similarity of these two contexts can assure the reasonable validity of some formalistic interpretations. For this reason, the formalistic schools have thrived mainly within the boundaries of modern European sensibility. As soon as their attempts are extended beyond these boundaries, they have tended to produce the sort of contextually disoriented formalistic results which clearly fail to illuminate historical or cultural objects in their own context.

I came to see this problem in formalistic programs not as an outside observer. I grew up in the Brooks-Wimsatt stronghold of New Criticism in New Haven, and cut my teeth on a New Critical interpretation of Dante's *Divine Comedy* in my *Fragile Leaves of the Sibyl: Dante's Master Plan*. I was just then coming under the joint spell of the New Criticism and European phenomenology, that is, their strikingly similar spirit of enabling the object to reveal its own structure through our unprejudiced formalistic or structural analysis. I could not think of any more effective occasion to test the true mettle of this phenomenological approach than trying it out for the structural understanding of the *Commedia*. In spite of the well-recognized surface grandeur of that renowned epic, every attempt to discover the master plan for the constitution of its famed three realms of damnation, purgation, and salvation had proven barren and futile. Consequently, Dante scholarship had long been resigned to episodic exegeses and fragmentary commentaries, while the comparison of the *Commedia* in its grandeur to a Gothic cathedral was becoming a pious but a hollow gesture among Dante admirers.

So I came to feel tempted to renew the barren and futile attempt and test the power of the New Criticism and phenomenology. I was astonished with the final result of my formalistic analysis of the *Commedia*; for I found a simple master plan that could bind together almost every feature of the great epic into one elegant whole. In my investigation, the structural principle of the *Commedia* turned out to be the Three Persons of the Holy Trinity and their actions in the creation and salvation of the universe. In traditional Dante scholarship, Dante the traveler had been taken to be representative of mankind; as such, he had been assumed to play the role of the epic hero in his own epic. In my figural interpretation, he is seen as only a traveling reporter faithfully recounting the epic actions of the Holy Trinity, which systematically permeate Dante's three realms. Hence my interpretation of Dante's allegory may be called "Trinitarian figuralism."

For a while, I remained pleased with the fortunate outcome of my phenomenological excursion into the *Divina Commedia*. A few years after the publication of my *Fragile Leaves of the Sibyl*, I began to develop some serious misgivings about the formalistic approach and came to conceive cultural contextualism in my effort to find a suitable remedy for its shortcomings. In adopting cultural contextualism, however, I have not abandoned the phenomenological motto "Let the object reveal itself instead of imposing one's preconception upon it." On the contrary, I have adopted cultural contextualism only because it alone can secure the requisite framework for the pheno-menological revelation of any historical object.

I came to appreciate the practical value of a contextual approach for the first time when I became engaged in a debate with Robert Hollander of Princeton. This debate began in the spring of 1970, when Thomas G. Bergin of Yale sent me a copy of Hollander's recent publication, *Allegory in Dante's "Commedia."* Through this book, I became acquainted with the figural program of the Auerbach-Single-ton school for unraveling Dante's allegory. Furthermore, I was convinced of the superiority of my figural reading of the *Commedia* over that of this school. In order to impart this conviction to Hol-lander, I wrote him at once; he then kindly invited me to his home. Thus began a long debate sustained over the past few years, in which we have truthfully tried to determine the comparative merit of my Trinitarian figural program vis-à-vis the figural program of the Auerbach-Singleton school.

At first in our debate, we both appealed to the text of the *Commedia*. This was in tune with the phenomenological spirit of the New Criticism, which allows nothing but manifest textual evidence and its formal analysis. On this score, my *Fragile Leaves of the Sibyl* had a decisive advantage over the works of the Auerbach-Singleton school. While the formal analyses of Dante's text in these works were rather haphazard, my *Fragile Leaves* was just one intricate network of textual arguments. So I thought at the outset that our debate would soon be resolved in favor of my Trinitarian figuralism. Contrary to this expectation, however, I failed to convince Robert Hollander of the validity of my theory for two reasons.

To begin with, my Trinitarian figuralism went bluntly against traditional Dante scholarship, which had never dreamed of viewing the Holy Trinity as Dante's epic hero. Any argument was bound to lose its subjective cogency to a considerable extent when it was pitched against the six-and-a-half-century-old way of reading and teaching the *Commedia*. The persistent force of a well-ingrained habit and long-established custom is always far more durable than our conscious estimation of it.

In addition to this force of habit and custom, I realized, my textual arguments met one more intractable obstacle in the very nature of allegorical exegesis. It is usually impossible to provide an overwhelming justification for any allegorical interpretation, especially for profound works of allegory. The function of profound allegory is very much like that of profound theology; their profundity is rooted in their ambiguity. Just as a God whose existence and operation can be easily proven seldom becomes the object of existentially meaningful faith, so an allegory whose reference and signification can be readily demonstrated rarely turns out to be a source of inexhaustible fascination. It is the very elusiveness of allegorical reference that assures the subtlety and versatility of its representation. My figural reading of the *Commedia* could not escape this common fate of allegorical interpretation; the textual arguments for my Trinitarian figuralism were obviously tenuous and fragile. For this reason, I had named my book *The Fragile Leaves of the Sibyl*.

When the textual arguments turned out to be inconclusive, I began to think of using contextual arguments in my debate with Robert Hollander. While I was writing *The Fragile Leaves*, I had been blissfully ignorant of contextual appeal in my innocent and fervent adherence to the textual (*solo textu*) spirit of the New Criticism. Since my arrival in Austin in 1966, however, I had been developing my program in cultural thematics with the enthusiastic encouragement of John R. Silber, then chairman of the University of Texas Philosophy Department. This program had been my attempt to overcome the formalistic defect of European phenomenology, and cultural contextualism had come about as one of the integral constituents of my cultural thematics. So I decided to test the efficacy of cultural contextualism by producing contextual arguments in support of my Trinitarian figuralism.

In the summer of 1973, I assembled most of my contextual arguments in one paper for the *Festschrift* in honor of Thomas G. Bergin. This book has recently been published by Yale University Press under the title *Italian Literature: Roots and Branches*, and my essay in it is called "Bonaventure's Figural Exemplarism in Dante." In slightly expanded form, this paper has become the first chapter of this book. I am grateful to the editors of the *Festschrift*, Kenneth Atchity and Giose Rimanelli, for their permission to use it in this manner.

In the meantime, I had sent Hollander the first draft of my *Festschrift* article, and received his objections and reservations in his long letter of 12 September 1973. This thoughtful letter became instrumental in my polishing that article and in prompting me to write what has become the second chapter of *Cultural Thematics*. Thus, the first half of this book has been generated from my debate with Robert Hollander, and it performs the triple maneuver of contextually grounding the *Commedia* in the development of Dante's ideas, Dante in the development of the medieval ethos, and finally my *Fragile Leaves* in the development of Dante scholarship. Whether my maneuver be well- or ill-conceived, I am sure of one thing at least: that is my friendship with Robert Hollander. If I have had the good fortune of grasping any truth through our debate, I will cherish it as a precious gift arising from this truthful relationship.

In the summer of 1974, I tried to extend my contextual hermeneutics from the domain of medieval allegorical sensibility to that of modern literal sensibility. In the course of this extension, I had to cope with the voluminous works of Petrarch and Boccaccio. Since I am an outsider to this illustrious field of the Italian Renaissance, I could not have mustered enough courage to plunge into this second phase of my project without the fatherly blessing and approval of my mentor, Thomas G. Bergin. This second phase of my inquiry produced contextually provocative interpretations of Petrarch, Boccaccio, Duns Scotus, and William of Ockham, just as its first phase had done for Dante, Augustine, Pseudo-Dionysius, Bonaventure, and Aquinas. Since I myself had no professional authority to assess, with confidence, the validity of these novel interpretations, I eagerly subjected them to Professor Bergin's perceptive judgment as soon as they cropped up in my mind. As a matter of fact, this entire volume contains not a single proposition that has failed to earn his authoritative endorsement. Hence this book is only one of the epiphenomena that have emerged from my enduring and edifying relationship with Thomas G. Bergin.

In our century, Gilsonian Thomists have contextually distorted our understanding of medieval theology as consistently as Auerbachian figuralists have done our understanding of medieval allegory. As I have tried to show in this volume, the Gilsonian distortion stems from the imposition of modern Catholic orthodoxy upon medieval scholasticism, while the Auerbachian distortion reflects the imposition of Protestant literal fundamentalism upon medieval literature. In my contextual approach, I have tried to correct the error of Gilsonian Thomists along with that of the Auerbach-Singleton school. In this endeavor, I have relied on the resourceful help of my colleagues Louis Mackey and Aloysius Martinich. Especially Martinich's meticulous observations and his judicious suggestions have saved me from committing some serious blunders.

A reasonable knowledge of Greco-Roman antiquity is essential to an adequate understanding of the Middle Ages and the Renaissance. A stranger to the vast domain of classical learning, I have managed to overcome my grave impediment through the generosity and versatility of my friend Karl Galinsky. I have also profited from John Peradotto's kind help during his brief stay at the University of Texas. I have relied on the expert counsel of my old friend Alexander Mourelatos on many technical questions in Greek philosophy.

In the course of their development, my ideas in this volume have taken quite a few unexpected turns. On almost every one of these occasions, I have sought my friend Alexander von Schoenborn's counsel on the strength and weakness of my new ideas. His discerning judgment has always stood as a responsive and reliable rein on the ramification of my program in cultural thematics.

Finally, I would like to thank my friend and colleague, Irwin C. Lieb, for his ceaseless concern with my project. I would also like to acknowledge the generous help I have received in preparing this manuscript from Dean Eldon Sutton of the University of Texas Research Institute, my friend Byung Hak Kim of IBM, and my secretary Gloria Fuentes.

Part 1

The Form of Life in Allegorical Sensibility

1

The Dantesque Enigma

If there is anything indisputable about *La Divina Commedia*, it is the assumption that this medieval epic is written in the allegorical mode. But the precise nature of Dante's allegory that has long been taken for granted is now coming to be recognized as a problem no less perplexing than any other medieval mystery. It is to this perplexing problem that Robert Hollander has lately addressed his *Allegory in Dante's "Commedia."*[1]

Hollander reports that Dante's *Commedia* had been interpreted as a personification allegory from the time of its publication to the beginning of our century, and claims that this way of reading it is really in conflict with Dante's own precepts expressed in his letter to Can Grande. He further claims that only in our century has the true nature of Dante's allegory begun to be appreciated through the labor of Erich Auerbach and Charles Singleton.[2] Thus at the outset Hollander declares his unmistakable allegiance to the Auerbach-Singleton school of figural realism, but his unique contribution is to elevate the debate between the school of personification allegory and that of figural allegory to the fully theoretical level. Hence it can be said to mark a new stage of theoretical consciousness in Dante scholarship.

Hollander assumes that Dante himself had clearly in mind the distinction between these two types of allegory when he proposed the distinction between the allegory of poets and the allegory of theologians in his *Convivio*. He further assumes that Dante's allegory of poets is the same as personification allegory, and that his allegory of theologians is the same as figural allegory.[3]

Two Types of Allegory

Personification allegory is exemplified in such works as *Psychoma-*

3

chia, The Romance of the Rose, The Faerie Queene, and *The Pilgrim's Progress.* Its modus operandi is to represent a certain universal truth or moral by some fictitious persons or events; fables and parables largely function in this mode of signification. Figural allegory or typology has been developed as an instrument of Biblical exegesis, namely, to establish the connection between the Old and the New Testaments. Its modus operandi is to represent one person by another or one event by another, by virtue of the similarity of the one to the other, for example, Isaac is a figure of Christ since the sacrifice of the former resembles that of the latter.

These two types of allegory may reflect two different types of onto-logical or epistemological outlook: nominalism and essentialism.*

Personification allegory cannot function without presupposing the reality of universals in at least two modes. The first of these two modes is the existence of the universal or moral (*unsversalis ante rem*) as the object of allegorical representation. The same universal or moral must also be reflected or manifested in the medium of allegorical re-presentation, and this reflected being of the universal(*universalis in re*) is its second mode of existence.† Thus the universal appears twice in personification allegory, first in its own being and then in its being represented.

*The medieval controversy between nominalists and realists was a scholastic debate concerning the existence of universals. Universals are abstract entities such as "triangu-larity," "circularity," "treeness," and "dogness;" particulars are concrete entities such as "triangles," "circles," "trees," and "dogs." Realism is the view that not only particulars but also universals are real (hence the labels of 'realism' and 'realists')—that is, they really exist in the world. Nominalism is the view that the world consists only of particulars and that universals are only mental products—that is, they exist only in the mind.

The label 'realism' is a bit confusing because it has been used to designate the position opposed to idealism as well as the position opposed to nominalism. In order to avoid this confusion, I will throughout employ the terms *essentialism* and *essentialist* rather than *realism* and *realist*.

†The medieval nominalism vs. essentialism debate has generally assumed the following distinctions between different kinds of universals: (1) *universalis ante rem*, (2) *universalis in re*, and (3) *universalis in mente*. The first kind is the Platonic or transcendent universal, for example, the Platonic Form of justice or a tree. The second kind is the Aristotelian or im-manent universal, for examples, the common essence or nature of the canine species shared by all dogs. These two types of universal are *real* (hence the term 'realism'), that is, their being is independent of the knowing mind. Hence to accept either of these two kinds of universal is to be an essentialist. In contrast to these types, the third kind is *unreal*, that is, its being is mind-dependent. The acceptance of this kind of unreal universal and no other kind is to regard universals only as labels or names for convenience, and this is the position of nominalism. To be sure, some extreme nominalists have repudiated even this third type of universal (the *flatus vocis* school), but they have been a small minority even among no-minalists.

Figural allegory does not require the existence of universals in either of these two modes, since the representing and the represented are both particulars in this type of allegory. The representational or allegorical link of these particulars is established, not by some universals that stand above them, but by the similarity that is immediately present between them. This immediate similarity-relation constitutes the essence of the only universal that nominalists can admit, the intramental universal (*universalis in mente*) or the *unreal* universal.

Some particulars in figural allegory may function like universals. Christ may be represented not only by one but by many figures, not only by Isaac but also by Joseph and Jonah. But even these cases do not presuppose the existence of the extramental universals, because the one-to-many relation in each of these cases is meant to reflect not the common essence shared by the particulars involved but only their many-termed similarity or resemblance relation. That is, there can be neither the Platonic Form of Christhood that stands above Christ and all the Christ-figures, nor the Aristotelian essence of Christhood that is shared by them. If there were such a Form or such an essence, Christ would be a derivative reality rather than an ultimate one. Not to recognize the ultimate reality of Christ would repudiate one of the central tenets in Christian teaching.

All that can be admitted about the relation of Christ to Christ-figures is that the latter resemble the former in some respect, which can be specified only in a nominalistic stipulation. Hence only particulars are admitted in figural allegory for the function of representing and that of being represented, just as only the reality of particulars is accepted in the nominalistic account of being and being known.

The relation of signifying and the signified in personification allegory is the vertical relation of the lower (or sensible) and the higher (or supersensible) worlds; in figural allegory it is the horizontal relation of the earlier and the later events of one and the same sensible world. The vertical relation is the relation of a copy or shadow and its original; the horizontal relation is the relation of promise and its fulfillment. One is a temporal or historical relation; the other is an atemporal or ahistorical relation.

Personification allegory reflects the highly atemporal Hellenic sensibility ("the timeless essence of things"); figural allegory manifests the highly temporal Hebraic sensibility ("the fullness of time").

As Robert Hollander points out, personification allegory was already being used in Homeric criticism in the fifth century B.C.[4] Plato makes extensive use of it in his "mythical account" of the higher truths, and then the Neoplatonists firmly establish it as a central method of exposition and instruction. Most of the great works in personification allegory, from *Psychomachia* to *The Faerie Queene*, have been written within the ambience of Neoplatonism.

As Beryl Smalley says, Philo of Alexandria was the first to adopt personification allegory for the exegesis of the Old Testament. As a Hellenized Jew who spoke and wrote not in Hebrew but in Greek, he was too sophisticated to accept the literal truth of some Biblical stories. Since these stories in their literal sense appeared to him either superstitious or fabulous, he tried to save their Biblical sanctity by reading them as the allegorical rendering of some Platonic truths.[5]

Smalley also says that, as a practising Jew, Philo accepted the literal significance of some Biblical stories as well as their allegorical meanings. Thus Philo's Biblical allegories fall into two groups: (1) the fabulous allegory, and (2) the literal or historical allegory. The former is a straightforward adoption of the Hellenic allegory; the latter is its adaptation for the Judaic tradition. Philo's example of the former is the Genesis story; his example of the latter is the Samuel story. The former has only allegorical significance; the latter describes a historical personage who probably lived as a compound of soul and body but allegorically represents a mind rejoicing in the service and worship of God.[6]

Even Philo's historical allegory is more firmly grounded in the Hellenic essentialistic ontology than in the Judaic nominalistic one. Like a true Platonist, he acknowledges only the *probable* truth for the historicity of the Biblical events: "Probably there was an actual man called Samuel." He expects to find the truths of universality and certainty only on the Platonic allegorical level.[7]

The difference between Philo's fabulous and historical allegories cannot become a matter of serious concern for Platonists. For they believe that the historical events of the corporeal world have no true reality: the corporeal world is no more than a copy or shadow of the supersensible world. Since true fables (or lies) are also shadowy manifestations of the same supersensible reality, the Platonists' distinction between fabulous and historical allegory amounts to no more than a distinction between one type of shadowy picture and another.

Hence, as Smalley says, there is always the queer sense of Alice-in-Wonderland logic hovering over Philo's demarcation between the Biblical passages which are only fabulously true and those which are literally as well as allegorically true.[8] This Alice-in-Wonderland aspect is a source of irritation and frustration only for those who presuppose the complete reality of history and the complete unreality of fiction. In the Platonic scheme, however, the manifestation of supersensible truths is not confined to the domain of fable and fiction. The entire sensible world is meant to reflect the supersensible. For example, St. Augustine's writings are filled with natural allegorical visions: the moon is a symbol of the Church, which reflects the divine light; the wind is an image of the Spirit; the number ten stands for the Ten Commandments. Hence, what counts for Platonists is not which of these two sets of shadowy entities has a greater semblance of reality, but how well they portray the true reality.

Since the question of historical truth and untruth is largely irrelevant for the efficacy of personification allegory, Philo's two kinds of allegory can be readily combined into a hybrid form. As Hollander points out, Prudentius does this in his *Psychomachia* by including at least one historical person in each of its episodes, for example, the appearance of Job in the train of Patientia during her struggle with Ira.[9]

As Hollander intimates, the function of personification allegory can be regarded as that of exemplification as manifested in the Roman rhetoricians' notion of exemplum. Ernst Robert Curtius says that Cicero and Quintilian urge the orator to gather his exempla not only from history but from myth and legend.[10] 'Exemplification allegory' is a little more accurate label than 'personification allegory.' Although most works in personification allegory do happen to employ persons rather than animals or things, it is not always persons per se that perform the function of exemplification. That function often falls not on persons but on events.

It has often been pointed out, especially by the champions of figural allegory, that personification allegory tends to be abstract while figural allegory tends to be concrete. We may invite some serious confusion in this matter unless we distinguish the concreteness or abstractness of the rind (the signifying) of allegory from that of its core (the signified). This medieval distinction between the rind or shell (*cortex*) and the core or kernel (*nucleus*) comes from Alan of Lille.[11]

It is obvious that the core or kernel of personification allegory is bound to be abstract since it is only an idea or a moral. What is not obvious is that the rind or shell of personification must also be abstract. To be sure, the fictitious persons in personification allegory do tend to be abstract simply because they are drawn up only to portray abstract ideas. But the historical persons used in personification allegory need not and cannot be any less concrete than the historical persons appearing in figural allegory.

Even the fictitious entities in personification allegory need not always be abstract since they can be rendered as concretely as historical entities. Hence we should bear firmly in mind that the concreteness or abstractness of the shell of personification allegory has no inherent connection with its factualness or fictitiousness. The same is true of the shell or rind of figural allegory.

While Philo adopts personification allegory for the Platonic reading of the Old Testament, St. Paul introduces figural allegory as his Christian way of seeing the relation of the Old to the New Testament. According to Paul's figural vision, the things of the Old Testament are the figures or types for the things of the New Testament. The two sons of Abraham prefigure the two Covenants, one of freedom and the other of bondage (Gal. 4:21–31); Adam is a figure of Christ (1 Cor. 15:21–22); the Crucifixion is the fulfillment of the animal sacrifices of the Jewish high priests (Heb. 9:11–14). To see everything in the context of the figure and its fulfillment is ingrained in the Pauline sensibility. It is, in fact, so firmly ingrained that its operation is unmistakable even in the cases where the word *typos* and its cognates are not even mentioned (e.g. 1 Cor. 15:21–22).

The figural way of seeing things does not remain a Pauline monopoly but becomes a common heritage of all the first Apostles of Christ. We can feel its presence not only in the Acts (e.g. 8:32), but even in the synoptic Gospels. For example, the long genealogy of Jesus at the beginning of Matthew's Gospel clearly carries the sense of promise and its fulfillment; the relation of John the Baptist and Christ is cast in the context of preparation and achievement (Matt. 11:2–9; Luke 7:18–35). According to Luke, the first act of Jesus after his resurrection was to give his disciples a figural account of himself: "And beginning with Moses and all the Prophets, he interpreted to them in all the Scriptures things referring to himself" (Luke 24:27). The very notion of the Messiahship had been built up as a figural way of perceiving Providence in history.

The conversion of Philo's vertical scheme of personification allegory into Paul's horizontal scheme of figural allegory was dictated by the this-worldly ethos of the Hebraic tradition. Yahweh is the god of this world, who has no other world; his covenant with Abraham is to be fulfilled in this world of mortality, whose perpetuation is the only form of immortality known to them. The Hebraic sensibility is so inexorably history-oriented that all the sacred writings of the ancient Jews have been cast in the form of historical chronicles. The horizontal schema of promise and fulfillment has grown out of this historical sensibility.

The decisively new element which the Christians bring to this figural sensibility is their firm belief in the Messiah—that is, the fulfillment is no longer to be looked for in the future because it is already here and now ("in the midst of us"; cf. Matt. 11:2–9, Luke 7:18–35). The moment of fulfillment that has been cast in the future tense for the Jews is now recast in the present-perfect tense by the Christians. Thus, the uniquely Christian principle of figural allegory takes its general form: the Old Testament prefigures the New Testament (*omnia in figura contingebant illis*).

The Pauline legacy receives further elaboration in two different cultural contexts: the Greek East and the Latin West.

The Fathers of Alexandria do not hesitate to retain both the Philonian and the Pauline methods of allegorical exegesis. As Erich Auerbach tells us, Origen is too much of a Platonist to believe in the bodily presence of the Lord. He is willing to admit that some Biblical stories, including even those from the New Testament, are no more than fabulous representations of supersensible reality.[12]

Side by side with this Philonian sensibility, Origen also develops the Pauline typology by classifying all the Biblical types into four kinds: (1) Christ and his Coming, (2) the Church and her sacraments, (3) the Last Judgment and the Kingdom of Heaven, and (4) the relation between God and the individual soul.[13]

As Auerbach shows, Tertullian puts a decisive stamp on the Pauline sensibility in the Latin West. He uses the Latin word *figura* for Paul's Greek word *typos* (e.g. Joshua is a figure of Christ). From Auerbach's documentation, it appears likely that Tertullian adopted the word *figura* from Quintilian's distinction between tropes and figures.[14] He may have thought that *figura* could be effectively used for the Christian notion of typology since *tropos* had been so closely associated with the Hellenic sensibility of personification allegory.

In a relentless opposition to the Alexandrian view of the Incarnation, Auerbach tells us, Tertullian argues that the Lord has come truly in flesh and blood.[15] This literally carnal conception of the Incarnation compels Tertullian to retain only figural allegory by completely dissociating it from personification allegory. Thus he restores the Pauline figural sensibility to its original purity by cleansing it of its Philonian accretion. With the triumph of Tertullian's position in the West, Auerbach says, both feet of the Christian allegory came to be firmly entrenched in historical reality, and the sense of reality and concreteness was fully restored in the Christian conception of history.[16] Through Tertullian the this-worldly sensibility of the Latin tradition came to reinforce the this-worldly sensibility of the Hebraic tradition in its waning days.

Although figural allegory has been indelibly stamped with the sign of historical reality in both its rind and its core since the time of Tertullian, it would be a mistake to assume that there is absolutely no room for poetic fiction in figural allegory. In the case of personification allegory, we have seen, its rind can be made of historical persons or events rather than fictitious ones. Conversely, we can see the possibility of using fictitious persons or events rather than historical ones for the rind of figural allegory. This type of allegory may be called fictitious or poetic figuralism. The most prominent example of this type of figural allegory for medieval Christians was the Song of Solomon; pious Christians from Augustine to Bernard of Clairvaux read it as a figural representation of the relation of Christ to his Church.

What appears to be a personification allegory may sometimes hide a figural core. For example, the Red Crosse Knight of *The Faerie Queene*, apparently a personification of the virtue of faith, may contain, in its ultimate figural core, Christ himself, the very foundation of Christian faith. The same thing can be said of Spenser's other personifications, such as *Una, Fidelia, Speranza, Charissa,* and so on. God is likely to be the ultimate figural core for most Christian personifications because he is believed to be the exemplary cause of all his creation, that is, all his creatures are only images or traces of his eminence. The core of this sort of allegory consists of two layers; its ultimate core is figural while its proximate core is personification. Hence it is a truly hybrid allegory.

Fictitious figuralism has survived as an important element in the tradition of the novel to our own day, as we can witness in Thomas

Mann's *Doctor Faustus*, a figural allegory of the decadent Faustian man, and in Günter Grass's *The Tin Drum*, a figural allegory of the Nazi superman.

In contrast to the abstract tendency of personification allegory, the concrete tendency of figural allegory has been well recognized. But the concreteness in question should be distinguished from historical reality. The kernel or core of figural allegory is always concrete since it is always historically real. However, the shell or rind of figural allegory, which need not be historically real, nevertheless may take on as concrete a texture as any other form of fiction.

The Auerbach-Singleton School

It has been Auerbach's signal thesis that the *Commedia* was written not as a personification allegory and not even as a fictitious figural allegory, but as a historically true figural allegory. At first sight this surely appears to be an implausible thesis. The *Commedia* was assuredly written as a poem which belongs to the domain of fiction rather than that of historical records. To give this obviously implausible thesis some air of plausibility has been the chief task for Auerbach and his followers.

Auerbach was, of course, the first courageous soul to try his hand at this impossible task. In recollection of his own performance in "Figura," he says,

> In the case of three of its most important characters—Cato of Utica, Virgil, and Beatrice—I have attempted to demonstrate that their appearance in the other world is a fulfillment of their appearance on earth, their earthly appearance a figure of their appearance in the other world.[17]

In Auerbach's interpretation, the historical Virgil is the figure and Dante's Virgil in the *Commedia* is its fulfillment. In order to maintain his figural realism, he advances the absurd view that Dante's Virgil is as real as the historical Virgil. It is one thing to grant the concreteness of Dante's Virgil, but quite another thing to claim his reality.

Following Charles Singleton, Hollander sensibly makes one concession in his own valiant attempt to uphold Auerbach's position: the persons and events of the *Commedia* are not truly real or historical, but they are presented as though they were.[18] What he calls "fictional pretense" is the only thing that is truly real in the *Commedia*.

But unfortunately this admission of the "as-if" tone, or fictional pretense, gives the whole show away. It is precisely the as-if tone of reality or fictional pretense that gives a fiction its fictitious character. I know of neither a fiction that is not written as if it were a true story, nor a fiction that is written as if it were a false story. To say that the *Commedia* has the as-if tone of reality is to admit that it is a fictitious work.

Hollander tries to inject some spirit into Auerbach's limp thesis by citing, on the authority of Ulrich Leo's *Sehen und Wirklichkeit bei Dante*, the amazingly frequent use of the word *see* and its cognates— namely, over four hundredtimes, an average of more than four per canto.[19] But the word *see* can be used to describe the pretense of seeing as well as the real act of seeing. The use of perception words never guarantees the reality of the perception in question. One sees in dream and fiction as much as one does in real life. The domain of *Sehen* is not always coextensive with the domain of *Wirklichkeit*. The designation of the perceptual contexts is never made by the perception words themselves, but always by their adjectival or adverbial qualifiers. Dante's extensive use of the word *see* would be a solid piece of evidence against Marshall McLuhan's thesis ("The medieval culture is more aural than visual"), but it is clearly irrelevant to the proving of Auerbach's thesis.

Even such a staunch follower of Auerbach's literal fundamentalism as Robert Hollander admits the patently fictitious character of the first two cantos of the *Commedia*, for example, Dante's getting lost in the dark wood, his encounter with the beasts of the mountainside, the coming of Virgil to his rescue, etc. Except for this brief interval, he is ready to uphold the literal truth and historical reality of Dante's journey, on the ground that the *Commedia* takes on an unmistakable aura of realism from the third canto on, that is, from the moment Dante and Virgil step into the Inferno.[20]

In my view, the aura of Dante's Hell does not appear to be any less or any more realistic than that of the first two cantos. Virgil's behavior inside Dante's Hell cannot be considered any less fictitious than his behavior outside of it; the beasts outside cannot be considered any less realistic than the beasts and monsters inside. Indeed, most of these monsters have been pronounced to be only fabulous or fictitious by the church authorities. According to Hugh of Saint-Victor, they belong to the category of *pictura*, an artificial and lying configuration of elements on the literal level.[21]

The difference between the first two cantos and the remainder of of the poem, then, is not that the former is fictitious while the latter is realistic. This way of reading it would only introduce a grievous textual fissure into the *Commedia*. Probably for this erroneous reason, Charles Singleton regrets "that somehow a curtain does not fall at the end of Canto II *Inferno* to mark off the first two cantos of the poem for the prologue which they are."22

The real difference between the two parts of the *Commedia* in question is that Dante provides clear enough pointers for the fictitious texture of his poetic world in the first two cantos, while he does not continue to do so after entering the gate of the Inferno. He provides those pointers in the first two cantos because they do indeed constitute the prologue of the *Commedia*. But the function of the prologue is not to *be* marked off, but to mark off Dante's poetic world from the world of reality. The prologue constitutes the frame for the world of Dante's poetic imagination, as it were.

That many of Dante's characters are derived from history makes no difference to their fictitious character; the Job of *Psychomachia* is as fictitious as any other of its characters. Their historical origins may indeed add to the concreteness they gain in the fictitious world, but the sense of concreteness should never be mistaken for the sense of true historical reality.

Fourfold Allegory

Singleton and Hollander try to shore up their position by citing Dante's own authority; they believe that Dante himself clearly stated the nature of his own allegory once and for all in his letter to Can Grande. According to this letter, the *Commedia* is a fourfold allegory that has the following senses: the literal, the allegorical, the moral, and the anagogical.23

Singleton and Hollander assume that this fourfold allegory is the same as what Dante has called the allegory of theologians. This assumption is prima facie justifiable, not only because Dante's fourfold scheme is only a recapitulation of St. Thomas's doctrine of fourfold allegory in Biblical exegesis, but also because Dante himself uses the fourfold exegesis of a Psalm (*In exitu israel de aegypto*) in his illustration of the fourfold allegory of his *Commedia*. If so, not to accept the literal truth of the *Commedia* would be to read Dante's work in contradiction to his own intention. Hence Singleton may be right in believing that to avoid this apparent contradiction has been the ulterior motive lurking behind the repeated attempts to prove the inauthenticity of Dante's letter to Can Grande.[24] Unfortunately, I have no textual competence to address myself to the question of the letter's authorship, but I do know which is the more sensible option to take if I am given the choice between the authenticity of that letter and the factuality of the *Commedia*.

Even if Dante's authorship of this problematic letter were conclusively established, I believe, it would still be of no use in justifying Singleton's position unless the link between paragraphs 7 and 8 of that document is rigidly construed. Here are the two paragraphs in question:

> 7. . . . the first meaning is that which is conveyed by the letter, and the next is that which is conveyed by what the letter signifies; the former of which is called literal, while the latter is called allegorical, or mystical. And for the better illustration of this method of exposition we may apply it to the following verses: 'When Israel went out of Egypt, the house of Jacob from a people of strange language; Judah was his sanctuary, and Israel his dominion.' For if we consider the letter alone, the thing signified to us is the going out of the children of Israel from Egypt in the time of Moses; if the allegory, our redemption through Christ is signified; if the moral sense, the conversion of the soul from the sorrow and misery of sin to a state of grace is signified; if the anagogical, the passing of the sanctified soul from the bondage of the corruption of this world to the liberty of everlasting glory is signified. . . .

> 8. This being understood, it is clear that the subject, with regard to which the alternative meanings are brought into play, must be twofold. And therefore the subject of this work must be considered in the first place from the point of view of the literal meaning, and next from that of the allegorical interpretation. The subject, then, of the whole work, taken in the literal sense only, is the state of souls after death, pure and simple. For on and about that the argument of the whole work turns. If, however, the work be regarded from the allegorical point of view, the subject is man according as by his merits or demerits in the exercise of his free will he is deserving of reward or punishment by justice.[25]

Paragraph 7 of the letter enumerates the four different senses in Biblical exegesis and illustrates them by the fourfold reading of the Psalm *In exitu israel de aegypto*. Paragraph 8 shows how fourfold allegory applies to the reading of his own poem.

Singleton and his followers take this application of the fourfold allegory to the *Commedia* in an obstinately rigid way: The *Commedia* must be literally true in the same way the Bible is believed to be. In fact, this sense of rigidity has been the hallmark of the Auerbach-Singleton school, and also its stumbling block. In that school the vice of rigidity is usually mistaken for the virtue of consistency. One can see historical irony in this rigidity, if one knows the historical fact that the chief motive for devising allegorical interpretation was to free the sacred and the profane texts from the rigid trap of literalism and fundamentalism. To be flexible and subtle is the life of allegorical sensibility; to be rigid and obtuse is its death.*

We can avoid many evils of rigidity by taking the link between paragraphs 7 and 8 in a flexible way: Dante is proposing an adaptation of the fourfold Biblical allegory to the reading of his own poem. All he has to do to make this adaptation is to change the literal or historical sense into the fictitious or poetic sense; he can leave intact all the other three senses. To be sure, Dante does not say so in paragraph 8. But once the fictional framework of Dante's poem is understood, the adaptation in question shows itself as too obvious to be mentioned.

The adaptation of the fourfold allegory to the reading of poetic works is not new even for Dante. He has already tried it in the *Convivio*, where he explains the fourfold allegory as a way of composing his own commentaries on his *canzoni*. He says that his commentaries will be made on four different levels of signification, that is, the literal, the allegorical, the moral, and the anagogical (*Convivio*, treatise 2, chap. 1).

Here Dante does not use the word *adaptation*. But what he does in his explanation of the four senses is clearly an act of adaptation. He explains the first two senses by taking an example from Ovid's story

*Incidentally, the flexibility of allegorical sensibility is not limited to the literal sense, but extends to every level of fourfold signification. St. Thomas says, "The four senses are attributed to Scripture, not so that we should give a quadruple interpretation of all its passages, but sometimes four, sometimes three, sometimes two, and sometimes only one" (*Quodlibet*. q. 7, a. 15, trans. John P. McCall, in William F. Lynch, *Christ and Apollo*, Supplement 4, p. 237).

of Orpheus: It hides a truth or a fable ("the wise man with the instrument of his voice maketh cruel hearts tender and humble")
beneath a mantle of fiction ("Orpheus with his lyre made wild beasts
tame"; *Convivio*, 2. 1).[26]

Then Dante points out that the second sense in this case is quite
different from the second sense in the practice of theologians. But he
does not take the trouble to explain the difference in question, probably because he regards it as too obvious. Whereas the second sense in
the allegory of theologians refers to concrete historical entities—let
us be clear on this—the second sense in his allegorical scheme conveys
abstract ideas or morals.

Dante's main purpose in this *Convivio* passage has been mistaken by
many Dante scholars; he is often assumed to be establishing the distinction between the allegory of poets and that of theologians. To be
sure, he does introduce the distinction in question. But it is introduced
not as a matter of theoretical comparison but as part of his practical
proposal for the adaptation of the fourfold allegory to the reading of
his canzoni.

His is a proposal for the ramification of personification allegory—
namely, that the allegory of poets be expanded to the same fourfold
scheme as that of the allegory of theologians. This is a noteworthy
suggestion to make, since the allegory of poets has been assumed to be
limited to only two levels of signification. If so, Dante's proposal is
probably meant to render personification allegory as complex and as
resourceful as figural allegory.

What is noteworthy in this proposal is that, on the level of literal
sense, Dante does not even mention the difference between the allegory of poets and that of theologians. There is a slim chance that he
might have done so in the famous textual lacuna. But the chance
appears to be so slim that we may safely discount it; this remote
possibility is not seriously entertained in any of the emendations of
that lacuna.

Since Dante does not assert the difference between the two types
of allegory on the literal level, should we then assume that he sees no
difference between the literal sense of his canzoni and that of the
Bible? It is just too obvious for him to say that his canzoni have only
the fictitious, literal sense because they are poetic works. If this point
is too obvious for him to belabor in the case of the *Convivio*, it cannot
be any less obvious in the case of the *Commedia*.

The Auerbach-Singleton school has the tendency to assume that "the literal sense" in medieval usage was synonymous with "the literal and historical sense." To be sure, this was the usual rule in the field of Biblical exegesis. But the expression "literal sense" enjoyed a far wider currency than this restricted one among Biblical commentators. In its general usage "the literal sense" just meant the immediate meaning of a sentence or text, which can be obtained by simply knowing the ordinary meaning of its words and their grammatical connection. The question of meaning in this general usage is completely divorced from the question of truth. The latter is always an extratextual problem; the former is always an intratextual problem.

The distinction between the intratextual problem of meaning and the extratextual problem of truth is equivalent to the distinction made by Hugh of Saint-Victor between the meanings of words and the meanings of things. He says that the meanings of words can be determined by the disciplines of the trivium, while the determination of the meanings of things requires the disciplines of the quadrivium.[27]

Hugh of Saint-Victor is evidently assuming that the disciplines of the trivium are the logical sciences of semantics and syntactics in the purely verbal domain, and that the disciplines of the quadrivium are the empirical sciences of real things and their relations in the factual domain. This division of labor is presumably applicable to the reading of not only the pagan but also the sacred writings. To be exact, the determination of the historical truth of sacred texts requires more than the use of the disciplines of the quadrivium, since it ultimately rests on the act of faith and revelation. Nonetheless, these extra elements surely belong not to the intratextual but to the extratextual domain.

At any rate, literal sense in its general usage should be understood as the common stage that one has to go through in the reading of both pagan and sacred writings. The understanding of literal sense is the first step one has to take whether one is a poet or a historian, a rhetorician or a theologian. Hence even St. Thomas, who adamantly refuses to accept any allegorical interpretation of pagan writings, readily recognizes their literal sense (*Quodlibet.* q. 7, a. 16).

Literal sense as a genus is context-neutral; it has no inherent connection either with the context of fiction or with that of fact. Only with the ascription of a respective differentia does it produce such species as the fictitious literal sense, the historical literal sense, or even the rhetorical literal sense. If Dante is using literal sense in this generic and neutral way in his *Convivio*, and if he assumes that the differentiae of its various species are dictated by the relevant contexts, then he has every reason to expect us to understand that the literal sense of the Bible is the historical literal one, and that the literal sense of his canzoni is the fictitious literal one. Thus, he sees no need to mention the difference between the allegory of poets and the allegory of theologians on its literal level.

Dante's adaptation of fourfold allegory in the *Convivio* amounts to replacing the first two senses of Biblical allegory by the two senses of personification allegory. He appears to leave intact the other two senses of Biblical allegory as they stand in the practice of theologians. Whereas he draws his examples from the pagan personification allegory in explaining the literal and the allegorical senses, he derives his examples from Biblical exegesis in explaining the moral and the anagogical senses. But the appearance in question hides a subtle change that Dante installs in the last two senses of fourfold allegory.

According to Dante's account of the third sense, the Biblical story that Christ took with him only three of his twelve disciples to the occasion of his Transfiguration conveys the moral "that in the most sacred things we should have but few companions" (*Convivio*, 2. 1). This third sense belongs to personification allegory as much as Dante's second sense; the function of both is to convey some moral that can be expressed in the form of a universal proposition. Their only difference appears to be that Dante's third sense conveys a religious moral, while his second sense conveys a nonreligious one.

According to his account of the fourth sense, the Exodus story expresses the spiritual meaning "that when the soul goeth forth out of sin, it is made holy and free in its power" (*Convivio*, 2. 1). A technical question we have to face is whether the elementary sentence in the quoted clause is meant to be a universal or a particular proposition. If it refers to a particular, existing soul, it is meant to be a particular proposition describing some particular historical event. If it refers to any soul, it is meant to be a universal proposition setting forth a universal truth. The sentence in question is ambiguous enough to be read either way, but in this case I am inclined to take it as a universal proposition. As is often the case, the definite article here operates as a universal quantifier. Thus Dante's fourth sense, along with his second and third senses, conveys a universal truth and can be readily accommodated within Philo's scheme of Biblical personification allegory just as much as Dante's second and third senses. Dante's fourth sense is not only religious but also concerns the affairs of the other world, or rather "the supernal things of eternal glory" (*Convivio*, 2. 1).

Dante's adaptation of fourfold allegory in the *Convivio* assumes in brief the following form: his first sense is literal and poetic, his second sense is nonreligious personification allegory, his third sense is religious personification allegory concerning this world, and his fourth sense is religious personification allegory concerning the other world. Through this adaptation he completely assimilates the fourfold Biblical allegory into the Philonian scheme of personification allegory.

Since all three spiritual senses in Dante's new fourfold scheme are given the form of personification allegory, they are hardly distinguishable from one another in their formal properties. His distinction between the three spiritual senses may indeed appear to be a distinction with little difference. As many Dante scholars have pointed out, Dante seldom appears to use the third and fourth senses in his own commentaries on his canzoni. Yet it may be closer to the truth to say that the third and fourth senses in his own practice are only formally indistinguishable from the second sense. For they can be materially distinguished.

When Dante comes to make another attempt toward adaptation in his Can Grande letter, he appears to reject his previous one. It is hard to detect anything like his previous attempt to transform figural allegory into personification allegory. In fact, the Can Grande letter gives the impression that Dante accepts the Biblical fourfold scheme in its entirety for the reading of his *Commedia*. Hence Singleton and Hollander are led to cite this letter in support of literal fundamentalism in their interpretation of this epic.

I am still convinced that in this letter Dante is using "literal sense" in its generic and context-neutral way, and that he leaves us to see its specific meaning in the light of relevant contexts. This is precisely the way he handled the matter in the *Convivio*; he regards this point as no less obvious in the Can Grande letter than in the *Convivio*. In the seventh paragraph of this letter, Dante describes the first sense of the fourfold scheme as literal (*literalis*) and defines it as the meaning conveyed by the letter (*per literam*). The meaning conveyed *per literam* is what I have called the intratextual meaning.

Toward the end of the seventh paragraph, where he demarcates the three spiritual senses from the first sense, Dante calls the first sense not merely literal but historical (*a literali sive historiali*). This designation of the first sense as *literalis sive historialis* may appear to be a casual restatement of St. Thomas's designation of it as *historicus vel literalis*—and may be taken as textual evidence to conclude that Dante's first sense in the Can Grande letter is meant to designate the sense that is historically true, just as St. Thomas believes it to be in the Bible. Thus the phrase *a literali sive historiali* appears to be the philological clincher for the argument of the Auerbach-Singleton school. In fact, such reputable translations as that of the Temple Classics or Singleton's translate the phrase in question as "the literal and historical sense."[28]

But the would-be clincher fails to clinch the argument; it has neither the muscles nor the teeth. The Latin word *historia* does not always mean history; its usual meaning is synonymous with the English word *story*. When Dante uses the Italian word *istoria* in the First Treatise of the *Convivio* (*la litterale istoria*), he is using it as the Italian counterpart of the Latin *historia*. Since *historia* is context-neutral just as "literal sense" is, the former is used simply as a synonym for the latter in Dante's *a literali sive historiali*. Thus his *sive* is the same as the English *or* of synonymity as it is translated by Paget Toynbee.[29]

To be sure, St. Thomas may have placed *historicus* before *literalis* in his *historicus vel literalis* in order to emphasize the historicity of Sacred Scripture by implicitly exploiting the special connotation of the word *historia*. If so, it is equally plausible that Dante has reversed the order of the two words in his *a literali sive historiali* in order to restore or retain the neutrality of the first sense. Probably for the same purpose he has completely dropped the word *historialis* on two of the three occasions where he names the first sense.

I have gone through all this to show that the Can Grande letter provides no textual evidence to support Singleton's literal fundamentalism. In support of his position, Singleton says that Dante may "imitate God's way of writing (i.e. the Bible)."[30] If it is claimed that Dante has adopted God's way of writing, I may have to concede that his literal sense must be historically true and not fictitious. But I cannot make the same concession as long as he is claimed to *imitate* God's way of writing.

The imitation in question is meant to carry one decisive element that resolutely prevents Dante's way from becoming identical with

God's way. Dante's imitation can be perfect and complete in the domain of three spiritual senses; but it is bound to fail to achieve the same perfection in the domain of carnal (literal) sense. Dante's words only describe while God's words create. Dante's way remains a mere imitation instead of becoming identical with God's way only by virtue of the unreality of Dante's literal sense. It is this unreality of his literal sense that Dante appears to admit openly by designating the form or mode of treatment (*forma sive modus tractandi*) of the *Commedia* as poetic and fictitious in paragraph 9 of the Can Grande letter.

If Singleton believes that Dante's words have the same historical reality as God's words have, he should say that Dante "adopts" God's way of writing. In fact, the adoption theory is much less misleading a label for his position than the imitation theory. The hypothesis I have advanced may be called an adaptation theory, that is, Dante has adapted the fourfold way of reading God's writings to the reading of his own poetic works. This adaptation theory appears to be far more sensible than the adoption theory. That Dante has made not one but two attempts toward such an adaptation is weighty prima facie evidence in favor of the adaptation theory.

Moreover, my adaptation theory may appear even more plausible than the adoption theory, if we consider the genetic relation of fourfold allegory to personification and figural allegories. In its designation of fourfold allegory as the allegory of theologians, the adoption school hastily assumes that fourfold allegory is the final formalization of figural allegory. It is this assumption that misleads the Auerbach-Singleton school to make a straight equation between fourfold allegory and God's way of writing.[31]

Fourfold Allegory and Biblical Exegesis

Now we have to inquire how the fourfold scheme of Biblical allegory has emerged vis-à-vis personification allegory on one hand and figural allegory on the other. The first clear formulation of the fourfold scheme comes from John Cassian: The literal sense of Jerusalem is the earthly city by that name, its allegory is the Church of Christ, its anagogy is the heavenly city of God, and its tropology is the soul of man.[32] The first two of these four senses are adopted from Tertullian's figural allegory, and the third one can be regarded as the extension of the second sense to the heavenly world. The second sense is the figural allegory concerning this world; the third sense is the figural allegory concerning the other world. In the Latin West this extension is chiefly due to St. Augustine's elaboration on Tertullian's figuralism. Since in the Greek East this extension had already been accomplished by Origen, Augustine may be said simply to have accepted Origen's typology.

As Auerbach shows, St. Augustine expands the two-term relation in Tertullian's figuralism into the three-term relation in his own.[33] Within Augustine's threefold figuralism, the New Testament is not only the fulfillment of the Old Testament but is also a new promise of the Last Judgment and the eternal glory of the heavenly world. To this threefold scheme of figural allegory, Auerbach says, Augustine adds the moral sense.[34] This is the fourfold scheme of allegory that Augustine uses in his Biblical exegesis.*

John Cassian's fourfold scheme may be regarded as the formalization of Augustine's fourfold allegorical sensibility or of the Origenian typology. The elements of Cassian's fourfold scheme are derived from both the tradition of figural allegory and that of personification allegory. Two of its three spiritual senses (allegory and anagogy) come from figural allegory; one of them (tropology) comes from personification allegory. Cassian may have called the moral sense "tropology" since he was aware of Quintilian's distinction between tropes and figures. We have already seen that Tertullian may have taken advantage of the same distinction made by Quintilian in his adaptation of *figura* for figuralism.

Cassian's fourfold scheme may be viewed as a two-to-one mixture of figural and personification allegory. But this ratio of two-to-one should be subject to the following consideration: Cassian's third sense (anagogy) has every right to be considered a Philonian allegory as much as a Pauline allegory. We have characterized the former as a vertical representation and the latter as a horizontal representation. Tertullian and Augustine often view the relation of this world and the other in horizontal perspective—that is, the everlasting glory of the heavenly kingdom will come for Christian souls in the future, or rather at the end of this mundane world. But the relation of the two worlds has also been viewed in vertical

---

*Incidentally, this fourfold scheme is quite different from another fourfold scheme Augustine gives in *De utilitate credendi*: history (*historia*), etiology (*aetiologia*), analogy (*analogia*), and allegory (*allegoria*). In the next chapter, it will be shown that this fourfold scheme represents Augustine's literal sensibility, which really overshadows his allegorical sensibility (see esp. pp. 90–92).

perspective, because the Kingdom of Heaven is an eternal reality which does not have to wait for the end of this world before it can come into being. To regard this world as a vague reflection of the other world has been one of the enduring Platonic legacies.

John Cassian's third sense can be viewed from a dual perspective: first as an extension of figural allegory and then as an extension of personification allegory. This perspectival ambiguity is adroitly reflected in its being placed between the second sense, which is clearly figural allegory, and the fourth sense, which is clearly personification allegory.

Cassian's fourth sense (tropology) bears wholly the Philonian stamp, while his third sense (anagogy) bears partly the Philonian stamp and partly the Pauline stamp. So the allegorical mixture bearing John Cassian's label turns out to be a half-and-half affair. The hybrid nature of fourfold allegory does not escape Auerbach's usually astute observation: "in the doctrine of the fourfold meaning of Scripture, it [personification allegory] wholly determined one of the four meanings, the ethical, and partly accounted for another, the anagogical."[35]

John Cassian's fourfold scheme can be called a synthesis of figural and personification allegory. In his own practice, he uses extensively not only figural allegory but also personification allegory, e.g., Egypt as the personification of gluttony.[36]

Incidentally, Dante was not even the first one to attempt to transform the fourfold scheme. The well-known precedent for his attempt is that of Hugh of Saint-Victor, who transforms the fourfold scheme into his threefold scheme of history, allegory, and tropology (*De sacramentis*, bk. 1, prol. 4; *Didascalicon*, bk. 5, chap. 2). This threefold scheme clearly gives equal balance to the two traditions of figural and personification allegory. Since Saint-Victor was an ardent Platonist, he must have thought that his threefold scheme gave a more accurate representation of the Platonic legacy in the medieval allegorical sensibility than the traditional fourfold scheme.

Some may be surprised to hear that St. Thomas's famous fourfold scheme came about as another way of transforming the traditional fourfold scheme. Because St. Thomas presents his own version in such a casual way that the transformation in question has usually been overlooked, I should cite the entire text:

> Therefore that first signification whereby words signify things belongs to the first sense, the historical or literal. That signifi-

cation whereby things signified by words have themselves also a signification is called the spiritual sense, which is based on the literal, and presupposes it.

Now this spiritual sense has a threefold division. For as the Apostle says (Heb. x. 1) the Old Law is a figure of the New Law, and Dionysius says (*Cael. Hier.* i) *the New Law itself is a figure of future glory*. Again, in the New Law, whatever our Head has done is a type [*signum*] of what we ought to do.

Therefore so far as the things of the Old Law signify the things of the New Law, there is the allegorical sense; so far as the things done in Christ, or so far as the things which signify Christ, are types [*signa*] of what we ought to do, there is the moral sense. But so far as they signify what relates to eternal glory, there is the anagogical sense. [*Summa theologiae*, pt. 1, q. 1, a. 10][37]

The order of the three spiritual senses St. Thomas gives in the first two paragraphs of this passage is exactly the same as is found in John Cassian's fourfold scheme: allegory, anagogy, and tropology, although he does not use these labels. He clearly regards the third sense (anagogy) as the extension of the second sense (allegory): he uses the word *figure* to describe both, citing the authority of Pseudo-Dionysius, whose figural language sounds exactly like that of St. Paul, and finally places both the allegorical and anagogical senses in one sentence.

St. Thomas places tropology in the fourth place just as in John Cassian's scheme, but he uses the word *signum* rather than *figura* in explaining its nature. The Latin word *signum* has as broad a usage as the English word *sign*. In the Dominican Fathers' translation of it as *type*, *signum* is assumed to mean "model" or "example." As a matter of fact, *signum* also means "signet" or "seal," that is, a model for making copies. St. Thomas himself uses *exemplum* as well as *signum* in explicating the moral sense (*Quodlibet.* q. 7, a. 15; *Commentary on St. Paul's Epistle to the Galatians*, chap. 4, lect. 7).

A model can be either original or derivative. While a derivative model exemplifies some Platonic Form or Aristotelian essence, an original model stands as the ultimate standard for itself and others. This ambiguity in the two senses of *model* is also inherent in the meaning of *type*. Since Christ cannot be a derivative model or type, the English word *prototype* would be the most accurate translation of *signum* in St. Thomas's exposition of the moral sense.

There is a decisive difference between the nominalist and essentialist conception of the prototype. For the essentialists, the prototype is always a universal; for the nominalists it is always a particular. In his typological description of the moral sense, St. Thomas regards the moral universal not as an ultimate prototype in itself but as an image or semblance of a nominalistic prototype, namely, Christ and his actions. If so, he is transforming Cassian's tropology from a personification into a figural allegory.

This is a perfectly respectable way of handling universals among the nominalists—indeed a disquieting thought for those historians who naïvely look upon Thomas Aquinas as a champion of essentialism in the prolonged medieval controversy between nominalists and essentialists. In fact his so-called essentialism is not any less ambiguous than his so-called Aristotelianism. At any rate, his nominalistic conception of the moral sense goes hand in hand with his figural conception of it.

Probably in order to accentuate his figural conception of the moral sense in place of Cassian's Philonian conception of it, St. Thomas shifts it from fourth to third place in the third paragraph of the quoted passage, where he gives his own enumeration of the four senses by their proper names. Since the allegorical and the anagogical senses have already been presented as *figural* in the first paragraph, to place the moral sense between these two firmly established figural senses is to give his conception of it an unmistakably clear figural frame.*

In the third paragraph St. Thomas further expands his conception of the moral sense which he has suggested in the second paragraph: the prototype of the moral sense is not limited to the New Law ("the things done in Christ"), but also extends to the Old Law ("the things which signify Christ"). Thus he completes his figural conception of the moral sense by treating it as a replica of the figural relation of the Old and the New Law.

In St. Thomas's scheme of fourfold allegory, the figural relation of the Old and the New Law is the prototype for the three spiritual senses. One and the same figural relation assumes the form of the allegorical sense on the macrocosmic level of human history, the form of the moral sense on the microcosmic level of the individual soul,

---

*As far as I know, this is one of the two instances where St. Thomas places the moral sense in the third place of the fourfold scheme. The other of these two instances is his reply to objection 5, *Quodlibet.* q. 7, a. 15. In other places beside these two, he places the moral sense either before or after the allegorical and anagogical sense, which are in turn kept together as a pair following the long tradition going back to Augustine and Tertullian (cf. *Quodlibet.* q. 7, a. 15; *Commentary on St. Paul's Epistle to the Galatians*, chap. 4, lect. 7).

and the form of anagogical sense on the supersensible level of eternal glory. The relation of the second and the third senses can also be regarded as the relation of the inner and the outer worlds; the relation of the second and the fourth sense can also be regarded as the relation of the temporal and the eternal worlds. Thus St. Thomas gives the fourfold scheme a systematic coherence by reconceiving it in a decisively figural mode.

This brief history of fourfold allegory has shown, first that Dante was not the first one to attempt to revamp the fourfold scheme, and then that the fourfold scheme has never been firmly associated either with figural or personification allegory alone. From Augustine and Cassian to Hugh of Saint-Victor, fourfold allegory has been clearly understood to be a mixture of both types of allegory. Only in the hands of St. Thomas does it receive a thoroughly figural texture. Once familiar with this historical background, one can see a rather hasty error in the straight equation of Dante's allegory of the theologians with figural allegory.

Since Dante was probably aware of the hybrid nature of the traditional fourfold scheme and the previous attempts to revise it, he saw nothing unusual in his own attempts toward its transformation or adaptation. The transformation he proposes in the *Convivio* turns out to be exactly opposite to that which St. Thomas presents in his *Summa theologiae*. Whereas the latter transforms fourfold allegory into a thoroughly figural scheme, the former transforms it into a pure personification scheme. It is hard to determine whether this diametrically opposite performance of Dante's to St. Thomas's was, or was not the reflection of his intention. But it is rather obvious that neither of them liked the hybrid nature of the traditional fourfold scheme and tried to change it into a purebred.

Since in his Can Grande letter Dante lists the four senses in the same order as St. Thomas's enumeration rather than John Cassian's, the Auerbach-Singleton school may argue, Dante should be presumed to retain St. Thomas's figural conception of all the four senses. But that would be a dubious presumption. As we have seen, Dante did not hesitate to transform completely the fourfold scheme into personification allegory in the *Convivio*, although he also retained the order of the four senses as he found it in St. Thomas's formulation. To be sure, Dante clearly presents the second sense as a figural sense in his Can Grande letter, but one can never be certain about his conception of the third and fourth senses. In his description of the moral and the anagogical senses, he uses neither the word *figura* nor its cognates.

His illustration of the moral and the anagogical senses is intriguingly the same as his illustration of the fourth sense in the *Convivio*, where he said that the Exodus story has the following anagogical sense: "to wit, when the soul goeth forth out of sin, it is made holy and free in its power" (*Convivio*, 2. 1). Now compare this with the illustration of the last two senses which Dante gives in his Can Grande letter, using the same Biblical passage:

> If the moral sense, the conversion of the soul from the sorrow and misery of sin to a state of grace is signified; if the anagogical, the passing of the sanctified soul from the bondage of the corruption of this world to the liberty of everlasting glory is signified.[38]

Since the anagogical sense in the *Convivio* was conceived as personification allegory, it is quite probable that the last two senses in this letter are also meant to be conceived as personification allegory. It is equally probable that the last two senses in the same letter are meant to be conceived as figural allegory, just as in St. Thomas's conception of the fourfold scheme. As it has been pointed out with Dante's description of his fourth sense in the *Convivio*, there is an inherent ambiguity in his use of the definite article ("the conversion of the soul" and "the passing of the sanctified soul") in paragraph 7 of the Can Grande letter. Because of this ambiguity, his third and fourth senses may be taken to express some universal truths or to describe some particular facts. Hence there is no conclusive evidence to assume that these two senses are meant to be either figural or personification allegory. Whereas Dante made a deliberate act of defiance against St. Thomas's figural conception of the fourfold scheme in the *Convivio*, it is likely that he is now, in this letter, making a conscious attempt to adopt St. Thomas's transformation *in toto*. It is also probable that he is now trying to restore the hybrid status of the fourfold scheme, since he has found inadequacies in both of its purebred versions wrought by himself and St. Thomas.

None of these probable conjectures can be confirmed by appealing to textual evidence because the text of the letter is hopelessly ambiguous.

Figuralism Free of Literal Fundamentalism

Auerbach's thesis concerning Dante's figuralism has two features: (1) the literal sense of the *Commedia* belongs to history and not to fiction (his literal fundamentalism); and (2) its spiritual senses are figural and not personification allegory (figural allegorism). Auerbach has assumed that these two features are inseparable from each other in figural allegory as they are supposed to be in Biblical exegesis. This assumption stems from an overgeneralization. Literal fundamentalism has never been maintained by theologians for every passage of the Bible; in fact, some of its passages have been read only figurally while others have been read both literally and figurally.

St. Augustine provides a flexible guideline for demarcating these two types of Biblical passages from each other in his motto of the promotion of charity—that is, whenever the literal reading of a Biblical passage is not conducive to the promotion of our love of God and neighbors, its meaning should be taken only on the figurative level (*De doctrina christiana*, bk. 3, chap. 10). Since then, very few pious Christians have thought that the literal meaning of the Song of Solomon is very conducive to promoting their charity.*

So even if it is conceded that Dante has *adopted* God's way of writing, this does not automatically assure the historical truth of his literal sense, since God's literal sense may or may not be true. As a matter of historical fact, St. Thomas did not regard the literal sense or its truth as the fundamental distinction between divine and human writings. For he holds that the only unique feature of Scripture is its spiritual sense while the literal sense is one thing shared by both sacred and pagan writings (*Quodlibet.* q. 7, a. 16). Hence he categorically denies even the very possibility of giving spiritual senses to human writings and regards all allegorical interpretation of pagan literature as an absolutely extraneous imposition. Aquinas's position on this point must have come about as a rather violent reaction against the prevailing tendency to allegorize the secular classics, but it surely constitutes an ironic contrast to the Auerbachian position of literal fundamentalism.

Furthermore, the truth of literal sense is not only inessential but also inconsequential in any program of figural interpretation. Whether the literal sense is true or fictitious has no relevance at all for its figural interpretation. For example, whether Dante's encounter with Virgil be taken as a matter of historical fact or a fictitious event has no

---

*Following this Augustinian guideline for Biblical exegesis, Hugh of Saint-Victor says that only the allegorical *sententia* of Scripture is always true, while its literal-historical *sensus* is sometimes false and sometimes even absurd (cf. *Didascalicon*, bk. 6, chaps. 10 and 11).

bearing at all in determining whether Virgil figurally represents Natural Reason, John the Baptist, or Christ. A fanatic obsession with literal sense has, indeed, the danger of blocking out all spiritual senses, as occurred with the Protestant Reformers.

The figural program Auerbach has proposed in his "Figura" consists of two sets of literal senses and nothing more, i.e. the literal sense of history and the literal sense of the *Commedia*. There he claims the latter literal sense as the figural sense of the former literal sense, leaving practically no room at all for any allegorical interpretation. This blinding obsession with literal sense inevitably leads to the contextual error of interpreting the *Commedia* in the context of modern, Protestant literal sensibility rather than in that of medieval allegorical sensibility. In order to avoid this contextual error, we must separate figural allegorism from literal fundamentalism and shift all the emphasis from the latter to the former. So we shall undertake a figural interpretation of the *Commedia* without unnecessary concern with its literal truth.

At the outset we must not be confused about our own motives. Some have favored the figural interpretation of the *Commedia* on the ground that it is a more interesting way to read the poem than seeing it as a personification allegory. This is just an expression of subjective preference; personification allegory would indeed have a greater appeal to Platonists than figural allegory. Subjective preferences and interests should have no place at all in our endeavor to find the right way of reading the *Commedia* only in light of its allegorical texture.

We cannot accept the traditional interpretation of Dante's Virgil as the personification of Reason, not because we are averse to personification allegory, but because, as Singleton rightly says, "Virgil cannot and does not always speak and act as Reason."[39] The most troublesome anomaly of Virgil as a representation of Natural Reason is that he guides Dante not only through the Inferno but right up to the top of Purgatorio. According to the Christian faith, Purgatorio as a realm of grace is inaccessible to Natural Reason. One may counter this objection by saying that Virgil is performing this and many other acts of grace as the personification of Natural Reason instructed and assisted by divine grace. But this rejoinder simply magnifies the initial anomaly: Natural Reason could not but cease to be natural as soon as it is instructed and assisted by divine grace. To receive grace in nature is the very essence of the infusion of grace into nature; there is, in fact, no vessel for the reception of grace other than that of nature.

It is quite easy to point out the unsatisfactory consequences of viewing Dante's Virgil as a personification allegory, but it is very hard to provide a figural interpretation of him. Auerbach proposes a simple solution: the historical Virgil is a figure of Dante's Virgil, or rather the latter is the fulfillment of the former.[40] The obvious trouble with this solution is the reversal of figure and fulfillment. Within Dante's poetic world his Virgil must be a figure that carries the literal sense, whatever figural senses it may contain.

Even such an enthusiastic follower of Auerbach as Singleton cannot accept this reversal of figure and fulfillment. He is content to accept the traditional view that Dante's Virgil is the rind (figure) of his allegory and not its core (fulfillment). He is even willing to accept the traditional interpretation of Dante's Virgil as an allegorical representation of Natural Reason, in spite of his vehement protest that Dante's Virgil is far from exhausted ("sometimes but not always") by this allegorical function.[41]

The excessive allegorical residual of Dante's Virgil—too much of him is left out in his allegorical interpretation—is indeed a reliable sign that his Virgil should be read not as personification allegory but as figural allegory. For the literal sense of figural allegory tends to have a greater amount of allegorical residual than that of personification allegory. But nowhere does Singleton appear to try to provide a figural interpretation of Dante's Virgil.

Thus Singleton's commitment to Auerbach's figural realism remains half-hearted in his handling of Dante's Virgil. Figural realism as conceived by Auerbach requires two solid wings, the wing of historical reality and that of figural allegorism. In Singleton's manipulation of it for the case of Dante's Virgil, it cannot even take off from the ground since it has to flutter on a pair of mismatched wings, the wing of historical reality and that of personification allegory.

The need for a figural interpretation is no less urgent in the case of Beatrice than in that of Virgil. As the personification of Revelation, her appearance on the top of Purgatorio would mean that Revelation does not come to mankind until it regains the lost Paradise, or that mankind is not given Revelation until it completes its purgatorial works. This would be a strange view of Revelation for any Christian. Read as personification allegory, the allegorical residual of Dante's Beatrice is as obtrusive as that of Virgil. Hence some critics, like Pierre Mandonnet, have been tempted to see her allegorical role on a much broader scale (*"ordre surnaturel"*) than that of Revelation.[42]

In his figural interpretation of Beatrice, Auerbach is more sensible than in that of Virgil. He does not insist on Dante's Beatrice being the fulfillment of the historical Beatrice; he readily admits her function in the *Commedia* as a figure rather than a fulfillment. He calls her a "*figura* or *idolo Christi.*"[43] But to regard Dante's Beatrice as a figure is quite inconsistent with his view that Dante's Virgil is a fulfillment and not a figure. Perhaps to amend this inconsistency, Auerbach in a subsequent essay insists on Beatrice's role as a fulfillment along with Virgil's corresponding role.[44]

Singleton almost develops a fixation with Auerbach's notion of Beatrice as a figure of Christ. There is something bizarre about this figural view of Beatrice: a feminine creature is singled out as a figural representation of a singularly masculine figure. Medieval theologians have always placed heavy stress on the masculine image of Jesus Christ, since Augustine consigned the feminine half of mankind to a lowly place somewhere between man and beasts. To the medieval understanding, Christ was the man of all men; he was the second Adam, the perfection of the first Adam, the first man. To the best of my recollection, I do not know of a single woman who has been numbered among the numerous Christ-figures—e.g. Adam, Isaac, Joseph, David, Solomon, Jonah, etc.—by medieval Biblical commentators.

I have singled out the two cases of Virgil and Beatrice because they are about the best touchstones for the evaluation of any allegorical theory proposed for the reading of the *Commedia*. For Virgil as the personification of Reason and Beatrice as that of Revelation are certainly the best-known examples of interpreting the *Commedia* as a personification allegory.

We have yet to consider the source of still greater embarrassment, Dante's third guide. Auerbach and Singleton are no different from many other Dante scholars in passing over this third guide in silence. He is seldom even mentioned in the voluminous allegorical exegeses on Virgil and Beatrice; he has long become a forgotten man. I refer to St. Bernard, who waits for Dante's arrival in the Heaven of the Empyrean and brings his journey to its consummation.

Virgil and Beatrice have been established so firmly as the two focal points in the interpretation of the *Commedia* that some scholars have even come up with the thesis of Dante's original or ultimate bipartite plan. For example, C. A. Robson seriously entertains the idea that Dante's original or real master plan for the composition of the *Commedia* is bipartite, the realm of Virgil and the realm of Beatrice, while

the tripartite plan is only a matter of surface adornment.[45] If Robson's thesis were true, it could surely offer a reasonable justification
for the consigning of Dante's third guide to the realm of silence and
oblivion.*

That the apparent triadic surface of the *Commedia* hides its truly
dyadic structure has indeed become a widely shared common premise
even among those Dante scholars who would not openly embrace
Robson's thesis. For they stand on this very premise, often unwittingly, when they subscribe to one of the most enduring assumptions
in Dante scholarship—i.e. that St. Thomas provides the substantive
theological ideas for Dante's poetic ornamentation. The fundamental
pattern of the Thomistic system is dualistic, as manifested in his
various dichotomies such as the natural vs. the supernatural and the
rational vs. the irrational. Of course, this pervasive dualistic pattern
is the Aristotelian legacy. On some occasions, to be sure, the Angelic
Doctor makes use of Plato's triadic pattern, but its role in the Thomistic system is no less incidental than in the Aristotelian system. If the
content of Dante's epic is derived from the dualistic Thomistic system, his epic is bound to have a dyadic structure despite its triadic
surface form.

In contrast to St. Thomas's dyadic pattern, St. Bonaventure's
sensibility is thoroughly molded in the triadic pattern. The Seraphic
Doctor sees everything in triple focus and feels everything in triple
rhythm. It is for this reason that I have called special attention to his
Journey of the Mind to God as one of the striking models for Dante's
epic journey.[46] Since very few have seriously taken up this suggestion
of mine, let me stress once more the indispensability of the Seraphic
Doctor's mystical theology for comprehending the triadic structure
of Dante's *Commedia*.

I myself have had to make a tortuous detour before coming to
appreciate the prodigious significance of St. Bonaventure for understanding not only Dante but also all of Gothic culture. I have had
much difficulty freeing myself from the prevalent view that St.
Thomas's achievement was the theological summation of the Gothic
ethos. Only recently have I come to realize that this view gravely

---

*Even those who would rather retain a triadic schema for the *Commedia* instead of em-
bracing outright a dyadic one are sometimes tempted to substitute someone else for St.
Bernard to anchor the third corner of the triangle. For example, Erich Auerbach is pleased
to make Cato of Utica the third partner of Virgil and Beatrice in their triune relationship
(cf. Auerbach, *Mimesis*, p. 195; "Figura," pp. 64 ff.).

distorts the real character of Gothic culture. It is not St. Thomas and his Dominican Brethren but St. Bonaventure and the Franciscans who constituted the mainstream of the Gothic ethos. The Angelic Doctor's contribution was no more than a tributary feeding the fresh currents of Arabian influence into this mainstream. These currents were often so overwhelming as to require a series of extraordinary surveillances culminating in the Condemnation of 1277. St. Thomas's dualistic system is simply incongruous with the very texture of the Gothic ethos. The Gothic cathedral is not a two-storied edifice, but a one-story structure despite its many-tiered windows—just like St. Bonaventure's mystical corpus.

The distorted view of St. Thomas's achievement has been an inevitable consequence of the Council of Trent, which adopted him as the official theologian of the Counter-Reformation. This view was further confirmed as "official" by the encyclical *Aeterni Patris* in 1879, and since then the exaltation of this official distortion has been the ultimate task of most contemporary Thomists, especially under the aegis of Étienne Gilson. The imposition of the Thomistic dualism on the *Commedia* is one of the contextual errors we moderns have made in reading Dante. The present Thomistic orthodoxy in the Catholic Church has induced most modern readers unconsciously to assume that the Thomistic dualism must have constituted the theological component of the cultural context in which the *Commedia* was written. Because of this erroneous assumption, the *Commedia* has been interpreted in the context of the Gilsonian medieval ethos rather than that of the Dantesque ethos.

Although I cannot here fully establish St. Bonaventure's as the central voice of the Gothic age, I will try to show that his mystical theology has a far closer affinity with Dante's epic than the dialectical theology of St. Thomas. The Seraphic Doctor's is a theology of allegory; the Angelic Doctor's is the theology of analogy. In spite of the instinctive assumption that allegory and analogy must somehow be intimately related to each other, the precise nature of their relationship still remains one of the most baffling medieval mysteries that have yet to be explored. Since we cannot here delve into this mystery, let us be content with observing one obvious difference: allegory is an intuitive mode while analogy is a discursive one.*

The discursive mode of analogy is the predominant form in the

---

*The relation of allegory and analogy will be examined in chap. 2, pp. 77–89.

organization of St. Thomas's system, while the intuitive mode of allegory is given only a subsidiary role in it. The insignificant role of the allegorical mode in his works is fully attested by the fact that he devotes only one article of his *Summa theologiae* to the explanation of this mode. Even that lone article is tucked in the first question of the first part, which is only a preface to his *Summa*. In his other *Summa* the topic of allegory fails to receive even this sort of cursory treatment. The only place where St. Thomas discusses the nature of allegory as an independent topic is his *Quodlibet*—that is, the haphazard assemblage of his miscellaneous ideas; even there he gives it only three articles, q. 7, aa. 14–16.*

The intuitive mode of allegory is what places St. Bonaventure's works securely in the tradition of mystical theology. The allegorical mode is not only the chief form of perception and exposition in his mystical opuscula, but is extensively used even in the *Breviloquium*, one of his obviously discursive works. He devotes the entire prologue of this work to the inquiry into the nature of Biblical allegory, and St. Thomas's exposition of fourfold allegory, which we have cited from his *Summa theologiae*, appears to be no more than a summary of this intricate exposition. In *De reductione artium ad theologiam*, Bonaventure exalts fourfold allegory as the universal schema for interpreting all human experience, ranging from sense perception to mechanical arts to natural and moral philosophy.

The allegorical mode is the very essence of Bonaventurian exemplarism, in which every creature is viewed as either a shadow (*umbra*), a vestige (*vestigium*), or an image (*imago*) of God. These three forms for the reflection of God come under the general category of resemblance or similitude (*similitudo*), which we have cited as the ontological foundation for figural sensibility. Throughout the prologue to the *Breviloquium*, Bonaventure clearly assumes the antonymity of 'the figural sense' to 'the literal sense' and its synonymity to 'the spiritual sense' on all levels. Hence it appears that St. Thomas's transformation of fourfold allegory into a purebred figuralism is most likely to have been a borrowing from St. Bonaventure.

In his figural perception, St. Bonaventure sees all of creation as the mirror of the divine perfections, or rather the poem that God writes with real things rather than with words. This is precisely what

---

*In scholastic disputations, quodlibetical questions were raised not by the master but by members of his audience (*quod libet*—whatever pleases the audience). Hence as a document a *quodlibet* usually turns out to be an unsystematic treatise on the issues which tend to reflect the concerns not of the master but of his audience.

is meant by "God's way of writing," which can be read only in the allegorical mode.* St. Bonaventure's mystical theology is to provide the proper way of reading this divine poem in allegory, and Dante composed his *Divina Commedia* in this mystical tradition of cosmic allegory·

It is the Bonaventurian sense of Trinitarian structure that compelled me to take seriously Dante's third guide, St. Bernard, in my *Fragile Leaves of the Sibyl: Dante's Master Plan*.[47] Following the Bonaventurian triadic schema, in which the third always plays the crucial role of bringing the first two into union, I was then convinced that the allegorical interpretation of Virgil and Beatrice would never be complete without tying it in with that of St. Bernard. As a matter of fact, the function and labor of the first two guides in the *Commedia* would amount to nothing until and unless they were consummated in the function and labor of the last guide. Thus I came to attempt a joint figural interpretation of all three of Dante's guides by proposing the simple thesis that they are figural representations of the Three Persons of the Holy Trinity.[48]

Trinitarian Figuralism in the *Commedia*

In my figural interpretation, Dante's Virgil is seen as a figure of the Second Person. Virgil comes to Dante lost in the *selva oscura*, just as Christ comes to mankind lost in this sinful world. Virgil shows Dante how to die in the world of sin (the Inferno) and how to be reborn in the world of grace (the Purgatorio)—that is, the way of the Crucifixion and the Resurrection. On Virgil's first appearance, Dante the poet gives us two rather prominent pointers to indicate the function of Virgil as a figure of Christ. He tells Dante that he was born *sub Julio* (*Inf.* canto 1, line 70) which is meant to be a veiled reference to the mission of the Second Person, from the Nativity (*nacqui*) to the Crucifixion (*sub Julio*—cf. *sub Pontio Pilato passus, et sepultus est*— the Nicene Creed). After Virgil's self-introduction, Dante describes him as "that fountain (*fonte*) which pours forth so rich a stream of speech (*parlar*)" (*Inf.* 1. 79–80).[49] Since John's Gospel, the Son has

---

*There are two senses to "God's way of writing." St. Bonaventure says, "Now, God speaks not with words alone, but also with deeds, for with Him saying is doing and doing is saying" (*Breviloquium*, prol. (4). 4, trans. José de Vinck, in *The Works of Bonaventure*, 2: 15). When God writes with words, he gives us the Sacred Scripture. When he writes with deeds, he creates the whole world (*Breviloquium*, 2. 12. 1). Hence there are two divine volumes: the Bible and the Book of Creation. These two divine books dictate two allegories: the Scriptural allegory and the universal or cosmic allegory. Cf. chap. 2, pp. 72–77, for a further discussion of this point.

been known as the Logos, the Primordial Word, or rather the Fountain of Speech.

Lest we may have missed these clues, Dante gives us one final one right after Virgil's departure: "Virgil, to whom I have given myself for my salvation (*mia salute*)" (*Purg.* 30. 51). As Hollander alertly points out, Dante does not use the word *salvation* lightly.[50] As a Christian, Dante knew that there were no other agents of salvation than the Three Persons of the Holy Trinity. "To give oneself over to Virgil for one's salvation" would be a blatant act of idolatry or stupidity on Dante's part unless his Virgil is conceived of as a figure of one of the Three Persons.*

The emphatic stress on Virgil's being a man of nature and not of grace might appear to be an insurmountable obstacle for his identification as a Christ-figure. But in truth the unmistakable stamp of *nature* on him is an indispensable figural means to convey the idea of the Incarnation; the human, or natural, aspect of the Son is as essential as his divine aspect in the dogma of Christ's dual nature.

In contrast to Dante's relationship with the ethereal Beatrice, the outstanding feature of his relationship with Virgil is its earthy dimension. As Thomas G. Bergin loves to remind us, Dante's Beatrice is in marked contrast to Petrarch's Laura. The latter is tangibly carnal; the former is thoroughly spiritual. Whereas Dante never grabs or hugs Beatrice, he is pushed and pulled by Virgil. This physical dimension of their relationship reflects Virgil's bodily nature. The same physical or carnal dimension of the Second Person is the essence of the Incarnation: "Behold the virgin shall be with child, and shall bring forth a son; and they shall call his name Emmanuel; which is, interpreted, 'God with us'" (Matt. 1:23). Through his physical dimension the Second Person comes to dwell among us and to be called Emmanuel. Dante's Virgil is a figure of Emmanuel.†

*That Dante's first guide must be a Christ-figure becomes quite obvious as soon as one recalls Christ's own remark to the Apostle Thomas: "I am the way, and the truth, and the life. No one comes to the Father but through me" (John 16:6). To be sure, the word *guide* is not contained in this remark, but Christ's role can be seen as that of a guide or a mediator to the Father. I do not know of any medieval theologians who have made use of the metaphor of a guide in explicating this Biblical passage, but I do know that St. Teresa of Avila indeed employed this metaphor in adapting this passage for the description of her own mystical journey (cf. *Interior Castle*, Sixth Mansion, chap. 7).

†The pagan Virgil is an Emmanuel-figure for Dante's universal allegory, in which both pagan and Biblical tradition are accepted as parts of the mirror of divine reflection. The very idea that Virgil the pagan is a Christ-figure is bound to produce a shock, quite similar to the shock produced by the dogma of the dual nature of Christ (how can a man be God?).

From the fourth century through Dante's own time, Virgil's Fourth Eclogue was believed to be the secular version of the sacred prophecy of the virgin birth of Emmanuel. Statius tells Virgil that he became not only a poet but also a Christian by following Virgil, and cites the prophetic passage from the Fourth Eclogue (*Purg.* 22. 70–73). He regretfully adds that Virgil himself did not benefit from his own light, which guided other people. Even this expression of regret carries a subtle reference to the role of Virgil as a Christ-figure. Christ neither draws any benefit from his own Incarnation nor becomes a Christian by following himself. Christ is not a Christian. Thus Statius's description of his relationship to Virgil turns out to be a deliberate case of figural or allegorical irony.*

In my figural interpretation, Beatrice is viewed as a figure of the Third Person of the Holy Trinity. She comes to Dante after the departure of Virgil; the Holy Spirit comes after the departure of the Son. Christ explained this relation between the Second and the Third Persons:

> But I speak the truth to you: it is expedient for you that I depart. For if I do not go, the Advocate will not come to you; but if I go, I will send him to you. And when he has come he will convict the world of sin, and of justice, and of judgment. [John 16:7–9]

On her arrival in the Terrestrial Paradise, Beatrice convicts Dante of his sin and judgment. After the ascension of the Griffin, she is adorned with the seven lights or gifts of the Holy Spirit while guarding the Chariot. This is clearly a figural representation of the Holy Spirit entrusted with the task of guiding the Church.

Auerbach and Singleton have just mistaken this Spirit-figure for a Christ-figure. This misidentification can be readily exposed by the presence of the Griffin, the mythical animal that comes to the Terrestrial Paradise with Beatrice. With its dual nature (half lion, half eagle), the Griffin clearly represents Christ in His dual nature. Beatrice as a Christ-figure would therefore duplicate the allegorical function of the Griffin, a duplication that would offend our sense of order and elegance since Beatrice and the Griffin come together in the same Procession.†

---

*A figural irony is a trap one gets caught in when one misses it. The notion of allegorical irony may turn out to be a highly fruitful instrument in allegorical studies, but its development as a critical instrument has yet to come. So far allegorical studies have been too earnest and too serious to reach the mature stage of playful reflection.

†Joseph Chierici has proposed an interesting revision to the traditional interpretation

The error of mistaking a Spirit-figure for a Christ-figure largely reflects two significant points in Christian theology which often fail to come to most Dante scholars' attention. First, there is always an intimate connection between Christ-figures and Spirit-figures, which in turn reflects the integral relation between the Second and the Third Persons. Second, there is a marked contrast between the medieval and the modern conceptions of God. Whereas the latter has been almost exclusively reduced to Christology, the former was always systematically amplified to Trinitarianism.

When the error of identification in question reflects the first of these two causes, it may produce some excusable consequences. However, when it reflects the second of the two, it can become a serious problem, since the initial error may lead to a still graver one—as in the pathetic case of mistaking Beatrice's Procession on the top of Purgatorio for the center of the entire *Commedia*.[51] Christ may indeed be regarded as the center of the Christocentric conception of God, but he cannot be taken to be any more of a center than the Father or the Spirit in the Trinitarian theology.

In the Heaven of the Sun, Beatrice becomes the center around which revolve the three circles of theologians under the inspiration of the Holy Spirit: "Oh vero sfavillar del Santo Spiro" ("Oh, the very sparkling of the Holy Spirit") (*Par.* 14. 76; also cf. *Par.* 10. 65). In the Heaven of the primum mobile, she herself explains the nine orders of the angelic ministers for the invisible mission of the Holy Spirit, while she leaves the task of explanation to other blessed souls in the other Heavens.

When Beatrice is relieved of her mission and goes back to her seat in the Mystical Rose, Dante changes the form of his address from *voi* to *tu*. This change is accompanied by a corresponding change in

---

of the Griffin. Whereas the Griffin has generally been understood as half lion and half eagle, Professor Chierici views it as half *dog* and half eagle (see *Il grifo dantesco*, Rome, 1967, p. 73). This identification of the Griffin as a winged dog rather than a winged lion enables him to suggest the intriguing association of the Griffin with the *Veltro* (Greyhound) of *Inferno* 1. Unfortunately, the *Veltro* is one of those enigmatic allegorical figures whose references are just impossible to determine with any degree of definiteness. Some have thought that the *Veltro* symbolizes Can Grande della Scala or some other political leader who is to establish the Universal Empire. In that event, the Griffin might not represent Christ and its allegorical function would not be duplicated by that of Beatrice as a Christ-figure. But then there are those who regard the *Veltro* as Christ in his Second Coming. In this view, the association of the Griffin with the *Veltro* only reinforces the traditional view of the Griffin as Christ in his dual nature. Professor Chierici himself seems to retain the ultimate function of the Griffin as a Christ symbol.

the syllabification of her name. As long as she stands as a figure of the Holy Spirit, "Beatrice" is syllabified as in *beatus* and *beati*. As soon as she returns to the Mystical Rose and assumes her private role, the first two vowels of "Beatrice," *e* and *a* are contracted into one syllable as in the normal pronunciation of Beatrice as a human name.

The Virgil of Limbo assumes the mission of guiding the lost Dante at the request of Beatrice, who is sent to Virgil by the Virgin Mary. This is probably meant to be a figural reference to the Miraculous Conception of the Son by the Holy Spirit: "Qui propter nos homines, et propter nostram salutem descendit de caelis. Et incarnatus est de Spiritu Sancto ex Maria Virgine"—"Who for us men, and for our salvation came down from Heaven and was made flesh, by the Holy Spirit of the Virgin Mary" (the Nicene Creed).

In my figural scheme of reading the *Commedia*, St. Bernard is understood as a figure of the First Person. The Father alone remains in the Kingdom of Heaven, while sending out his Son on the visible mission and his Spirit on the invisible mission. St. Bernard waits for Dante's arrival in the highest heaven, while he is being recovered from the dark wood by Virgil and brought to the Empyrean by Beatrice. St. Bernard is not only described as looking like a tender father (*tenero padre*), but he is addressed as the holy father (*santo padre*; *Par.* 32. 100).

The visible mission of the Son is to establish faith; Virgil constantly talks of faith. The invisible mission of the Spirit is to strengthen hope; Beatrice comes crowned with olive and her eyes are emerald. The function of the Father is to consummate the missions of his Son and his Spirit by receiving the sanctified soul into the bower of love. In this world St. Bernard was already well known as an eloquent exegetical expert on the nature of love, through his *Sermons on the Song of Songs* and *On Loving God*. Thus the Three Persons in their function are related to the three theological virtues of faith, hope, and love.

On his first appearance St. Bernard tells Dante that his intention is to bring Dante's journey to its consummation. This should remind us of the promise which Saint Benedict, another Father-figure, gave Dante in the Heaven of Saturn—that is, to grant Dante's wish to see his face unveiled (*Par.* 32. 61–63). To see the Holy Father's face unveiled is the very essence of Dante's beatific vision, which brings his love to its consummation.

In *The Fragile Leaves of the Sibyl*, I present this figural interpretation of Dante's three guides, not as complete in itself, but as an integral part of my systematic figural reading of the entire *Commedia*. In this systematic figural program I maintain the thesis that every person and every event in the three realms of Dante's other world are figural representations of the Holy Trinity in their works of salvation on the macrocosmic and the microcosmic levels. The figural roles of the three guides constitute only one (surely the most prominent) fragment of this overall figural representation of the Three Persons throughout the entire epic.

I do not set forth my figural reading of various persons and incidents one after another in an ad hoc sequence, but show how Dante presents them in a systematic sequence of three successive circles of the Son in his visible mission, the Spirit in his invisible mission, and the Father in his mansion.

The figural way of seeing the Holy Trinity in their works of salvation is to see the history of mankind from the perspective of Providence. The providential perspective had been firmly engrained in the medieval sensibility since Augustine's *City of God* and *On the Trinity*. In contrast to the Eastern Fathers' abstract doctrines of the Trinity, the unique feature of Augustine's Trinitarian doctrine is its concreteness, which reflects his figural sensibility. He tries to show us the nature and function of the Trinity as figurally manifested in the history of mankind.

It is such a figural view of God in history that Dante adopts from St. Augustine for the spiritual sense of his epic.* The *Commedia* is ostensibly a literal account of the other world ("the state of souls after death"), but its spiritual sense is meant to be "a story of the living world," as Bergin says in his succinct restatement of Dante's own intention in his letter to Can Grande. "A story of the living world" is precisely the history of mankind which is referred to in the opening line of the *Commedia*: "Nel mezzo del cammin di nostra vita" ("Midway along the journey of our life").[52] As in St. Thomas's fourfold allegory, the history of mankind functions in the *Commedia* as the common prototype for all three levels of figural signification: the macrocosmic, the microcosmic, and the supersensible.

Dante's figural vision of the Trinity turns out to be a poetic version of Augustine's figural view of God and his Providence. Hence Augustine's *City of God* and *On the Trinity* are as prominent models for Dante's epic as Virgil's *Aeneid*. Perhaps Dante adopted the *Aeneid* as

---

*That this adoption is not a direct one will be explained in chap. 2, esp. pp. 62–66.

one of his models mainly because he looked upon it as a secular forerunner of his own poetic version of Augustine's providential vision.

My figural reading of the *Commedia* leads to the astonishing conclusion that the actions of the Trinity constitute the ultimate theme of Dante's epic. As long as one does not accept this, one has to conclude instead that the *Commedia* is an epic devoid of an epic hero. Chiefly to forestall such an absurd consequence, critics have often presented Dante the traveler as the epic hero, who allegorically represents the Christian, or even mankind.

But Dante the traveler makes an awkward epic hero. Whereas the traditional function of such a hero is to perform a sustained heroic action, Dante's chief function is to see and report, the function of a traveling reporter. Of course there are a few things he does on his own, but all of them are the instinctive actions one might expect from any attentive, involved observer. It is in perfect accord with the medieval conception of a true Christian primarily as a receiver of grace that Dante the traveler plays the passive role of observer rather than the active one of gallant hero. As Meister Eckhart says, "We are made perfect by our passivity rather than by our activity" (Sermon 2). So the *Commedia* is bound to remain essentially a travelogue without an epic hero, as long as we fail to see the action of the Trinity as its main theme.

To be sure, Virgil's *Aeneid*, one of the conscious models for Dante's epic, is cast in the form of a travelogue. But Virgil's is a travelogue not merely of a traveler but of an epic hero. The failure to see the epic action of Aeneas in the *Aeneid* would be the same gross oversight as the failure to see the epic action of the Divine Trinity in the *Divina Commedia*.

Once the epic model of the *Commedia* is understood and it is placed in the Augustinian figural sensibility, my thesis that the Trinity is the epic hero for Dante's work emerges as inevitable. In a perceptive review of my *Fragile Leaves*, Father Kenelm Foster of Cambridge University grants this point:

> If Dante's poem is about God and man, we should expect it to present the divine nature as the dominant ordering principle of the whole. And so in fact it does; and in this sense Mr. Swing is perfectly right to say that the Trinity is the 'main theme of Dante's epic.' Few critics, however, have ever said this of the

Comedy; and none that I know, apart from Swing, has made anything like a convincing effort to show that it is true.[53]

To see the figural presence of the Trinity in Dante's poetic mirror is indeed a novel way of reading his epic, but it is by no means incompatible with the traditional way. To be sure, even the traditional reading has its own mode of seeing the Trinity in Dante's poetic world by observing the pervasive effect of divine power and justice. But that mode provides only an indirect reflection of God in Dante's mirror, while the other presents his direct reflection in it. To see God's reflection through his effect is an indirect mode; to see his reflection in his action is a direct mode. It is these two ways of seeing the divine reflection that St. Bonaventure systematically employs in his use of the mirror of the whole world. According to him, the direct reflection is to see God "in the mirror (*in speculo*)," while indirect reflection is to see him "through the mirror (*per speculum*)." Furthermore, to see God *through* the mirror is only the stage preparatory to seeing him *in* the mirror. Thus, to see the working or effect of God's justice in the *Commedia* is no more than the preparatory stage of seeing God's reflection *through* Dante's poetic mirror, which must be perfected in the ultimate stage of seeing God's figural presence and action *in* that mirror.

It is by no means easy to see the figural presence of the Trinity in the *Commedia*. Although man is an image of God and as such reflects his glory, Augustine says, this divine reflection in the human mirror is indeed obscure (*enigma*; *De trinitate*, bk. 15, chaps. 8 and 9). He goes on to explain that an enigma is one species of allegory, that is, the obscure allegory. Dante's allegorical mirror is as obscure as Augustine's. Both of them are so obscure, indeed, that the figural reflection of the Trinity is supposedly visible only to the eyes of the faithful. Even a fleeting glimpse of it is meant to be an act of faith and a gift of grace.

Dante is keenly conscious of this obscurity of his poetic mirror. Throughout the *Commedia*, in fact, he is almost obsessed with the fear that the vivid realism of his poetic creation may mislead his readers to mistake it for an ultimate reality and fail to perceive its obscure, figural function. In order to forestall this grievous misunderstanding on our part, he ceaselessly draws our attention to the "veiled" (*ombra*) or "figural" (*figura*) character of his visionary world.

For the sake of consistency in my figural reading, I do not make the obstinate claim that there is no personification allegory in the *Com-*

media. I readily admit that Dante's three worlds are organized in accordance with the medieval table of seven natural virtues (humility, mercy, meekness, fortitude, liberality, temperance, chastity) and three supernatural virtues (faith, hope, and love), and their contraries. In that respect Dante's epic belongs to the medieval tradition of representing virtues and vices in personification allegory. Dante's unique contribution to this tradition has often been pointed out—i.e. that he gives his regions of virtue and vice a strong sense of concreteness by populating them with concrete persons and their behavior. But this concerns the concreteness of the rind of Dante's allegory; I have shown the concreteness of its core by demonstrating that the abstract attributes of the various virtues and vices are not the ultimate but only the proximate core of Dante's figural allegory—which in turn figurally represents, severally or jointly, the Three Persons of the Trinity.

These virtues and sins can be taken on three different allegorical planes: (1) as independent entities ascribed to no particular persons either human or divine; (2) as attributes of human beings; and (3) as attributes of the divine being. The first of these three positions is taken in the reading of the *Commedia* as a personification allegory, while either the second or the third position can be taken in its figural reading. The first position is incompatible with the central tenet of Christian ontology, since it exalts abstract entities as the ultimate reality. This is one of the overriding reasons that forbid all personification reading of the *Commedia* and dictate its figural reading. The second position would indeed encourage a figural reading, but would render the *Commedia* an epic of humanity rather than that of divinity. This is roughly the direction in which Robert Hollander moves by emphasizing the role of universal history in his figural reading of the *Commedia*.

The role of humanity and its universal history are indeed important in the *Commedia*, but they should be taken as the proximate core of its figural sense rather than its ultimate core, if we are to preserve the *Commedia* as an epic of divinity rather than converting it into an epic of humanity. Thus, the third position alone is left as a viable way of reading the *Commedia*, since it alone regards the virtues and sins in Dante's three worlds as figural representations of the virtues and actions of the Three Persons of the Holy Trinity. It is this figural reading that I have systematically presented in my *Fragile Leaves of the Sibyl*.

The table of virtues and vices that is used as the ground plan for the construction of the Inferno, the Purgatorio, and the Paradiso constitutes the ladder of grace for Dante's descent and ascent. This triple ladder of grace consists of two sections, the natural and the supernatural. The seven natural virtues and their contraries become the seven rungs of the natural section; the three supernatural virtues and their contraries become the three rungs of the supernatural section. The natural section of the ladder is used for separate representations of the Three Persons in the following figural schema: the first and second rungs (humility and mercy) for the Son; the third and fourth rungs (meekness and fortitude) for the Spirit; and the fifth, sixth, and seventh rungs (liberality, temperance, and chastity) for the Father.[54] The supernatural section of the ladder is used for combined representations of the Trinity in the following figural schema: the eighth rung (faith) for the Son with the Father; the ninth rung (hope) for the Spirit with the Father; and the tenth (love) for the Father with the Son and the Spirit.[55]

Even such attentive readers as Hollander may have received the misleading impression that the ultimate objective of my Dante book is to clarify the topography of virtues and vices in the three realms of Dante's other world.[56] But this clarification is only a means, a methodic framework, to provide a systematic figural reference to the *Commedia* as a whole. Without such a systematic framework as mine, the figural interpretation of Dante's epic always turns into an arbitrary succession of fragmentary illuminations of one scene after another, one episode after another, in the endless course of which Dante's vision in its totality is likely to recede farther and farther into obscurity.

I had better once more stress the indispensability of a systematic procedure for reading Dante's allegory. The ad hoc procedure is liable to produce tangled trails of allegorical interpretation, whose unreliability can be well described by the German word *Holzweg*, a meandering trail in a deep forest, which usually leads a lost traveler to a clearing but seldom out of the forest. We may have the Auerbach trails, the Barelli trails, the Croce trails, the Dunbar trails, the Hollander trails, the Singleton trails, etc., and some of them may even lead to one of the clearings, each of which may be claimed by some to be the center of the entire forest. But, unfortunately, any clearing may appear to be the center to anyone who can command no overview of the entire forest. Thus, without a systematic framework that can assure a comprehensive perspective for the entire *Comedy*, one can easily become lost in a maze of tangled trails, which is no less distressing than getting lost in the *selva obscura*.

The traditional reading of Virgil and Beatrice as personification allegories is another case of fragmentary interpretation that can be rounded out only in a systematic figural framework. It is sometimes feasible to see Virgil as a personification of Reason, because he is a figure of the Son, whose attribute is Wisdom or Reason; it is also sometimes feasible to see Beatrice as a personification of Revelation, because she is a figure of the Holy Spirit, in whose province lies the function of Revelation. Nevertheless, as long as one remains on this abstract personification level, one has mistaken the proximate core of Dante's allegory for its ultimate core.

Now it should be instructive to compare my figural program for the interpretation of the *Commedia* with that of the Auerbach-Singleton school. We have already seen that Auerbach's own program has two elements: (1) the carnal sense of Dante's epic must be construed as historically true; and (2) its spiritual sense must be construed as figural allegory rather than personification allegory. He wants to maintain the indispensability of both elements even at the expense of reversing figure and fulfillment.

Singleton is as emphatic as Auerbach in maintaining the historical truth of the carnal sense, but he is willing to accept some personification allegory along with figural allegory on the level of spiritual sense (e.g. Virgil does sometimes represent Reason). In our discussion of Dante's letter to Can Grande, we entertained the possibility that his fourfold scheme in that letter may consist of both figural and personification allegory on the level of spiritual sense. Singleton understands Dante's fourfold scheme in this hybrid form when he takes it as Dante's own explanation of the nature of his allegory in the *Commedia*.

Singleton's hybrid version is a considerable revision of Auerbach's approach, which leaves no room for personification allegory on any level of interpretation. Robert Hollander subscribes to Singleton's revised version rather than Auerbach's original program, eagerly admitting other kinds of allegory than that of figuralism for the *Commedia*.[57] Faithfully accepting the personification allegory of Beatrice as Theology or Revelation and Virgil as Reason, Hollander is also intent on finding their figural references, thereby fully acknowl-

edging "the mixture of the two kinds of allegory."[58] He also assumes
that the moral sense in Dante's allegory belongs to the abstract
allegory of personification.[59]

Hollander's unique stand in the furtherance of Auerbach's figural
program is his insistent stress on the importance of relating the
figural references of the *Commedia* to the secular tradition. This
persistently shows up in most of his ingenious figural interpretations,
for example, the comparison of *Inferno* 1 and 2 to Aeneas's shipwreck
in the *Aeneid* 1, and that of *Paradiso* 2 to Jason's voyage.[60] His performance almost counterbalances that of Singleton, whose chief
concern has been to elucidate Dante's figural references to the
sacred tradition.

In the *Divina Commedia* the two traditions of the sacred and the
profane are, in fact, pronounced to be two complementary features of
one universal history: I have already stressed this point as an expression of Dante's universal spirit in *The Fragile Leaves of the Sibyl*.
Hollander's truly remarkable contribution lies in rounding out
Dante's vision of universal history by illuminating its secular dimension, which is usually overshadowed by its sacred dimension in most
commentators' exegeses. He appropriately calls the central chapter
of his book "The Roots of Universal History."[61] His secular-oriented
figural reading may long remain as durable a guide for Dante
readers as Singleton's sacred-oriented one.

My identification of Dante's Virgil as a figure of Christ should
have been welcomed by Hollander in his secular-oriented figural
interpretation of the *Commedia*. But he has not given it serious thought
in his reading of my book. Instead, he proposes the hypothesis that
Virgil is a figure of John the Baptist.[62] This hypothesis is a natural
consequence of accepting the Auerbach-Singleton thesis that Beatrice
is a Christ-figure: Virgil may appear as the preparation for the coming of Beatrice just as John the Baptist was for the coming of Christ.

In support of this hypothesis, Hollander cites Dante's first words in
describing Virgil, "Quella fonte / che spandi di parlar sì largo
fiume" ("that fountain which pours forth a river of speech").[63] Then
he entertains the idea that this "river of speech" may be figurally
related to the River Jordan for John's baptism. Unfortunately, he
fails to see that what cannot fit into this apparently neat figural
schema is the most important phrase in Dante's description of Virgil,
quella fonte. Dante calls Virgil not simply a river of speech, but its very
fountain. This metaphor of the fountain, especially in conjunction

with that of a river, has long enjoyed the unique function of representing God, the fountain of all creation, in Christian Neoplatonic thought. It is this Neoplatonic metaphor that led Augustine to describe Christ as the Word of God, that is, the fountain of wisdom (*De trinitate*, bk. 15, chap. 11). It would simply be sacrilegious to use that metaphor in describing the role of the Baptist.

So Virgil's preparation of Dante for the coming of Beatrice should be understood as a figural representation of the mission of the Second Person in preparing for the mission of the Third Person. Perhaps in order to avoid any misunderstanding of this figural relationship, Dante presents both Virgil and Beatrice as the agents of salvation, as Hollander carefully observes:

> The last words of Dante concerning Virgil (*Purgatorio* xxx, 51) are these: "Virgilio a cui per mia salute die'mi" ("Virgil, to whom I gave myself up for my salvation"). And, contained in Dante's last words to Beatrice are these: "O donna . . . che soffristi per la mia salute / in inferno lasciar le tue vestige" ("O lady . . . who for the sake of my salvation bore the leaving of thy footprints in Hell") (*Paradiso* xxxi, 79–81).[64]

Mia salute (my salvation) is the common element that appears in Dante's last words to both Virgil and Beatrice. We should once more repeat Hollander's astute observation that Dante does not lightly use the word *salute*. For it is the crux of the Christian *Credo* that the agents of salvation are none other than the Three Persons of the Holy Trinity.

The one feature that revisionists Singleton and Hollander share with their master Auerbach is their insistence on the historical truth of the *Commedia* on the level of literal sense. Evidently, Singleton and Hollander believe that the first of the two elements in Auerbach's program is far more important than the second: they assume that the historical truth of literal sense is the sine qua non of figural realism. In diametrical opposition to these revisionists' position, I dismiss as inessential the first element in Auerbach's program and retain the second as the only essential one. I fully grant the fictitious character of Dante's epic on the level of literal sense, but always insist on finding the figural interpretation of every passage on all three levels of spiritual sense. Whenever I find any personification allegory in any part of the poem, I assume that the interpretation in question is bound to be only provisional or proximate.

In my figural program, all three spiritual senses revolve around the Three Persons of the Holy Trinity: the allegorical sense is the figural representation of their works in this world (the macrocosmic dimension); the moral sense is the figural representation of their works in the individual soul (the microcosmic dimension); and the anagogical sense is the figural representation of their works in the Kingdom of Heaven (the supracosmic dimension).

My thoroughgoing figuralism is not meant to neglect the significance of the poem on its carnal (literal) level. On the contrary, the literal sense of the poem should be stressed as the very foundation on which the superstructure of spiritual senses stands. Furthermore, figural allegory assures the existence of sufficient allegorical residual, whose chief function is to remind us that the poem as a carnal entity has its own independence and can never be exhausted by any assemblage of spiritual readings. This perpetual tug-of-war between the carnal and the spiritual senses, which may be called allegorical dissonance, is the same kind of simultaneous relation of attraction and repulsion or dependence and independence as one can find in St. Thomas's conception of the natural and the supernatural orders, in the musical relation of the tenor (lower voice) and the upper voice(s) in the organum, or in the medieval interaction between the Empire and the Church. It is this inner tension (war of love and love of war) that gives Dante's work its unique vitality and its inexhaustible fascination.

After reading through my systematic figural interpretation of the *Commedia* and generously calling it "a grand design," Kenelm Foster says, with his usually astute perception, "There are obscurities in the *Comedy* which resist—I would rather not say contradict—the critic's system [i.e. my interpretative system]."[65] These resistant obscurities are precisely the manifestations of the struggle between the carnal and the spiritual senses of the poem. They can be generated neither by a wrong-headed interpretation that can produce a patent contradiction with the text of the poem, nor by a superficial interpretation that can assure a hollow harmony with it. It is only a profound interpretation that can induce and sustain the perpetual tug-of-war in question. So allegorical obscurity functions just like Socratic ignorance: its presence can be distinctly seen only beneath a penetrating illumination.

We may call my figural program of interpretation figural fictionalism or poeticism in order to distinguish it from Auerbach's figural realism. Figural poeticism is precisely the way St. Bernard reads the

Song of Solomon in his *Sermons*. This is why I said that his *Sermones in cantico canticorum*, along with his other works, constitute a "chief model for the architectonic construction of Dante's *cantica* of divine love."[66] In truth, it is almost impossible to think of a more appropriate model for the composition of Dante's own *cantica* of divine love than the *Canticum canticorum* as explicated in St. Bernard's *Sermons*.

In the *Commedia* Dante gives clear enough pointers toward his own conception of poetic figuralism. First, Dante the poet is welcomed into the elect company of the classical poets in the Noble Castle (*Inf.* 4. 101). Then, in the Heaven of the Sun he is accepted into the sacred school of theologians by virtue of his being with Beatrice, around whom the circles of theologians revolve (*Par.* 10. 65 ff.). By this joint affiliation with poets and theologians, he is asking us to understand the *Commedia* as a fusion of the allegory of poets (fictionalism) and the allegory of theologians (figuralism)—that is, his work is a theological poem. It is perhaps to stress the importance of understanding the dual nature of his poem that Dante assigns Solomon, the father of all theological poems, the role of explaining the equal importance of body (carnal sense) and soul (spiritual sense) in human nature (*Par.* 14. 34 ff.).

In my reading of the *Commedia* I have spared no effort in trying to peel off every layer of its rind and to find its innermost figural sense.* In this I have followed Meister Eckhart's advice: "If you want the kernel, you have to break the shell" (Sermon 11).[67] I have adopted my figural program not as an end in itself but as the necessary means for grasping the ultimate signification of the *Commedia*. With my conviction of the inseparability of form and content, I have assumed that there can be no other way into the sanctum sanctorum of Dante's allegorical domain than that of figural understanding. Thus, by simply following this figural path to the innermost core of Dante's allegory, I have, at the same time, come to see the Trinity as the epic hero and as the ultimate spiritual sense of his epic. I am now convinced that his *Divina Commedia* is the finest embodiment of Bonaventure's exemplarism in its figural mode, which enables us to see God not only *through* but also *in* the mirror of divine reflection.

*In his appraisal of the various efforts made to interpret the *Commedia* figurally, Hollander singles out "one German and one American" for special praise (p. 18). I was disappointed to find that he had not even recognized *The Fragile Leaves of the Sibyl* as an endeavor toward the figural reading of the *Commedia*—in truth, the only comprehensive and consistent reading to this day. That the consummation of the figural reading of the *Commedia* may take even one Korean may be seen as an eloquent testimony to the universality of Dante's genius.

2

The Dionysian Tout Ensemble

Petrarch on the Mount of Allegory

In the opening lines of his famous letter "The Ascent of Mount
Ventoux," Petrarch explains his motive for climbing that mountain:
"My only motive was the wish to see what so great an elevation had
to offer."[1] The verb *to see* in this sentence may appear to contain only
a literal sense to any casual reader; Petrarch may seem to be interested only in the physical view from the mountain top. However,
Petrarch's literal account of the ascent becomes progressively loaded
with allegorical meaning.

Probably the first sign of intruding allegorical signification is given
in Petrarch's description of the mountain as "a very steep and almost
inaccessible mass of stony soil" and his recitation of the moral: "But,
as the poet has said, 'Remorseless toil conquers all.' "[2] Then he goes
on to explain how, in the first stage of the ascent, his brother took a
straight path up the ridge while he himself got lost three times in the
valleys because he was looking for an easier path. The allegorical
significance of this passage may easily be lost on those unacquainted
with Petrarch's concern about his choice of a secular career in contrast to his brother's entering the monastic life. But immediately
following this passage, Petrarch establishes a definite allegorical
frame of reference for his ascent:

> I finally sat down in a valley and transferred my winged
> thoughts from things corporeal to the immaterial, addressing
> myself as follows: "What thou hast repeatedly experienced to-
> day in the ascent of this mountain, happens to thee, as to many,
> in the journey toward the blessed life. But this is not so readily
> perceived by men, since the motions of the body are obvious and
> external while those of the soul are invisible and hidden. Yes,

50

the life which we call blessed is to be sought for on a high eminence, and straight is the way that leads to it. Many, also, are the hills that lie between, and we must ascend, by a glorious stairway, from strength to strength. At the top is at once the end of our struggles and the goal for which we are bound. All wish to reach this goal. . . . Thou certainly dost ardently desire. . . . What, then, doth hold thee back? Nothing, assuredly, except that thou wouldst take a path which seems, at first thought, more easy, leading through low and worldly pleasures. But nevertheless, in the end, after long wanderings, thou must perforce either climb the steeper path, under the burden of tasks foolishly deferred, to its blessed culmination, or lie down in the valley of thy sins, and (I shudder to think of it!), if the shadow of death overtake thee, spend an eternal night amid constant torments.[3]

Petrarch calls his ascent of the mountain and his wanderings in the valleys "the journey toward the blessed life." This journey seems to be loaded with allegorical resonances of Dante's journey. In the first canto of the *Commedia*, Dante the pilgrim struggles to climb a delectable mountain (*dilettoso monte*) only to run into the obstacle of the three fierce beasts. At the moment of despair, however, Virgil appears on the scene to rescue him and takes him through the valleys of sin and death and then to the top of Mount Purgatory.

When we compare Petrarch's journey with Dante's, we can immediately detect the former's divergence from the latter. Petrarch's mountain is a real one that can be located on a map, whereas Dante's cannot be so located. Petrarch does not run into any allegorical beasts; his wandering through the valleys is his own choice. He does not wait for the arrival of some heavenly aid, but makes it all on his own to the top of the mountain once he has decided to put an end to his dawdling.

Once on the top of Mount Ventoux, the divergence of Petrarch's behavior from Dante's becomes even more dramatic. It is impossible to speculate upon what Dante would have done on top of the delectable mountain since he never got there. But when he reaches the top of Mount Purgatory, he is enthralled with the beauty of the Terrestrial Paradise and Beatrice's Procession unfolding therein. When he enters the Terrestrial Paradise, he leaves the entire domain of earthly concerns completely behind and below him. Hence his last act just before admission into the Terrestrial Garden is to bid farewell to Virgil, symbol of the earthly or natural existence.

On reaching the mountain top, Petrarch says, he stood momentarily stunned. The source of this moving experience is the view, not of the mountain top or what goes on there, but of what lies below. He sees the clouds under his feet and the snow-capped Alps far away; they remind him of the skies of Italy, which in turn provokes in him a violent desire to see his friend and his native land. This chain of perception, association, and provocation shows how his attention is shifting from the external to the internal (feeling) world. Forgetting the stunning view for a while, he engages in another soliloquy, in which he reviews his spiritual struggle of the past ten years. He admits that his struggle is far from over and that his heart has become a battleground for the struggle between his love of this world and that of the other world. He says, "These two adversaries have joined in close combat for the supremacy, and for a long time now a harassing and doubtful war has been waged in the field of my thoughts."[4]

When Petrarch wakes from this meditation as though from a sleep, he is seized with the idea of looking into Augustine's *Confessions* and opens it at random. His eyes fall on the following passage: "And men go about to wonder at the heights of the mountains, and the mighty waves of the sea, and the wide sweep of rivers, and the circuit of the ocean, and the revolution of the stars, but themselves they consider not."[5] Thereupon Petrarch becomes ashamed and angry with himself for having admired earthly things and forgotten the cardinal lesson that there is nothing wonderful or great outside the soul. So he decides to shift his gaze from the external to the internal world and descends Mount Ventoux in a silence of embarrassment.

This last soliloquy of Petrarch's is a complete reversal of his first. During the ascent he tries to see the physical journey as an allegorical representation of his spiritual journey, but he is compelled to reject this possibility once he experiences the view from the top. This dramatic reversal is caused by the violent clash of his experience with his expectation. Since his expectation has been cast in the Dantesque mold, the reversal may be considered the Petrarchan repudiation of the Dantesque sensibility.

"The Descent from Mount Ventoux" would have been a more revealing title than "The Ascent of Mount Ventoux." Petrarch makes the ascent in the Dantesque sensibility, which he hopes will give him the blessed unity of his inner and his outer worlds. Instead of this blessed unity, however, he experiences an uncomfortable disunity once he reaches the mountain top. He believes that the Augustinian sensibility which preaches this disunity has been proven true by his experience, while the Dantesque sensibility which assumes its contrary has proven false. Hence the ultimate consequence of the entire journey is to reject the Dantesque sensibility and to assert the Augustinian sensibility in its place.

What precisely is the reason for the violent clash between the Augustinian and the Dantesque sensibilities? The clash in question may be explained in terms of the dialectic between the inner and the outer, or the spiritual and the corporeal. The Dantesque sensibility stands on the premise that the corporeal world can be used as an allegorical medium for portraying the spiritual world, and Petrarch expresses this point in the opening lines of his first soliloquy during the ascent of Mount Ventoux: "What thou hast repeatedly experienced today in the ascent of this mountain, happens to thee, as to many, in the journey toward the blessed life. But this is not to be so readily perceived by men, since the motions of the body are obvious and external while those of the soul are invisible and hidden." The essence of the allegorical sensibility is to portray what is invisible and hidden through what is readily visible and external. Hence the allegorical sensibility requires a certain degree of consonance or parity between the inner and the outer, the spiritual and the corporeal. But Saint Augustine is too obsessed with the inner world to accept this parity.

Augustine is the saint of Christian interiority. His famous *noverim te, noverim me* (*Sol.* 2. 1)—"to know thee, to know myself"—clearly shows his ultimate concern. He conceives his God and his soul only as interior realities; all he wants to know is these two and nothing else. He is a master of soliloquy, the most appropriate form of discourse for the interior man; even his *Confessions* is no more than a series of soliloquies. In *De magistro* (On the Teacher) he argues that the only teacher the soul can have is its Interior Teacher. The two cities in *De civitate dei* (The City of God) are meant to be understood not as external or political institutions but as spiritual or internal realities. One of the main reasons for his vehement stand against the Pelagians may have been the latter's emphatic concern with the exterior world; *De civitate dei* was written partly as one of the many treatises against the errors of the Pelagians.

It is this obsession with his own interiority that prevents Augustine from overcoming his sickly attitude toward the bodily world, and that makes it difficult for him to accept the doctrine of the Incarnation. He eventually accepts it and acknowledges the goodness of the Creation, but he does it as an act of faith rather than out of true conviction. To the bitter end of his life, Augustine never seems to have succeeded in cleansing his sensibility of the taint of Manicheanism.

In his deprecation of the world of flesh and his exaltation of the world of spirit, Augustine believes, he is true to the spirit not only of the Christian but also of the Platonic tradition. But there are really two sides to the Platonic tradition as well as to Christianity: there is the Plato of exteriority as well as the Plato of interiority. His *Republic* is a treatise on the nature of the state as well as on that of the soul. His interest in cosmology is as intense as his interest in psychology. Despite its emphatic belief in the immortality of the soul and the mortality of the body, the true Platonic spirit is not to exalt spiritual reality at the expense of corporeal reality, but to bring the latter into harmony with the former and to maintain their delicate balance.

Two Streams of Platonism

With its emphatic stress on interiority, Augustine's Platonism is very much like that of Socrates, who was so obsessed with the life of his soul that he became almost indifferent to the life of his polis. Augustine is likely to have inherited this rather one-sided Platonism from the Cynics and the late Stoics. It may be safe to call his Platonism "dualistic Christian Platonism." If Augustine is regarded as the chief medium for the transmission of the dualistic wing of Christian Platonism, Pseudo-Dionysius may be considered the chief source for the transmission of its monistic wing. Through his erroneous identification as *Dionysius Areopagita* throughout the Middle Ages, he was believed to have been one of St. Paul's disciples, and his writings carried an immense authority, almost like that of the Bible. It is now generally believed that he was a disciple of the fifth-century Platonist Proclus (A.D. 410–85).[6]

Proclus' unique contribution to Neoplatonism was to provide a dialectical account for its doctrine of emanation. His dialectical method is highly mathematical. A competent mathematician in his own right, he wrote a fine commentary on Euclid's *Elements of Geometry*, which is now believed originally to have been his lectures given at the Platonic Academy in Athens.[7] When he wrote *The Elements of Theology*, he stuck to the Euclidean format of enumerating propositions and their demonstrations.[8] So he predates Spinoza in adopting the geometrical method by about twelve hundred years.

Proclus may not fully live up to the rigorous ideal of the geometric method, but his acceptance of it introduces a decisive feature to Neoplatonism. As E. R. Dodds says, Plotinus's *Enneads* are not and were not meant to be, either individually or collectively, an orderly exposition of a system, because they were a collection of occasional essays or lectures.[9] He also points out that even the works of Porphyry and Sallustius do not present Neoplatonism as a coherent system and that these works were written for the purpose of ethical persuasion rather than logical demonstration. He further says that Proclus's *Elements of Theology* is the only systematic exposition of Neoplatonism that has come down to us. It is an austere logical treatise, just like a mathematical proof, containing little for moral persuasion or spiritual edification. It is this chilling, austere spirit of logical demonstration that constitutes Proclus's method of a priori deduction.

In the prologue to his *Commentary on the First Book of Euclid's Elements*, Proclus discusses the metaphysical implication of mathematical objects and methods. He stresses the Platonic notion that mathematical objects occupy an intermediate position between the intelligible and the sensible spheres by partly sharing the attributes of both.[10] Then he notes that the two features of the mathematical procedure— namely, the analytic and the synthetic processes—resemble the two features of the Neoplatonic cosmic movement—namely, the "progression" from the One and the "reversion" to the One.[11] From these two propositions naturally follows the conclusion that the mathematical procedure is eminently suited to rendering a dialectical account of the Neoplatonic cosmology. This conclusion becomes the principle that governs Proclus's construction of his *Elements of Theology*.

Since Proclus adopts the mathematical notion of mediation, his dialectical logic turns out to be a triadic movement. This triadic logic comes into dramatic contrast with Augustine's logic. Because Augustine emphatically stresses the chasm between the inner and the outer, his logic tends to be a dyadic affair. Proclus's triadic logic is the fountainhead of Hegel's logic of both/and; Augustine's dyadic logic is the fountainhead of Kierkegaard's logic of either/or. The former is a logic of continuity; the latter, the logic of discontinuity. The former implies a monistic view of the self and the world, and the latter a dualistic one.

The contrast between the logic of continuity and that of discon-

tinuity shows up not only in the relationship between the interior
dimension of human existence (the soul) and its exterior dimension
(the world), but also in the relationship between God and his creation. The latter relation takes the form of necessity ("The emanation of the world from the One is a necessary process of diffusion")
for the logic of continuity, and the form of contingency ("The
creation of the world is a contingent act on the part of God in his
absolute freedom") for the logic of discontinuity.

This contrast, which may be regarded as two opposite ways of
accounting for "progression," is naturally expected to show up in
two opposite ways of accounting for "reversion." In the logic of
continuity, the soul has the inherent power to make the flight to, and
become one with, the One. In the logic of discontinuity, the soul is
inexorably faced with the unfathomable gulf between itself and God.
Reflecting these two modes of relation with God, Christian mysticism
consists of two distinct traditions. One of these may be called the
mysticism of meditation; the other may be called the mysticism of
ecstasy. The former is to endure in the anguish of longing for God;
the latter is to exult in the ecstasy of union with him. The former
is exemplified by Peter Damian and Bernard of Clairvaux; the latter
was enjoyed by Meister Eckhart and St. Teresa of Avila. The
mysticism of ecstasy is inspired by the Proclusian logic of continuity;
the mysticism of meditation is encouraged by the Augustinian logic
of discontinuity.

Augustine's theory of human knowledge comes in as a handy
case to illustrate this contrast a little further. He accepts the Platonic
doctrine that the human mind can behold eternal ideas, and this
seems to create a grave problem for him, since he believes that these
eternal ideas are in the mind of God and constitute its essence. So
Augustine appears to be committed to an un-Christian view that the
human mind in its cognition of eternal ideas becomes identical with
the divine essence. This is generally called "ontologism."[12] Quite
often Augustine has been subject to the charge of ontologism, and
sometimes he talks so casually and so imprecisely as to invite this
charge. But this casualness and carelessness reflect, more than anything else, his gnawing sense of the immense gulf between the human
mind and the divine essence.

In his logic of discontinuity, Augustine's constant problem is not
that one may get too close to God, but that one may never get close
enough to him. So he never feels the need to guard himself against the

kind of careless language that has invited the charge of ontologism. On the contrary, he is far more concerned with the problem of finding the extraordinary means of bridging the immense gulf between man and God. Thus, his emphatic accent falls on his doctrine of grace, the only means for overcoming the Augustinian chasm.

If one really wants to find clear enough statements that can exonerate Augustine from the charge of ontologism once and for all, one can find them easily in many of his works. One typical example of these statements can be found in his *De trinitate*, book 15, chapter 9, where he says that the inner word of the human mind is only an obscure image of the Divine Word, the locus of eternal ideas. That is, the human mind never comprehends eternal ideas directly, but sees only their obscure copies.

So Augustine's God is never the God of immanence but always the God of perpetual transcendence. For this reason, he has been the most formidable authority for those Christians seeking the transcendent God in defiance of immanentism. For example, Martin Luther always invoked the authority of St. Augustine in his battle against Renaissance immanentism.

As the logic of disjunction, Augustinian logic is well suited to the rejection of this world for the sake of the other. In fact, Augustinian logic served well as the logic of renunciation, or contempt of this world, for the medieval Christians. As the logic of conjunction, Proclusian logic cannot easily allow the disjunction of this world from the other world, but must dictate the acceptance of both. Hence Proclusian logic has been a useful instrument for the manifestation of secular concerns since the Carolingian Renaissance.

To dualistic Augustinians, Proclusian monism may appear to be devoid of interiority since it lacks the interior dimension that is completely shielded from the exterior world. Hence the Proclusians, from Joachim of Floris to Hegel, have sometimes been branded as champions of exteriority who are ostensibly pitched against the champions of Augustinian interiority. But this label is more or less an expression of the Augustinian revulsion toward monism. Strictly speaking, Proclusian monism is not any more devoid of interiority than it is of exteriority, because interiority and exteriority constitute the two sides of Proclusian triadic schema.

Pseudo-Dionysius and Christian Neoplatonism

I have gone into all these details to set up the dialectical framework for the interplay of the Augustinian and the Pseudo-Dionysian wings of Christian Platonism. I have used Proclus rather than Pseudo-Dionysius himself because the logic of continuity is not so readily visible in the latter as in the former. Pseudo-Dionysius could not accept the Proclusian metaphysical framework outright and still remain within the fold of Christian orthodoxy, since Proclusian monism is alien to the notion of a personal God and his free creation of the world. Nonetheless, it is the spirit of Proclusian logic that inspires all his works, *De divinis nominibus* (On the Divine Names), *De caelesti hierarchia* (On the Celestial Hierarchy), *De ecclesiastica hierarchia* (On the Ecclesiastical Hierarchy), *De mystica theologia* (On the Mystical Theology), etc. As M.-D. Chenu says, the concept of *hierarchia* and *ordo* is the keystone of the Dionysian system.[13] I suppose that this concept of *ordo* and *hierarchia* is Pseudo-Dionysius's adaptation of Proclusian monism.

John Scotus Erigena of the ninth century was the first man in the Latin West to attempt the systematization of Pseudo-Dionysian ideas; his *De divisione naturae* was a metaphysical rendition of the Pseudo-Dionysian idea of the hierarchy of beings. It is quite instructive to note that John Scotus's attempt was made during what is generally known as the Carolingian Renaissance. Naturally his work was condemned by the Church for its heterodox tendency. While Pseudo-Dionysius himself managed to escape censure by avoiding the language of Proclusian metaphysics, John Scotus almost invited it by formally adopting that language. Pseudo-Dionysius himself remained uncondemned partly because of the immense authority he enjoyed through his mistaken identity. Nonetheless, the condemnation of John Scotus had the natural consequence of reinforcing the position of the Augustinian wing of Christian Neoplatonism as the official spokesman for Christian orthodoxy in the Latin West. Gilson and a few other historians attach such enormous significance to this condemnation that, without it, they speculate, the development of the Latin West would have taken quite a different course.[14]

But the condemnation of John Scotus did not turn out to be the destruction of the Dionysian wing of Christian Platonism. Since the Dionysian wing was a dialectical counterpart of the Augustinian wing, the former could not be eliminated as long as the latter was retained as an orthodoxy. With the condemnation, as Gilson says, the Pseudo-Dionysian wing, and especially John Scotus Erigena, became the undercurrent of the Latin West.[15] I will go a little further and propose the hypothesis that the development of the Latin West after the ninth century may be viewed as a dialectical interplay between the Augustinian upper current and the Dionysian undercurrent. Although I cannot here substantiate this hypothesis, I will try to show how the flowering of allegorical sensibility during the twelfth and thirteenth centuries drew its main impetus from the steady ascendency of the Dionysian undercurrent. In this attempt I will partly rely on the patient labors of the brilliant historian M.-D. Chenu.

One of the fascinating books to mark the twelfth-century Renaissance is Bernard Sylvester's cosmological treatise, *De mundi universitate* (On the Universe of the World). The title of the book itself is intriguing because it reflects the revival of the ancient notion of the universe (*universitas*) as a unitary entity. As Chenu points out, it was John Scotus Erigena who had initiated this revival: "Universitatem dico Deum et creatum" ("by 'universe' I mean God and creation"; *De divisione naturae*, 2. 1).[16] The novelty of this was to view God and the various grades of his creation as the well-ordered constituents of one systematic universe.* This picture of reality was a metaphysical implementation of Pseudo-Dionysius's notion of universal hierarchy. This hierarchical conception of the universe rapidly gained a great popularity during the twelfth century, and *De mundi universitate* was one of the many works inspired by this novel idea. Chenu says:

> From the middle of the century on, the 'hierarchial' conception of the universe would cast over men's minds a spell comparable to that cast by the scientific *mythos* of evolution in the nineteenth century. The key to the understanding of the universe, and of man in the universe, was taken to be the ordered, dynamic, and progressive chain of all beings—a chain in which causality and meaning fall together, and in which each being is a "theophany," a revelation of God.[17]

The Dionysian cosmology exults in the order and beauty of the world. This produces a notion quite contrary to the orthodox Christian notion of the *contemptus mundi*, when order and beauty are

---

*In *De divisione naturae*, John Scotus Erigena recognizes four levels of being or reality (*natura*): (1) that which creates but is not created (*natura quae creat et non creatur*); (2) that which is created but creates (*natura quae creatur et creat*); (3) that which is created and does not create (*natura quae creatur et non creat*); and (4) that which neither creates nor is created (*natura quae nec creat nec creatur*). These four levels constitute one hierarchical chain for the *egressus* and *regressus* of the divine power.

extended to the mundane world. Chenu says that this extension is brought about by the followers of Gilbert of La Porrée, the Porretani, who go even far beyond John Scotus Erigena:

> Under the influence of Platonic ambivalence prone to see matter as an unmitigated force of disorder, John the Scot supposed that God had not originally intended his creative power to descend as far down the scale as corruptible matter, and that the subsequent descent of that power followed upon a defeat or fall. Man had been intended to have a spiritual body only, without animal needs. As against this projection of sin onto the cosmos, the masters of the twelfth century, resting their case on the interpretation given the *Timaeus* and the pseudo-Dionysian hierarchy at Chartres, proclaimed that the possibility of participating in the divine reality belonged expressly to matter as well as to everything above it.[18]

According to Chenu, the Platonism of the *Timaeus* that thrived at Chartres was inspired by the Pseudo-Dionysian cosmology.[19] The *Timaeus* available in the twelfth century was Chalcidius's translation, which omitted that part of the dialogue concerning man. Through this omission, Chenu says, the *Timaeus* became eminently suitable for the Pseudo-Dionysian monistic cosmological outlook. The highlight of this Chartres cosmology is to preach the order and the beauty of this mundane world.

It is this Pseudo-Dionysian cosmic sensibility that produces the most fascinating man of letters of that century, Alan of Lille. A disciple of Gilbert of La Porrée, Chenu says, he took intellectual nourishment from the *Timaeus* and from Proclus.[20] In his *De planctu naturae* (The Complaint of Nature), Alan of Lille exalts the position of Dame Nature as "Child of God and Mother of Things." This exaltation was in tune with the worship of ladies in the tradition of courtly love on the one hand, and the adoration of the Blessed Virgin on the other. This Dionysian elevation of the feminine principle presents a dramatic contrast to the Augustinian denigration of it. Since Augustine identified femininity with the flesh, the corporeal, and the corruptible, he felt obliged to downgrade it while exalting masculinity, which he identified with the spirit, the incorporeal, and the incorruptible. Of course, this neatly fit into his logic of exclusion and discontinuity.

In *Anticlaudianus de antirufino*, Alan of Lille pursues his argument for the goodness of Nature to the end. As Ernst Robert Curtius says, this work is not a refutation but rather a counterpart of Claudian's poem *In Rufinum*.[21] Rufinus was an odious evil genius, who became Theodosius's all-powerful minister. Curtius goes on to say, "Over against this utterly evil Rufinus, Alan, in his *Antirufinus*, sets the ideal man." If Rufinus is the model for humanity as an object of contempt, Antirufinus is its model as an object of wonder. The former (though a pagan creation) happens to dramatize the medieval conception of man as the creature of original sin and depravity; the latter is a forerunner of the Renaissance concept of man as the greatest wonder of all creation.

Alan's works embody a new poetics, in which the scientific and the literary sensibilities are fused into one integral whole. This new poetics is inspired by the Proclusian mathematical sensibility and may be called the Pseudo-Dionysian poetics. Alan's famous geometric description of God as an intelligible sphere whose center is everywhere and whose circumference nowhere, is sufficient to show his Proclusian sensibility. He calls his *Anticlaudianus* a scientific poem and a *summa* of seven *artes* (sciences). Since he brings together all the accomplishments of human science and art in his poem, he rightly deserves his title of the *Doctor universalis*.

Alan of Lille does not limit his Pseudo-Dionysian cosmic sensibility to the portrayal of Nature but extends it to the account of the Trinity, in his *Regulae caelestis iuris*:

> Unity begets unity from itself, from itself produces equality. So God exists from nothing, and each person exists from him, so he begets a second self, that is, the Son; and from himself he produces one equal with himself, that is, the Holy Spirit. . . . In the Father is Unity, in the Son Equality, in the Holy Spirit the bond of Unity and Equality.[22]

As Chenu says, this is meant to be Alan's restatement of Augustine's account:

> Thus there are the Father, the Son, the Holy Spirit, and each is God, and at the same time all are one God; and each of them is a full substance, and at the same time all are one substance. The Father is neither the Son nor the Holy Spirit; the Son is neither the Father nor the Holy Spirit, the Holy Spirit is neither the Father nor the Son. But the Father is the Father

uniquely; the Son is the Son uniquely, and the Holy Spirit is
the Holy Spirit uniquely. All have the same eternity, the same
immutability, the same majesty, and the same power. In the
Father is unity, in the Son equality, and in the Holy Spirit a
concord of unity and equality. [*De doctrina christiana*, bk. 1,
chap. 5][23]

As Chenu points out, the concluding sentence of this passage is
almost identical to the concluding sentence of Alan's restatement.
The striking divergence between the two versions appears in what
Augustine and Alan respectively start out with. Whereas Augustine
begins with three distinct Persons of the Holy Trinity, Alan begins
with the One (*unitas*) and then traces the generation of the Second
and then the Third Person from it. The latter account is an attempt to
restate the doctrine of the Trinity in Proclus's dialectical language of
emanation.

The Pseudo-Dionysian sensibility even invades the school of
Saint-Victor, the twelfth-century stronghold of Augustinian Pla-
tonism. Hugh of Saint-Victor writes a commentary on the *Celestial
Hierarchy*. Chenu observes:

> It is fascinating to watch the Augustinian Hugh of Saint-Victor
> at work commenting on the *Celestial Hierarchy*: not only did he
> have to purge from it all taint of emanationism, but he made a
> desperate effort to hold on to the ontological naturalism found
> in the work while at the same time preserving a personal, free
> and freely given relationship between the soul and God as
> envisioned in Augustinian theology with its "inward" em-
> phasis.[24]

Godfrey of Saint-Victor adopts the idea of man as a microcosm from
the school of Chartres, and writes his *Microcosmos* in the language of
the Fathers rather than in that of the physical scientists at Chartres.
Most important of all, the entire school of Saint-Victor becomes
permeated with Dionysian optimism rather than Augustinian pes-
simism.

The acceptance of the Dionysian spirit in the framework of Augustinian orthodoxy becomes most prominent in the conception of
universal history. Augustine compared the history of mankind to the
growth of a single individual (*De civitate dei*, bk. 10, chap. 14). A host
of twelfth-century theologians try to implement this suggestive idea

of Augustine's in their periodization of universal history.[25] Whereas Augustine intended his metaphor of maturation solely for the description of sacred history, the twelfth-century theologians extend it to the entire history of mankind. For example, Hugh of Saint-Victor exploits the Augustinian schema of periodization in establishing an integral relation between sacred and secular history: he sees a continuity, not only between the history of the Bible from Adam to Christ and the history of the Holy Roman Empire, but also between the latter and the history of ancient Rome.[26] Thus the Roman Empire comes to take on a significant role in the history of salvation. This Dionysian view of Roman tradition is in outright contradiction to Augustine's own venerable view. The traumatic experience of witnessing the sack of Rome, which provoked him to write his *City of God*, had convinced Augustine that the Roman Empire, along with Assyria, was a vivid embodiment of the City of Babylon.

The new conception of universal history resolved the dualism in Augustine's idea of the two cities. This dualism is twofold. First, there is the conflict between the two cities. Then, there is the tension between the inner realities of these two cities in the heart of the human soul and their external manifestation in political and social institutions. The Dionysian conception of universal history not only places the earthly city within the fold of the heavenly city, but also considers the universal city or empire as both a spiritual and a political entity. In spite of his even temperament, Chenu cannot conceal his astonishment at this drastic transformation of Augustine and exclaims: "This was political Augustinianism—unfaithful to Augustine!"[27]

The transformation in question is really an anti-Augustinian revolution in the guise of an Augustinian move. The Augustinian schema for the periodization of world history appears only as a casual observation in Augustine's own thought, which is dominated by the perpetual battle between the *corpus christi* and the *corpus diaboli*. The Dionysians of the twelfth century projected this rather peripheral idea in Augustine to the forefront of their own thought, thereby shifting the arena of revelation and sanctification from the souls of individual Christians to the history of mankind. It was through this anti-Augustinian revolution that Christianity began to be reconceived as the religion of the world-historical progress.

The Dionysian concept of Christian history received its consummate formulation at the hand of Rupert of Deutz. In *De sancta trinitate et operibus eius* (On the Trinity and its Works), he states his view of the three world "weeks"; that is, the entire history of mankind is divided into three periods: (1) the time of the Father (Creation) from the creation of the world to the fall of Adam; (2) the time of the Son (Salvation) from the Fall to the Crucifixion; and (3) the time of the Holy Spirit (Sanctification) from the Resurrection to the end of the world. In this, Rupert of Deutz reduces the customary six or seven ages to three, each of which is further divided into seven parts. What is unique to him is his linking of the three major periods to the Three Persons of the Holy Trinity for their proper works or functions. It is this correlation that is emphasized even in the title of his book.

The revolutionary feature of Rupert's thought is his Trinitarian schema. From the time of the Church Fathers, it had been the usual practice to divide history into two periods, which roughly corresponded to the Creation by the Father and the Redemption by the Son. In spite of some differences in the demarcation of the two periods, the second period had almost unanimously been assumed to last until the end of the world. This had been especially the case with the twofold division of history corresponding to the Old and the New Testaments. In the meantime, the role of Sanctification by the Holy Spirit had been conceived of as the final phase in the vertical schema of the soul's ascent to God. Rupert of Deutz transfers this final phase in the vertical schema to the horizontal schema of world history and transforms it into the age of the Holy Spirit, which is to succeed the ages of the Father and the Son. This exaltation of the Third Person makes its historical function truly coequal with those of the First and Second Persons of the Holy Trinity. Hence Rupert's achievement may be called the Revolution of the Spirit. Only with this revolution are the prodigious significance of the Holy Spirit and its role fully appreciated for the first time in the history of Christianity.

The Revolution of the Holy Spirit is the radical movement of Dionysian immanentists. Whereas Dionysian transcendentists expect to achieve the full sanctification of their souls by transcending this world, Dionysian immanentists are confident in witnessing it as the final phase in the development of this world. What has been a spiritual movement with the former now becomes a secular movement with the latter. It is again this Dionysian immanentism that Joachim of Floris propounds in his famous triadic schema of universal history: the Age of the Father, the Age of the Son, and the Age of the Holy Spirit. The doctrine of the three states (*status*) presented in his *Concordia veteris et novi testamenti* (The Concordance of the Old and the New Testaments) is very much like that of Rupert of Deutz except in the demarcation of the three ages. Whereas Rupert of Deutz regards the Fall as the demarcation point between the first and the second ages, Joachim of Floris moves this point from the Fall to the Incarnation. In Joachim's schema, the traditional demarcation between the two epochs of the Old and the New Testaments is retained as the demarcation between the reign of the Father and the reign of the Son. In defiance of the traditional belief that the epoch of the New Law is to last to the end of the world, however, Joachim proclaims that the reign of the Son is to be succeeded by the reign of the Spirit, which will see the establishment of the Kingdom of God on earth.

The proclamation of this new and final age is the radical element that Joachim of Floris boldly injects into the Trinitarian schema of universal history. Furthermore, he makes this proclamation in an urgent tone of great expectation, by claiming that the Age of the Holy Spirit has been in preparation for a long time and is about to burst forth into the open. This claim becomes the clarion call to take the spirit of Christianity out of the monastic cloisters into the open world. The Benedictine notion of building walls against the world to create a shelter for a true religious life had been dictated by the Augustinian logic of discontinuity; the Joachimian notion of tearing down the monastic walls was inspired by the Dionysian logic of continuity. Of course, the Joachimian sensibility prepares for the emergence of the new breed of this-worldly monks, the Franciscans and the Dominicans.

Joachim of Floris transforms the traditional figural view of Biblical history in accordance with his doctrine of the three ages. In the traditional view, the Old and the New Testaments are believed to stand in the relation of figure and fulfillment. To this dyadic schema Joachim adds the third stage; the reign of the Spirit will be the final fulfillment for which the reign of the Son is only a figure, just as the reign of the Father is for the reign of the Son. In this maneuver, the *anagogia* of fourfold allegory is transferred from the vertical to the horizontal scale and the traditional dyadic schema of historical figuralism is expanded into the Joachimian triadic schema. This triadic schema is the framework of the Trinitarian figuralism which Joachim works out in his *Liber figurarum* (Book of Figures). This fabulous work becomes the fountainhead of the Trinitarian figural sensibility that comes to full bloom in Bonaventure and Dante.

If 'universalism' is an appropriate label for the Dionysian sensibility, 'particularism' is a suitable one for the Augustinian sensibility.* Augustine's logic of discontinuity becomes his logic of election and exclusion. He believes that only Israel is a chosen tribe while all others are condemned, that only the Bible records sacred history while all other books are records of profane history, and that only the Church is a divinely instituted organization while all other institutions are excluded from divine guidance. In contrast to this, the Dionysian wing believes that Israel is only a member (albeit a special one) of the entire human race, that the history of Israel is only a part (of course, a special part) of universal human history, and that, the Church is only a segment (albeit an especially exalted one) of the cosmic hierarchy.

This is a brief sketch of the overpowering influence of Pseudo-Dionysian Neoplatonism during the twelfth century. But we may find some unmistakable signs of its emergence even during the

---

*Augustinian particularism and Dionysian universalism constitute the two dialectical poles in the internal struggle of medieval Christendom. The historical development of Christendom since the Middle Ages can be viewed as a further continuation of this thematic dialectic. The Protestant Reformation may be regarded as the revolt of Augustinian particularism against Dionysian universalism; the particularism of the Reformers appears to be fully manifested in the proliferation of their sectarian movements.

In her battle against the Reformers, the Catholic Church was led to adopt her own version of particularism. The Counter-Reformation can be viewed as the proclamation of Catholic particularism. The Catholics' *sola ecclesia* ("*extra ecclesiam nulla salus*—outside the Church there is no salvation") embodies the logic of exclusion as adamantly as the Reformers' *sola fide* ("salvation comes through faith alone"). After the Council of Trent, furthermore, the authority of the Catholic Church comes to be almost identified with that of the pope rather than with that of the council. The conciliar conception of Church authority appears to embody universalism; the papal conception of it, particularism.

The ecumenism of Pope John XXIII should be understood as an attempt to revive the spirit of universalism; with Vatican II, the council started to regain some of its long-lost authority for the first time since the Counter-Reformation. Furthermore, the spirit of Pope John's ecumenical movement was to seek reconciliation and eventual reunion with "the separated brethren": "The Counter-Reformation is over" was the favorite slogan of the radicals at Vatican II.

The resurgence of universalism among the Protestants appears to be most emphatically heralded by Dietrich Bonhoeffer. His theology of "religionless Christianity" can be construed as his rejection of the logic of particularism that has excluded the secular from the sacred. The same spirit of resurgent universalism appears to underlie the recent position the World Council of Churches has taken in recognizing the validity of the other great religions of the world, which have long been condemned as institutions of idolatry or superstition by Christian orthodoxy.

eleventh century. Let us take the two cases of Anselm of Canterbury and the rise of nominalism.

As a faithful follower of Augustine, Anselm is generally believed to have been immune to Dionysian influence. According to Joseph Pieper, the name of Dionysius the Areopagite is mentioned only once in the entire body of Anselm's works, and this is no way to pay a tribute to the Areopagite.[28] If one carefully reflects on the general format of Anselm's *Proslogion*, however, one is bound to have second thoughts. The format of this celebrated work is to deduce the divine attributes one after another, and even his renowned ontological proof of divine existence is presented as the logical deduction of the first divine attribute. This format appears to be an adaptation of that of Pseudo-Dionysius's *De divinis nominibus*, which is to enumerate the various divine names and to discuss the different modes of their signification. In Anselm's work, to be sure, the divine names are replaced by the divine attributes, but this replacement is quite natural because Pseudo-Dionysius's divine names are the names of divine attributes.

Furthermore, Anselm of Canterbury brings about the shift of interest from the domain of words (what the divine names signify) to that of things (what divine attributes can be demonstrated). This entails the shift of emphasis from the negative to the positive phase in Dionysian theology. As Pieper points out, Anselm's unique contribution lies in stressing positive theology, and this positive tendency may appear to be in sharp conflict with Dionysius' emphasis on negative theology. But this shift from the negative to the positive side is the most decisive hallmark of the Dionysian ethos that governs the twelfth-century Renaissance, and Anselm may very well have been one of the first Dionysian pioneers to initiate this shift of emphasis.

The most striking feature of Anselm's thought is his penchant for deductive rationalism, which is dramatically manifested in his celebrated ontological proof. In his *Proslogion* Anselm does not limit his deductive demonstration to the attribute of divine existence but extends it to all other divine attributes. He will go even further and claim that even such Christian mysteries as the Incarnation and the Trinity can be demonstrated by necessary reason. This is surely against the Augustinian spirit, but clearly in tune with the dialectical spirit of Proclusian logic.

Perhaps the most celebrated philosophical event of the eleventh century is the emergence of Roscelin's nominalism, namely, the claim

that names are mere external labels which can never capture the
unique essence of an object. This nominalism appears to be nothing
but Roscelin's transference of what Pseudo-Dionysius says about the
divine essence to finite objects. So the debate between the nominalists
and the essentialists (realists), the scholastic debate par excellence,
may be regarded as a battle between the Dionysian and the Augustinian wings of Christian Platonism. St. Augustine has often been
quoted, in this debate, as the foremost champion of essentialism. For
example, St. Thomas accepts the Platonic doctrine of the divine ideas
on the authority of St. Augustine, even at the expense of destroying
the integrity of his Aristotelianism (*Summa theologiae*, pt. 1, q. 15, aa. 1
and 2). At the same time he is fully aware that this goes against the
teaching of Pseudo-Dionysius: the acceptance of divine ideas as a
part of the divine essence is incompatible with the unity and the
simplicity of God. When Meister Eckhart claims that God has no
ideas, needs none, and surely despises all ideas, he invokes the authority of Pseudo-Dionysius (Sermon 1).

The real picture of the medieval debate between the essentialists
(realists) and the nominalists is a little more complicated than this,
chiefly because Dionysian universalism can easily swallow up Augustinian particularism as a moment in its vast system. In the case of
divine ideas, the Dionysians can still accept them not as a part of the
divine nature but as a phase in the universal emanation. In this
spirit of accommodation, John Scotus Erigena accepts the divine
ideas as the second division of "nature (the universe)," that is, created
and yet eternal. In spite of this complication, it is known as historical
fact that Dionysius and Augustine have been regarded as the champions of the two respective camps.

Even the enthusiastic introduction of Aristotelianism and Averroism into the Latin West appears to have been prepared and
consolidated by the emerging Dionysian ethos. Obviously, Aristotelianism and Averroism are in harmony with the Dionysian ethos. Albert the Great, who was a principal instrument for this movement,
appears to have been an enthusiastic Dionysian Platonist. As Joseph
Pieper points out, Albert wrote commentaries on all the Areopagite
writings, with the firm belief that the Holy Spirit itself was their true
author.[29] *Expositio in dionysium de divinis nominibus* is one of the important works that St. Thomas, Albert's star disciple, wrote during his
formative years (probably 1258–65). On this task he spent a long
period of about seven years. In addition to this, Joseph Pieper says,

there are more than seventeen hundred quotations from Dionysius the Areopagite in the works of the Angelic Doctor.[30]

The Aristotle that came to the Latin West was not the Hellenic original but the Arabian version of it. This version had already been assimilated into Arabian Neoplatonism, which shared many features with Dionysian Neoplatonism. This is probably why the introduction of Aristotle into the Christian West was championed by such a great electic Platonist as Albertus Magnus.

The Gothic culture of the thirteenth century may be regarded as a systematic attempt to tame the rampant Dionysian ethos beneath the Augustinian yoke. Of course, in the vanguard of this battle were the followers of St. Francis and St. Dominic, the new breed of monks who had emerged into the open world. In theology, the taming of the Dionysian ethos assumes two forms, that is, to reinforce the sagging authority of the Augustinian yoke, and to impose the old yoke on the new bull. St. Thomas takes the latter course, while St. Bonaventure takes the former.

St. Thomas takes the bull of Aristotelianism and Averroism by the horns and brings it firmly under the Augustinian yoke, which is his demarcation between the natural and the supernatural orders. This demarcation is alien to Aristotelianism; the only demarcation in the Aristotelian cosmology is the one between the sublunary and the superlunary world. The Thomistic distinction between the natural and the supernatural orders is Aquinas's adaptation of the Augustinian logic of discontinuity.

To the casual observer, the effort of St. Bonaventure may appear to be a straightforward attempt to buttress the sagging authority of Augustinian Platonism. But in this process of reinforcement he injects a heavy dose of Pseudo-Dionysian ethos into the Augustinian corpus. Let us take his distinguished work, *Itinerarium mentis in deum* (The Journey of the Mind to God). This journey is described in two extended metaphors, the ladder for ascent to God and the mirror for divine reflection. Bonaventure makes use of three elements in the construction of the divine ladder and the divine mirror: (1) the vestige of God (*vestigia dei*), (2) the image of God (*imago dei*), and (3) the name of God (*nomen dei*). He further divides each of these into two phases of *per* and *in*. For example, God can be seen first *through* (*per*) his vestige and then *in* (*in*) his vestige. Thus the journey turns out to be climbing six steps of the divine ladder, or seeing God in six successive mirrors.

The entire journey may appear to be purely Augustinian, chiefly because Bonaventure's key terms, such as *vestigia dei, imago dei*, and *nomen dei* can all be traced back to Augustine. In fact, the format of *Itinerarium* can be traced back to books 11 through 14 of Augustine's *De trinitate*. In book 11, Augustine shows how the Trinity is reflected in the material or external world (*vestigia dei*). In books 12 through 14, he explains how the Trinity is reflected in the human soul (*imago dei*). When these four books of *De trinitate* are compared with Bonaventure's *Itinerarium*, the divergence of the latter from the former is obvious. While Augustine assigns one book to *vestigia dei* and three books to *imago dei*, Bonaventure not only gives equal emphasis to both but also establishes a firm continuity between the two. This surely reflects his acceptance of the Dionysian sensibility.

The third element in Bonaventure's journey, the mirror of divine names, cannot be traced back to Augustine's *De trinitate*. So we have to assume that this element comes from Dionysius's treatise, *De divinis nominibus*. The introduction of this third element carries the Bonaventurian journey way beyond the Augustinian gulf between the soul and God; this is surely a Dionysian flight. Bonaventure concludes this flight with his recitation of Pseudo-Dionysius's mystical utterance:

> As for you, my friend, in regard to mystical visions, with your course now well determined, forsake sense perception and discursive reasoning, all things visible and invisible, every non-being and every being; and, as much as possible, be restored, naked of knowledge, to union with the very One who is above all created essence and knowledge. Thus, in the boundless and absolute rapture of the unencumbered mind, above yourself and above all things, leaving all and free from all, you will rise to the super-essential radiance of divine darkness. [*Itinerarium*, chap. 7, sect. 5][31]

The metaphors of the ladder and the mirror which Bonaventure uses throughout his *Itinerarium* have their roots far deeper in the Dionysian ethos than in the Augustinian one. The metaphor of the ladder embodies the Dionysian idea of *hierarchia* and manifests the Dionysian logic of continuity. So it is definitely a Dionysian product. The metaphor of the mirror is a little more complicated. Augustine says that the human soul (*imago dei*) is an obscure mirror of the Trinity, but Bonaventure extends the metaphor of the mirror to the material world (*vestigia dei*). This extension comes about from the acceptance of the Dionysian view that every creature, spiritual or material, is a theophany of God. Of course, the same is true of his extension of the same metaphor to the divine names. Bonaventure's distinction between the two modes of the divine reflection (*per speculum* vs. *in speculo*) again shows the influence of the Dionysian ethos. Since Augustine insists on the obscurity of the divine reflection in the mirror of the *imago dei*, he appears to recognize only the *per speculum* mode. If so, the *in speculo* mode appears to come from the Dionysian sensibility.

The most prominent mark of the Dionysian infusion into Bonaventure is, however, the ever-present triadic schema in his works. As I have already said a few times, Augustine's logic is dyadic, a structure which is clearly manifested in his conception of the two cities (*De civitate dei*). The logic that is operative even in his treatise on the Trinity is still the dyadic logic of discontinuity, insofar as the soul's relation to God is concerned. But it is the triadic logic of continuity that enlivens most of Bonaventure's works. Obviously this triple rhythm of Bonaventurian sensibility is a Proclusian legacy.

The Journey of the Mind to God is Bonaventure's supreme work as a Dionysian transcendentist. His thought as a Dionysian immanentist is also governed by the same Trinitarian structure, but Bonaventure the immanentist has been rather overshadowed by Bonaventure the transcendentist. Joseph Ratzinger has recently done a remarkable deed in drawing our attention to this usually neglected side of Bonaventure. He shows that, in the *Hexaemeron*, Bonaventure appropriates the tripartite view of history developed by Joachim of Floris in his *Concordia veteris et novi testamenti*.[32] He says that as a Franciscan, Bonaventure shared the common belief of his order that St. Francis was not simply another saint but a sign—or rather the John the Baptist—of the final age, sent by God.[33] In this vein of Dionysian immanentism, Bonaventure conceives of even mysticism as a historical development of the divine revelation rather than as an individual act of contemplation and intuition apart from the historical manifestation of God.[34]

The irony of the entire historical development is that St. Bonaventure, presumably a straightforward champion of Augustinian Platonism,* wound up with the indelible triadic sign of the Proclu-

*That Bonaventure is a straightforward champion of Augustinian Platonism is perhaps the most firmly entrenched premise in Bonaventure scholarship. Most works about him

sian logic, while St. Thomas, accused of disrespecting the authority of St. Augustine, emphatically stamped his works with the dyadic sign of the Augustinian logic. It was chiefly this dyadic sign of the Augustinian orthodoxy that induced the Council of Trent to take up Thomas Aquinas rather than Bonaventure as its theological weapon for the Counter-Reformation—that is, the battle against the Lutherans, who had initially opened their campaign of restoration with the Augustinian bugle call.

Allegory of Words and Allegory of Things

The two traditions of Christian Platonism have produced two distinct types of theology. Adopting Chenu's labels, we shall characterize the Augustinian theology as the theology of "signs" and the Dionysian theology as the theology of "symbols."[35] According to Augustine's theory of signs, signs are for the external manifestation of the interior movement of the soul. External words, which are heard or read, are the signs not of things but of internal words (*De trinitate*, bk. 15, chap. 11). Thus the soul can reflect on the divine nature only through the working of its internal words, which obscurely reflect the Divine Word.

---

have numerous references to Augustine but only a few to Pseudo-Dionysius, and even these few are seldom quite essential. For example, the index to Gilson's *Philosophy of St. Bonaventure* lists thirty references to Augustine and three references to Pseudo-Dionysius. If we take another example in J. F. Quinn's exhaustive study, *The Historical Constitution of St. Bonaventure's Philosophy*, its index shows no fewer than four hundred and twenty-three references to Augustine and no more than fifteen references to Pseudo-Dionysius. In contrast to this, St. Bonaventure in his own writings seems to refer to the works of the Areopagite as often as to those of Augustine. This point is roughly borne out by José de Vinck's faithful editorial work in establishing Bonaventure's nonscriptural references in *The Works of Bonaventure*, 5 vols.

The Gilsonian interpretation of Bonaventure has been challenged by F. Van Steenberghen (cf. *Aristotle in the West*, pp. 89 ff. and 147 ff.). He has shown that the study of Aristotle was one of the integral features of the standard preparation for students going into the faculty of theology in Paris during the time of Bonaventure, and that Bonaventure's theology should be understood as Augustinizing Aristotle rather than as repudiating Aristotle for the sake of Augustine. This challenge to Gilson still remains within the camp of "Bonaventure the Augustinian," since it is a dispute on the question of whether Bonaventure's Augustinianism should be understood as exclusive or inclusive of Aristotelianism.

Joseph Ratzinger is one of the rare Bonaventure scholars who have seriously tried to identify the influence of Pseudo-Dionysius on Bonaventure (cf. *The Theology of History in St. Bonaventure*, pp. 88 ff.). But unfortunately he does not make the extensive claim that the Dionysian sensibility is the chief inspiration for Bonaventure's entire outlook. To the best of my knowledge, no Bonaventure scholar has yet proposed the epithet "Bonaventure the Dionysian."

If the Augustinian theology is called the theology of words, the Dionysian theology should be called the theology of things.* The Creation is a theophany, a manifestation of the hidden divine essence, which in itself (without such a manifestation) cannot be known even to God himself. Every object in the world is a "symbol" of the ultimate divine reality. Hence the entire universe takes on a sacramental texture, and cosmology in this sacramental perspective becomes one with soteriology. Hence the separation between the knowledge of the soul and that of the world becomes inadmissible for the Dionysian sensibility. For example, Bernard Sylvester's *De mundi universitate* is a treatise on the nature of the world and of the soul at the same time. This is the Dionysian way of *scientia*, diametrically opposed to the Augustinian way of *sapientia*, which emphatically exalts knowledge of the interior depth of the soul over and above knowledge of the external world.

The Dionysian idea of theophany becomes common currency in the metaphor of "mirror" during the twelfth century, and from then on the word *speculum* becomes one of the most popular elements in many book titles, for example, *Speculum naturae* (Mirror of Nature), *Speculum historiae* (Mirror of History), *Speculum astronomiae* (Mirror of Astronomy), etc. It is this conception of the divine mirror that underlies the vast works of lapidaries and bestiaries—in other words, even stones and beasts reflect the divine glory.

So the difference between the theology of things (*res*) or their symbolic function, and the theology of words (*verba*) or their signatory function, rests on the difference between the mirror of things and the mirror of words. The Augustinian mirror of words provides the medium for the allegory of words; the Dionysian mirror of things provides the medium for the allegory of things.

The contrast between the theology of words and the theology of things shows up in the difference between the two conceptions of the sacraments. According to the universalistic Dionysian view, Chenu

*The centrality of words to Augustinian Neoplatonism may very well reflect the tradition of Roman rhetoric in which Augustine grew up. He imbibed his share of Platonic ideas chiefly through the works of such Roman rhetoricians as Cicero and Seneca; rhetoric is the art of words par excellence. The emphasis on things in Dionysian Neoplatonism may in turn reflect the tradition of geometric reasoning which Pseudo-Dionysius inherited from Proclus. In addition to logical precision and clarity, the outstanding feature of geometric reasoning is its intimate connection with space or the physical world. In traditional geometry, every definition requires spatial or physical instantiation and every proof can be given a spatial or physical illustration. For this reason, the distinction between pure and physical geometry remained quite unimportant until recently.

says, the entire cosmos takes on a sacramental character, producing the "sacralization of the seasons, hymns to the day and night, the multiplication of blessings for profane objects."[36] According to the particularistic Augustinian view, the sacraments are the special remedies instituted by the divine authority for the healing of fallen man and administered by the priestly utterance of some magic words. The former is a positive view of the sacraments, whose power resides in the goodness of creation. The latter is a negative or remedial view of the sacraments, whose raison d'être lies in the evil of the world.

The medieval doctrine of transubstantiation is a mixture of these two views, in which the sacrament of things—the transformation of bread and wine into the flesh and blood of God—plays only a subservient role to the sacrament of words—the pronouncement of *Hoc est enim corpus meum* ("For this is my body") and *Hic est enim calix sanguinis mei* ("For this is the chalice of my blood"). In their attempt to be even more true to the Augustinian spirit than the Catholics, the Reformers came to reject all traces of the sacrament of things and to accept only the sacrament of words.

Since Augustine chiefly relies on the mirror of words rather than that of things, he attaches extraordinary significance to the Bible, a record of the revealed Word. Hence the Augustinian theology is tantamount to a Biblical theology. The Dionysians are compelled to incorporate this Biblical theology into their theology of things; so Bernard Sylvester regards the entire universe as a single volume for the revelation of the divine nature and glory. Following Bernard Sylvester, Alan of Lille says, "Every creature in the world is, for us, like a book and a picture and a mirror as well."[37] In this scheme of the universal revelation, the Bible is only one part (albeit a special part) of the universal volume.

What is amazing in this current of thought is that even Hugh of Saint-Victor, a stout champion of the Augustinian wing, is swept off his feet by this idea and calls the sense world a sort of book written by the finger of God. Even St. Bonaventure comes to accept this idea of two books of revelation, one special and one general, and gives priority to the latter by saying that the special book has been given only because the general book has become illegible to the sinful man.

It is in the same spirit of universalistic revelation that Hugh of Saint-Victor and Robert of Melun recognize the continuity between Scripture and the Fathers. Joseph Ratzinger explains this point:

As Grabmann has expressed it, for Hugo, Scripture and the Fathers flow together into one great *Scriptura Sacra*. This basic orientation appears even more clearly in Robert of Melun, who distinguishes four types of *auctoritas*.[38]

The four types of *auctoritas* cover what is now known as the noncanonical writings (for example, Origen, Augustine, Jerome, etc.) as well as the canonical writings. Furthermore, the difference of these four types is meant to be a difference of degree rather than of kind. Ratzinger says that in the *Hexaemeron* Bonaventure adopts this universalistic notion of *Scriptura Sacra* developed by Hugh of Saint-Victor and Robert of Melun.[39]

The spirit of Bonaventurian universalism appears perhaps most dramatically in his historical theology. Historical theology is distinguished from "scientific" or scholastic theology. The former had been the chief model for theological writings throughout medieval Christianity until the arrival of the latter with the schoolmen. Historical theology is built on the study of historical events as recorded in the Sacred Scripture. The most prominent model in historical theology has been the interpretation of the *Hexaemeron*, that is, a series of commentaries on the six days of Creation in the opening chapters of Genesis. It is the historical or chronological order of sacred events that governs the unfolding of historical theology.

The singular feature of historical theology is that it is meant to be a theology of believing rather than of understanding, because historical events can only be "believed" and cannot be "understood." The scientific or scholastic theology emerges as a theology of understanding, which is to render intelligible to some degree what has been merely believed. For this reason, Joseph Pieper is right in calling Boethius the first scholastic for his valiant attempt to prove or demonstrate matters of faith in his *Consolation of Philosophy* and for his speculations on the Trinity.[40] It is the same scientific spirit of understanding that Anselm of Canterbury expresses in his famous mottoes, *fides quaerens intellectum* (Faith desiring understanding) and *credo ut intelligam* (I believe in order to understand), and implements in his "proofs" for the necessity of the Trinity and the Incarnation. This incipient spirit of scientific theology may very well be the descendent of Proclusian geometric theology.

Up to the middle of the twelfth century, historical theology remained the prevalent mode among the vast majority of theologians while scientific theology was attempted only by a few daring souls like Boethius and Anselm. But during the twelfth century, as Chenu says, Abelard and Peter Lombard brought about a theological revolution by abandoning the historical order as the primary principle of organization and reorganizing theological inquiries in a "scientific" framework.[41] This revolution prepared for the emergence of the *Summa* as the most colorful form of theological treatise during the thirteenth century.

Even with the emergence of scholastic theology, however, it was impossible for Christian theologians to ignore completely the historical dimension of their faith, because the ultimate locus of their faith, the Incarnation, was a historical event. Hence, according to Chenu, the urgent problem which the builders of the *Summae* faced was how to "transform sacred history into an organized science."[42] Aristotle, whose introduction to the Latin West had certainly encouraged the emergence of scientific theology, could offer no help, because the domain of history had been completely left out of the perimeter of the Aristotelian sciences. Chenu says that St. Thomas solved this problem by adopting as the plan of his *Summa* the Neoplatonic scheme of *exitus* and *reditus*—that is, the going out of all creatures from God as Creator and their coming back to him as their end:

> Part I [of his *Summa*] tells of the emanation of creatures from God as their source. Part II deals with their return to God as last end. And because God has freely and in an utterly gratuitous manner decreed that this return should be effected through Christ, Who is the Word made flesh, Part III studies the "Christian" conditions of man's going back to God. Quite obviously, it is in the Third Part, more than anywhere else in the *Summa*, that history comes to the foreground and plays its most magisterial role.[43]

Since St. Thomas relies on the Neoplatonic historical schema rather than the Biblical historical schema, his *Summa* fails to regain the original model of historical theology. In the third part, to be sure, he brings history to the foreground, but even there he simply concentrates on one privileged moment of history, the Incarnation, instead of attempting to incorporate the entire sacred history into his *Summa*. St. Bonaventure goes much further than St. Thomas in his effort to incorporate the tradition of historical theology into the new edifice of scientific theology. In his *Hexaemeron*, he reactivates the most

ancient format of historical theology and boldly assimilates Joachimism into this ancient format (cf. collation 13, sect. 2; collation
15, sect. 10). In this tour de force, he transforms historical theology
into a scientific system.

According to Joachim, the cosmic course of *egressus* and *regressus*
is identical with universal history, which is in turn coextensive with
sacred history. Since the cosmic course of *egressus* and *regressus* is a
logical or rational system, the sequence of events in sacred or universal history ceases to be a contingent and unintelligible chain and
takes on a systematic coherence and intelligibility, once these events
are understood in the cosmic context of *egressus* and *regressus*. Since
Bonaventure accepts this rational notion of history, Joseph Ratzinger
says, for him the history of the world is an infinite circle of ordered
movement, or the *circulus intelligibilis* from God through Christ to
God.[44] Ratzinger goes on to say that this Bonaventurian view of
history is Bonaventure's historical adaptation of Alan of Lille's
definition of God as the intelligible sphere whose center is everywhere
and circumference nowhere.

This conception of God as the intelligible sphere has been, perhaps,
the favorite geometric metaphor among Proclusians from Pseudo-
Dionysius through Alan of Lille (the poet of Dionysian geometric
sensibility par excellence), down to Nicholas of Cusa. In spite of the
perpetual fascination which this metaphor and other forms of
geometric thought had for Proclusians, not many of them made the
daring attempt to assimilate the apparently contingent domain of
history into the systematic mold of geometric thought. Bonaventure
belongs to this elite. His attempt to absorb sacred history into the
elegant mold of geometric thought is probably the most evident
precursor of Hegel's attempt to expand Spinoza's geometric cosmology and theology for the dialectical appropriation of universal
history.

From Theology of Allegory to Theology of Analogy

Exemplarism is perhaps the truly unique theme of Bonaventurian
theology. The exemplar, or the exemplary cause, is the model or
prototype which its copies imitate. While the resemblance of the copy
to the original is called imitatory, the resemblance of the original to
the copy is called exemplary. It is this exemplary relation that Bonaventure employs in explaining the relation of God to the cosmic

volume of his Creation. That is, the universe is like a book reflecting the divine exemplar (cf. *Breviloquium*, pt. 2, chap. 12, sect. 1; *Collationes in hexaemeron*, 12. 14). But what is intriguing is that Bonaventure's exemplarism is conceived in two different ways that may correspond to the allegory of words and the allegory of things. For the sake of distinction, let us call these two ways formal exemplarism (or exemplarism in its formal mode) and figural exemplarism (or exemplarism in its figural mode).*

Exemplarism in its formal mode is anchored in the Platonic Forms, which function as exemplars for the creation of the world. Since these Platonic Forms are the divine ideas belonging to the Second Person of the Trinity, exemplary causation is regarded as the characteristic function of the Son, while efficient causation and final causation on the cosmic scale are attributed respectively to the First and the Third Person. This point shows up in Bonaventure's frequent enumeration of the Efficient Cause, the Exemplary Cause, and the Final Cause, which are interchangeable with the Father, the Son, and the Holy Spirit.

Exemplarism in its figural mode neither requires the service of divine ideas nor has any special connection with the Second Person. For, in figural exemplarism, the Three Persons of the Trinity function jointly and equally as the ultimate exemplar for all creation. Figural exemplarism can be manifested on many different levels of existence, which Bonaventure calls the shadows, the vestiges (or traces), and the images. As an image of God, for example, the human soul consists of the three faculties of memory, understanding, and will, which exemplify the Trinity (*Itinerarium*, 3. 5). Even a purely corporeal object that can be regarded only as a trace or vestige of God consists of weight, number, and measure, which exemplify the Trinity. Every being is determined by three principles, that is, matter, form, and their union, which again reflect Three Persons.

Both versions of exemplarism are theories of resemblance. Formal exemplarism claims the resemblance of creatures to the divine ideas, and figural exemplarism, the resemblance of creatures to the Trinity itself. Figural exemplarism expresses the central notion of the allegory of things; creatures can be regarded as the mirror of things for the

---

*Most Bonaventure scholars include only the formal mode in Bonaventure's exemplarism, excluding figural exemplarism from it. For example, Gilson calls figural exemplarism Bonaventure's "universal analogy" and distinguishes it from his exemplarism (see Gilson, *The Philosophy of St. Bonaventure*, pp. 127 ff. and 185 ff.).

reflection of divine attributes. On the other hand, formal exemplarism belongs to the domain of the allegory of words. If creatures
resemble divine ideas, they can be considered as the mirror of words,
because divine ideas are divine words, or rather belong to the Word.
Thus figural exemplarism is Bonaventure's adaptation of the Dionysian allegory of things, while formal exemplarism is his extension of
the Augustinian allegory of words.*

Figural exemplarism states outright the creatures' resemblance to
the Creator, but formal exemplarism does not make this outright
claim of direct resemblance. That creatures resemble eternal ideas
or archetypes in the divine mind does not, in and by itself, assure
that the creatures resemble the Creator. This is the important difference between formal exemplarism as the theory of the creatures'
resemblance to divine ideas and figural exemplarism as the theory of
their resemblance to divine attributes. But Bonaventure's common
concern in both versions of his exemplarism is to demonstrate the
resemblance of the creatures to the Creator.

In formal exemplarism, Bonaventure assures the resemblance of
the creatures to God himself by emphatically insisting on the real
unity of divine ideas with divine essence. There appear to be many
ideas rather than one in any discourse about divine ideas, and this
multiplicity of divine ideas is obviously incompatible with the unity
of the divine mind that is claimed to contain them. Augustine himself
is fully aware of this incompatibility and sees the need to stress the
unity of divine ideas in the divine mind. But he is also fully aware of
the need to recognize their multiplicity. J. F. Quinn says, "But
Augustine also teaches that the divine ideas are eternal and un-
changeable forms; so it would seem that, for Augustine, the divine
ideas are not really one."[45] This is the Augustinian dilemma on the
divine ideas, which Bonaventure resolves by rejecting categorically
their multiplicity. For Bonaventure, as Efrem Bettoni says, the
multiplicity of divine ideas only reflects the external view of the

*There are really two kinds of Augustinian mirror: (1) the mirror of human words (or
ideas) reflecting the eternal ideas in the Divine Word, and (2) the mirror of created things
reflecting the same eternal ideas (cf. De trinitate, bk. 15, chap. 11). The former kind may
be regarded as exclusively verbal or mental. Both components of the former (i.e. the reflecting and the reflected) are made of words or ideas, while only one component of the
latter (i.e. the reflected) is made of verbal or mental elements. The latter kind can be
viewed as a hybrid of the strictly Augustinian and the Dionysian mirrors. This hybrid
type is also fully recognized by Pseudo-Dionysius in his doctrine of exemplary or archety-
pal ideas (cf. De divinis nominibus, chap. 5, sect. 8).

divine mind, that is, the view the finite mind takes in trying to understand the infinite nature of the divine mind in terms of the multiplicity of created things.[46] So the multiplicity of divine ideas is not real but only apparent.

According to Bonaventure, divine ideas are not only one with each other but also one with the essence of the Divine Word. That is, God does not simply possess divine ideas, or they are not simply located in his mind, but rather he *is* them or they *are* his mind. Through this unity of divine ideas and their identity with the divine mind, Bonaventure's exemplarism in its formal mode comes to have the same result as his exemplarism in its figural mode. To say that creatures resemble divine ideas would amount to saying that they resemble the divine mind or the Second Person, because divine ideas in their real unity are the divine mind, which is in turn the same as the Second Person. Thus Bonaventure's formal exemplarism is an indirect way of expressing what is directly stated in his figural exemplarism. Thus, the Augustinian allegory of words is assimilated into the Dionysian allegory of things in Bonaventure's exemplarism.

This assimilation of the Augustinian sensibility into the Dionysian sensibility in Bonaventure's exemplarism becomes most vivid in his doctrine of *expression*. Bonaventure calls the Son the *similitudo expressiva* of the Father, that is, the Father expresses his complete self or the sum total of his power in the Son, or rather in the totality of the divine ideas (*Collationes in hexaemeron*, 1. 13). Things are, in turn, created to express these divine ideas. Hence, the apparent multiplicity of divine ideas and the real multiplicity of created things are two stages in one continuous process of divine expression. This notion of divine expression seems to be Bonaventure's adaptation of the Neoplatonic notion of emanation; in fact, it greatly resembles John Scotus Erigena's and Alan of Lille's notion of the divine procession and creation.

When formal exemplarism is seen in this context of the divine expression, it is hardly distinguishable from figural exemplarism. Hence exemplarism in its figural mode should be taken as the central theme in Bonaventure's mystical theology. In Bonaventure's writings, in fact, formal exemplarism is quite overshadowed by figural exemplarism. It is figural exemplarism that animates most of his mature mystical works, such as *Itinerarium mentis in deum* (The Journey of the Mind to God), *De triplici via* (The Triple Way), *Lignum vitae* (The Tree of Life), and *Vitis mystica* (The Mystical Vine). These works seldom have recourse to the divine ideas; the exemplar is usually the Trinity itself.

There is one striking difference between Dionysian *anagogia* and Bonaventurian figural exemplarism. Pseudo-Dionysius is much more concerned with the One than with the differentiation of Persons; Bonaventure is chiefly intent on understanding the distinct roles of the Three Persons. In the transition from Dionysian *anagogia* to Bonaventurian exemplarism, consequently, the emphasis shifts from the One to the Three Persons as the ultimate exemplar of all things. This entails a corresponding shift of interest from negative to positive theology. As long as the One is accepted as the ultimate exemplar, the highest stage of *anagogia* remains the "darkness of unknowing" because the One allows no distinction and no knowledge. But the acceptance of the Three Persons opens up a vast new domain of positive theology because the Three Persons permit the distinction of their attributes. In short, Bonaventure places far greater stress on the immanent stage of the Dionysian *anagogia* than Pseudo-Dionysius himself.

This shift of interest with Bonaventure may be regarded as an Augustinian influence, because it is made with the acceptance of the Three Persons as the ultimate exemplar, and because Augustine clearly asserts the distinction of the Persons to be a matter of divine essence rather than of its manifestation. But the same shift of interest may also be regarded as a dialectical movement within the Dionysian camp, that is, as the emergence of a new concern with the immanent stage of *anagogia* in reaction against the old concern with its transcendent stage. This view is certainly plausible because as we have just seen, the reaction in question had already set in with the twelfth-century Dionysians and because the dialectical move can be executed within Dionysian theology, which accepts the Three Persons on the plane of divine manifestation.

These two different accounts of the change of interest are by no means incompatible with each other. In fact, they can reinforce each other, that is, the shift of interest from the transcendent to the immanent may have taken place as a dialectical development of the Dionysian *anagogia*, and the Augustinian doctrine of the Trinity may have been found to be a useful conceptual instrument for articulating this development. At any rate, what counts here is the transfer of emphasis from the transcendent to the immanent. For it is with this transfer that the Dionysian allegory of things blossoms into Trinitarian figuralism in the hands of Bonaventure, as it did in those of Joachim of Floris.

St. Bonaventure's exemplarism as a theory of divine resemblance prepares for St. Thomas's analogy of names or words. How can we use the human language, which has been developed to describe finite beings, in naming the infinite divine attributes? This is the question St. Thomas tries to answer in his theory of analogy. At the outset, he recognizes two modes of using names or words: the intrinsic and the extrinsic denominations. In intrinsic denomination, words are used to designate some attributes directly. For example, the sentence "John is healthy" directly refers to John's attribute of being healthy. In contrast to this, words used in extrinsic denomination do not directly name some attributes. For example, the sentence "This medicine is healthy" does not name the attribute of being healthy enjoyed by this medicine, but refers to the attribute of being healthy which can be induced in some persons, like John, by this medicine. The attribute of being healthy referred to by this sentence resides not in the medicine but outside it. Hence the denomination is extrinsic.

Aquinas knows that God can be named from creatures either in intrinsic or extrinsic denominations (see *De veritate*, q. 21, a. 4 ad 2). When we say "God is good" as a shorthand way of saying "God is the cause of good," we are not really naming the attribute of divine goodness in intrinsic denomination (*Summa theologiae*, pt. 1, q. 13, a. 2). In his doctrine of analogy, St. Thomas wants to justify the use of human words like *good, wise, power*, etc. in intrinsic denomination (*Summa theologiae*, pt. 1, q. 13, a. 1). This intrinsic use of human words to describe the divine attributes is precisely the problem that Pseudo-Dionysius has confronted in his *De divinis nominibus*. This problem comes to be the central concern of St. Thomas after the formative years he spent writing his commentary on *De divinis nominibus*.

St. Thomas knows that God can be named from creatures intrinsically only if God and creatures share a certain set of attributes. It is St. Bonaventure's exemplarism that assures this sharing of some common attributes between Creator and creatures. If the creatures resemble the Creator, the former can be said to share or reflect the attributes of the latter. But the resemblance between God and creatures is not simply a matter of similitude but also one of dissimilitude; the resemblance in question is precisely what Pseudo-Dionysius has called the *similitudo dissimilium* (*De divinis nominibus*, 9. 6

and 7). The *similitudo dissimilium* is a degree of resemblance too great to be contained within the Aristotelian boundaries of species and genera, and this ontological fact poses a serious semantic problem which Pseudo-Dionysius has already wrestled with in his doctrine of positive and negative theology.

It is one of the cardinal rules in Aristotelian semantics that words can retain their univocal meanings only as long as they are used to describe the similitude contained within the boundaries of species and genera.* Does our language retain its univocity when we extend it to describe the divine attributes whose similarity with finite beings surely transcends the boundaries of species and genera? Moses Maimonides of the twelfth century emphatically claimed that our language becomes completely equivocal in such an extension. This doctrine of equivocity is a restatement of Pseudo-Dionysius's designation of the Godhead as "the darkness of unknowing," which can never be fully described (negative theology) in human language but can be approached (mystical theology) only through the mystical flight of the soul.

Like St. Bonaventure, St. Thomas is too much a child of Dionysian immanentism to accept this absolutely transcendent view of God. He knows that the doctrine of equivocity would lead him into the uncomfortable position of agnosticism in which our language of theology would become only a cluster of meaningless words. Neither can he accept the doctrine of univocity, because it would fail to recognize, in its anthropomorphism, the singular disparity between God and his creatures. While the doctrine of equivocity would give us too little understanding of God (negative theology), the doctrine of univocity would give too much of it (positive theology). The former entails the absolute transcendence of God from creatures (or his complete dissimilitude from them); the latter entails his absolute immanence (or his complete similitude with them). It is to avoid these two evils of extreme that St. Thomas proposes his golden mean of analogy, that is, our language can be used in the analogical description of God. This Thomistic golden mean becomes the ladder

---

*A word is said to be univocal when it has one meaning only; for example, the word *house* means a building in which people live. A word is said to be equivocal when it has more than one meaning; for example, the word *pen* means both an instrument for writing in ink and a small enclosure for domestic animals. Univocity is the claim that our words (e.g. *being, wisdom, power*) retain the same meanings when describing human and divine atributes. Equivocity is the claim that these words have entirely different meanings in these two usages.

for the theological descent from Dionysian transcendentism to Dionysian immanentism.

Thomistic analogy can be taken either as a doctrine of names or words or as one of beings (attributes).* In the former role, Thomistic analogy is an epistemological or semantic theory. In the latter role, it is a theory of the analogical likeness between infinite and finite beings which is the ontological counterpart to the semantic or epistemological feature of Thomistic analogy. We can further clarify this ontological dimension by elaborating on St. Thomas's conception of the analogical likeness between God and creatures, or rather their proportional likeness (*similitudo ad invicem proportionum*; *De veritate*, q. 23, a. 7 ad 9).

St. Thomas distinguishes between two kinds of resemblance: the resemblance of one to another (*unius ad alterum*) and the resemblance of many to one (*duorum vel plurium ad unum*) (*Summa contra gentiles*, bk. 1, chap. 34). The resemblance of many to one is also called the resemblance of two to a third (*ad aliquid tertium*) (*De potentia*, q. 7, a. 7). The resemblance of many to one is a case of indirect resemblance involving a tertium quid; for example, two dogs may resemble each other by virtue of their resemblance with the Platonic Form of "dogness" or of their sharing the common nature of the canine species. In contrast to this indirect resemblance, the resemblance of one to another is direct and immediate, and as such allows no room for mediation by a tertium quid.

St. Thomas repeatedly claims that the analogical likeness between God and his creatures is always the direct resemblance of one to another and never the indirect resemblance of many to one (*De potentia*, q. 7, a. 7). In the latter case, as Pseudo-Dionysius points out, God and creatures would resemble each other through a superior principle of similarity which is common to both (*De divinis nominibus*, 9.6). This principle of similarity would be the tertium quid that would abrogate God's ontological primacy over all other beings, since its ontological status would be higher than that of both God and his

---

*This should not be confused with *analogia entis*, a label which modern Thomists have adopted in their exposition of Thomistic analogy. By using this label, they have tried to incorporate Gilson's thesis into St. Thomas's theory of analogy, and have claimed that the category of being or existence is the central divine attribute in Thomistic analogy. In my view, this is an unnecessary distortion. To the best of my knowledge, *analogia entis* is a label that St. Thomas seldom uses in his own exposition of analogy, and his theory of analogy is meant to be applicable to all divine attributes without any special discrimination among them.

creatures. It is this absolute unavailability of any tertium quid above God and creatures which renders it impossible to describe univocally the analogical likeness between God and creatures. The univocal likeness of creatures to each other can be described precisely because their likeness is determined by a tertium quid, such as a Platonic Form or an Aristotelian essence, which serves as the univocal meaning of a given term. The analogical likeness, which does not refer to any tertium quid as a common standard, is like the divine resemblance in Bonaventure's exemplarism in its figural mode, which directly asserts the resemblance of God and creatures without the mediation of divine ideas.

Although St. Thomas accepts the doctrine of divine ideas on the authority of St. Augustine, this celebrated doctrine plays no significant role in his theology of analogy. If divine ideas (e.g. the idea of wisdom or being) were available for the common understanding and description of both God and creatures, these ideas would assure the semantic foundation for a univocal theology, thereby forestalling the genesis of the problem of analogy. So we have to assume that the divine ideas St. Thomas does accept concern only finite entities and never infinite being; that is, the operation of these ideas is confined to the domain of the finite. In contrast to these finite ideas, those divine ideas whose operation could encompass the infinite as well as the finite might be called "infinite divine ideas." It is the absence of these infinite ideas that produces the Dionysian *similitudo dissimilium* in the relation of the finite and the infinite and creates the problem of analogy.

The exclusion of divine ideas from the domain of the infinite attributes presents an intriguing and embarrassing problem to the advocates of Platonic Ideas or Forms. According to Plato, the most essential function of an idea is its universality; for example, every instance of justice, divine or human, exemplifies and derives from one and the same Idea of Justice. The divine ideas have to lose this absolute universality as soon as they are brought to bear upon the infinite Christian God by the champions of Dionysian figural sensibility.

This development cannot take us by surprise if we bear in mind that the doctrine of divine or eternal ideas is a Hellenic legacy. With the Greeks, to be finite or definite is the very essence of being and being real; hence their way of being and being known is always anchored in the doctrine of finite Ideas or Forms, whether it takes the shape of transcendent Platonic Ideas or that of immanent Aristotelian Forms. The inadequacy of the finite divine ideas as a Christian theological instrument could be overcome by converting them into infinite ideas, but this would jeopardize the absolute sovereignty of the Christian God. The acceptance of the infinite ideas, which could stand as paradigms for both the finite and the infinite attributes, would surely relegate even God to the level of derivative realities.

To be sure, there is a way of investing eternal ideas with infinite scope without jeopardizing God's absolute ontological primacy, and this is to make all divine ideas identical with the infinite divine essence. As we have seen, this is precisely what St. Bonaventure claims in his insistence upon the real unity of divine ideas. But this absolute unity can be attained only at the expense of their multiplicity; that is, the divine ideas have to lose their distinctness from each other. Without their distinctness, the divine ideas would become totally useless as an instrument of discrimination and discourse. So the divine ideas are destined to remain a nonfunctional Hellenic legacy for Christian theologians, whether these ideas are accepted in their original finite form or are converted into their new infinite form.

Thomistic analogy emerges precisely because the divine ideas can render no help at the most critical juncture of Thomistic theology, and these ideas can be readily dispensed with without endangering any essential feature of the Angelic Doctor's theological outlook. The divine ideas are also ultimately dispensable in Bonaventure's exemplarism. As we have seen, his formal exemplarism, which relies on the divine ideas, can be reduced to his figural exemplarism, which does not require those ideas. Both Bonaventurian exemplarism and Thomistic analogy are theories of seeing and understanding the finite and the infinite beings in their immediate relation with one another rather than through the mediation of divine or eternal ideas. In this regard, they are scholastic formalizations of figural sensibility, or rather its nominalistic ontology and epistemology, which have germinated from the Dionysian theology of the *similitudo dissimilium*.

Although both Bonaventurian exemplarism and Thomistic analogy are meant to be elaborations on the Dionysian theology of the *similitudo dissimilium*, there is one fundamental difference between these two elaborations. Bonaventure's exemplarism claims the resemblance of a creature as a whole to the Creator; Thomas's analogy admits the resemblance in question only in a highly selective manner. St. Thomas distinguishes between the names of simple perfections (*perfectiones simpliciter*) and the names of mixed perfections (*perfectiones secundum quid*). Words like *being, wisdom, power,* and *goodness* are examples of the former; words like *stone, lion,* and *angel,* examples of the latter. The attributes of simple perfections are not contained within the boundaries of species and genera, whereas the attributes of mixed perfections are limited within such boundaries. The former are unlimited perfections; the latter are limited perfections. St. Thomas claims that only the names of simple or unlimited perfections can be admitted in the analogical description of divine attributes (cf. *Summa contra gentiles,* bk. 1, chap. 31; *Summa theologiae,* pt. 1, q. 13, a. 3).

The attributes of simple perfections are contained in the creatures that are referred to by the names of mixed perfections, for example, the attribute of being or goodness is contained in the things that are called lions or stones. This concrescence of simple and mixed perfections in creatures renders it possible to name God from the creatures, because God embodies simple perfections in the most eminent way. But this analogical description of divine attributes requires the careful process of discriminating the names of simple perfections from those of mixed perfections in the language of the creatures, because the names of mixed perfections can never be analogically attributed to God. St. Thomas says that the attribution of mixed perfections to God is only a metaphorical usage of our language (cf. *Summa contra gentiles,* bk. 1, chap. 30).

The discrimination of simple perfection from mixed perfection is the refinement that St. Thomas introduces into Bonaventure's exemplarism. Instead of making this sort of discrimination, Bonaventure views every creature, in its concrete whole or in its concresence of both simple and mixed perfections, as a mirror of the Trinity. For example, every finite being reflects the Trinity because its three principles of form, matter, and their union correspond to the Three Persons. St. Thomas would never allow any perfection inherently connected with matter or its union with form into the domain of his analogy, because such a perfection would be surely a mixed perfection rather than a simple one.*

---

*Using Cajetan's distinction, Bonaventure's exemplarism may be called the analogy of improper or metaphoric proportionality, while Thomistic analogy may be called the analogy of proper proportionality. But the former expression has a built-in ambiguity; the metaphoric use of a word like *lion* in naming God may be assumed to contain either only

The names of simple perfections are really coextensive with the Dionysian divine names. Hence we can recognize three distinct stages in the development of Dionysian theology. In the first stage, Dionysius concerns himself with the semantic problem of divine names (what do we mean by these names?) and ends up stressing the negative way. In the second stage, Bonaventure tries to shift the emphasis from the negative to the positive way, by establishing the semantic ground of divine names allegorically in the names of creatures. In the third stage, Aquinas refines this Bonaventurian semantic maneuver by discriminating the names of simple perfections from the names of mixed perfections, since the names of creatures include both.*

Since St. Thomas admits only the names of simple perfections, he has to abstract these attributes from the concrete wholeness of the creatures. It is this abstraction that gives Thomistic theology a much more precise and definite mode of reasoning and expression than Bonaventurian theology. Gilson expresses this point:

> Where the reader expects syllogisms and formal demonstrations, St. Bonaventure usually offers him only correspondences, analogies and conformities, which seem to us hardly satisfactory but which seem to satisfy him entirely. Images cluster together in his thought and follow one another indefinitely, evoked by an inspiration the logic of which is far to seek, so that even neoscholastic philosophers and theologians turn nowadays with a sigh of relief to the clear and succinct expositions of St. Thomas.[47]

But this Thomistic refinement in precision and definiteness is accomplished with the loss of the concreteness of Bonaventurian mystical theology. In contrast to the abstract attributes of simple

---

the lion's mixed perfections, or both its simple and mixed perfections. If the metaphoric usage is taken in the latter, or rather inclusive, sense, the analogy of improper proportionality would contain more than the analogy of proper proportionality. If the same usage is taken in the former, or rather exclusive, sense, the analogy of improper proportionality would contain nothing of what is employed in the analogy of proper proportionality. It is this ambiguity that has generated and sustained the debate on the similarity vs. dissimilarity of the two analogies of proportionality (e.g. Ralph M. McInerny, "Metaphor and Analogy," *Sciences Ecclésiastiques* 16 (1964): 273–89; J. F. Quinn, *The Historical Constitution of St. Bonaventure's Philosophy*, pp. 468 ff. and 482 ff.).

*This final stage can also be characterized as the derivation of the Dionysian divine names from Bonaventurian exemplarism, and as such it can establish the continuity between the first two mirrors (*vestigia dei* and *imago dei*) and the last mirror (*nomen dei*) in Bonaventure's *Itinerarium mentis in deum*.

perfections in Thomistic analogy, St. Bonaventure in his *anagogia* always employs the mirror of creatures in their concrete wholeness. That is why I have, in the last chapter, called St. Bonaventure's a theology of allegory in distinction from St. Thomas's theology of analogy. In spite of this difference, both theologies belong to the grand tradition of the Dionysian theology of "progression" and "reversion," or "ascent" and "descent." Of his doctrine of analogy, St. Thomas says:

> This clearly brings out the truth that, as regards the assigning of the names, such names are primarily predicated of creatures, inasmuch as the intellect that assigns the names ascends from creatures to God. But as regards the things signified by the names, they are primarily predicated of God, from whom the perfections descend to other things. [*Compendium theologiae*, 27][48]

As a ladder of ascent and descent, the theology of analogy belongs to the Dionysian mirror of things as much as the theology of allegory does.

Dionysian Allegorical Realism

It is the Dionysian mirror of things that anchors the raging allegorical sensibility of the twelfth century. When Bernard Sylvester champions the allegorical reading of pagan literature, he is merely extending the way of reading his own *De mundi universitate*—that is, the allegorical reading of the whole universe—to pagan literature. This Dionysian allegory of things has a tendency to ignore the intrinsic role of words, while recognizing only their instrumental role of designating things in their allegorical context. This Dionysian stance becomes widespread and even invades the Cistercian fortress, where Bernard of Clairvaux becomes so obsessed with the allegorical senses of the *Song of Songs* that he completely discounts its literal sense.

This rampant tendency to disparage the meaning of words in their own right naturally provoked a violent protest from the Victorines, the twelfth-century custodians of the Augustinian theology of words. Hugh and Richard of Saint-Victor insist on the primacy of the literal sense of the Bible and make it their cardinal rule never to yield easily to its allegorical interpretation alone.

In spite of this fictitious tendency on the literal plane, the Dionysian allegory is insistent on the *reality* of its allegorical core. This principle of allegorical realism, which is quite obvious in works portraying the transcendent reality, also governs the composition of allegorical works dealing with such an immanent reality as Nature or Man. That is, the hidden reality of Nature or Man is the ultimate object which these allegorical works try to capture through the various, partial projections or reflections of that hidden reality. For example, Bernard Sylvester allegorically portrays, in *De mundi universitate*, Nature as the partner of Noys in the ordering of Chaos, and Alan of Lille further elaborates on this allegorical device in *De planctu naturae*. In either case, the personification of Nature is made in imitation of the reflection and diffusion of the One in the universe. Nature in her depth and totality is not available for direct confrontation and intuitive inspection, just like the reality of the Creator, and this hidden reality of Nature demands her allegorical representation.

This allegorical principle of diffusion and projection is rendered explicit in the *Romance of the Rose*. When the Dreamer comes to the Fountain of Narcissus, he says that he can see a vivid reflection of the Garden in the Fountain. But he emphatically points out that none of the reflections shows the entire Garden at once (*Le roman de la rose*, lines 1537–70). That every mirror image is bound to be only a partial reflection of its object is what underlies the principle of diffusion governing the personification allegory in the *Romance of the Rose*. So the sovereign self, who is never encountered in a direct confrontation, is represented in the personification of its various attributes.* Here

---

*This principle of diffusion and projection is further manifested in the systematic perspectivism which governs the successive discourses of various speakers, the so-called *Digressions*, in the second part of the *Romance of the Rose*. These speakers can render only partial accounts of the nature of the sovereign self and its love, because their perceptions and understandings are limited by their individual perspectives. Hence the succession of these *Digressions* looks like a sequence of mirror images of one and the same object from various angles. Thus, in the second part of the *Romance*, Jean de Meun transforms the idea of diffusion and projection which Guillaume de Lorris explains through his metaphor of Narcissus's mirror in the first part. That is, the principle of diffusion and projection, which underlies the personification of the various attributes of the sovereign self for Guillaume de Lorris, is used to generate the various perspectival discourses on the nature of the sovereign self by Jean de Meun. This, in turn, explains the transformation of the *Romance* from allegorical into literal mode in the transition from its first to second part. The allegorical framework retained from the first part is used largely for the successive presentation of literal *Digressions* in the second part.

As it were, Jean de Meun employs speaking-mirrors while Guillaume de Lorris relies on picturing-mirrors. Although both kinds of mirrors perform the same function of reflection, the role of speaking-mirrors appears to be far more active than that of picturing-mirrors. This transition from the passive to the active role of mirrors seems to reflect one of the central elements in the transformation of medieval into modern sensibility. While

again, personification allegory stands on the idea that the under-standing of a person demands the allegorical projection of his hidden reality, because there is no way to encounter it directly any more than the divine reality.

So the central principle of Dionysian allegory appears to be its realism, that is, the ultimate object of allegorical representation is always the hidden reality, whether it be the reality of the One, Na-ture, or the Self. If there is any personification allegory that appears to represent only an abstract moral rather than a concrete hidden reality, I feel, that sort of allegory should be regarded as a simple fable or exemplum in the Dionysian sensibility. Insofar as allegorical realism is concerned, the question of personification vs. figural alle-gories is of little consequence in the domain of allegorical shells, because both personification and figural allegories can be readily employed to represent hidden concrete reality. For the same reason, the historical truth of the literal sense in Dionysian allegory is incon-sequential for its allegorical realism. The only thing that counts is the *reality* of the allegorical referent; the allegorical medium is only a shadow, whether real or fictional.

It is this Dionysian allegorical realism that dictates the Trinitarian figural reading of the *Commedia*. If Dante's allegory is really about the Christian world, no other being than the Three Persons of the Holy Trinity can be admitted as the referent of the poem's ultimate figural sense. To do otherwise would amount to failing to recognize the Trinity as the ultimate reality in Dante's epic. Thus, the Trinitarian reading of the *Commedia* becomes inevitable once it is placed in the context of its own allegorical ethos.

Fourfold Allegory Again

It is about time to clarify the relation of fourfold allegory to the Dionysian sensibility on the one hand and to the Augustinian sensi-bility on the other. Of the four senses, the anagogical sense is clearly Dionysian, not only because it is an allegory of things, but also because the word *anagogia* is uniquely Dionysian.[49] The allegorical sense may appear to be rooted in the Hebraic notion of promise and fulfillment, but the relation of promise and fulfillment cannot be

medieval sensibility was largely passive and receptive, modern sensibility becomes em-phatically active and constitutive, that is, it forms its own view of things rather than re-ceiving it from someone else.

transformed into the relation of figure and fulfillment until the promise is seen not only as a promise but also as a partial fulfillment. For example, Isaac can be regarded as a figure of Christ only when Isaac is seen as a partial embodiment of Christhood. If so, the allegorical sense also belongs to the allegory of things. Whereas the anagogical sense is an allegory of things in a vertical scheme, the allegorical sense is an allegory of things in a horizontal scheme.

The horizontal allegory of things comes about by the extension of the vertical allegory of things, and this extension is made possible by the Incarnation. As long as God remains the transcendent deity, he can be represented only in the vertical scheme. But once he comes down to the earth and lives among us, his immanence dictates the extension of vertical anagogy into horizontal allegory. Since St. Thomas is clearly aware of the presence of the Dionysian allegory of things in the figural exegesis of the Bible, he always cites the authority of Dionysius the Areopagite in his exposition on the figural interpretation of the Bible (cf. *Summa theologiae*, pt. 1, q. 1, aa. 9 and 10; *Quodlibet*. q. 7, a. 15).

The literal sense clearly belongs to the Augustinian theology of words. It is hard to determine whether the moral sense, or tropology, belongs to the allegory of words or that of things. I have already shown that some theologians like St. Thomas tried to conceive tropology in a figural mode, while many others have regarded it as more like a fable or exemplum. That is, the moral sense can be claimed by both the allegory of things and that of words. Thus the fourfold allegory turns out to be a conglomeration of the Augustinian allegory of words and the Dionysian allegory of things. Of course, it would be quite anachronistic to assume that Augustine adopted the allegory of things contained in the fourfold allegory from Dionysius himself, who is believed to have lived about a century after him. But Augustine did receive it from Origen, the common father of the allegory of things for all of Christendom.

Since Augustine's is a theology of words rather than things, he primarily relies on the literal sense in his interpretation of the Bible. The ultimate guideline Augustine offers for the reading of the Holy Scripture in *De doctrina christiana* can be summed up in one sentence: "the true spirit of the Bible is in its literal sense." The Bible is written for the sole purpose of educating and edifying the Christians about faith, hope, and love. Augustine claims that this Christian spirit of the Bible is openly stated in its literal sense and that its obscure passages should be interpreted in accordance with the manifest spirit of its clear passages (*De doctrina christiana*, bk. 2, chap. 9).

Since Augustine believes that the literal sense of the Bible contains its spiritual sense, his conception of literal sense is radically different from Origen's. Whereas the Augustinian spiritual sense is contained in the literal sense, as Gerhard Ebeling points out, the Origenistic spiritual sense is systematically excluded from the literal sense and is transferred to the allegorical senses.[50] These two different conceptions of spiritual sense reflect respectively two different ways of understanding the Incarnation: Augustine accepts the Incarnation in its literal sense whereas Origen sees it only figuratively.

Augustine develops the identity thesis of the literal and the spiritual senses mainly for the reading of the New Testament, the official record of the Incarnation. It is this Augustinian identity thesis that Auerbach unwittingly imposes upon the *Commedia* by claiming literal truth for both figures (e.g. Virgil of history) and their fulfillments (e.g. Virgil of the *Commedia*). Auerbach inherited this identity thesis via Martin Luther, through whom the Augustinian unity of literal and spiritual senses became a central feature of the Protestant sensibility.

Augustine expects and explains the divergence of the Old Testament from this identity thesis, since it is meant to be a historical record of the pre-Incarnation period. Only then does he adopt the allegorical reading and make *allegoria* one of the four senses in *De genesi ad litteram*. As Hollander points out, the other three senses in this fourfold scheme—history, analogy, and etiology—are three different features of literal sense.[51] When Augustine enumerates the four senses once more in *De utilitate credendi*, he gives the same four with a slight change in the order of their enumeration. So Augustine's persistent emphasis always falls on the literal sense.

With Augustine, allegorical exegesis serves two functions: (1) the emergency device, or rule of exception, for reading those Biblical passages which are quite unedifying on the literal level; and (2) the routine device for enriching the literal and spiritual senses of the New Testament by illuminating its figural nexus with the Old Testament. In either case, Augustine's allegorical sensibility remains subservient to his literal sensibility.

The fourfold allegory, which is heavily loaded with Dionysian sensibility, is thus a little too much for the Augustinian theology of words; the operation of a fourfold scheme in Augustine's writings is almost as skimpy as in the works of the Angelic Doctor. Of his numerous writings, Augustine does not assign even one to the discussion of the fourfold allegory as a central topic. The fourfold allegory has to wait for the arrival of the Seraphic Doctor on the Dionysian scene before it is formally accepted as the principal way of reading, not only the Bible, but also the Book of all Creation.

Dante in the Dionysian Tradition

Dante's poetic sensibility is developed in the Dionysian school of *dolce stil nuovo*, and the Beatrice of *La Vita Nuova* clearly belongs to the allegory of things. But this first important work of Dante also bears a few marks of the Augustinian stamp. The arrival of the heavenly spirit in the form of Beatrice immediately produces a harsh conflict with the natural spirit of Dante (cf. *Vita Nuova*, chap. 2). The new life that begins with the coming of Beatrice exacts the death of the old life, and the perpetual conflict of life and death permeates the entire *Vita Nuova* (see chaps. 8, 15, 21, 22, 23, etc.). In addition to these typical forms of Augustinian logic, Dante uses the form of Augustine's *Confessions* for the composition of the *Vita Nuova*.

The death of Beatrice finally leaves Dante in the care of the *donna gentile*, Lady Philosophy, for whom he writes the *Convivio*. With the clear intention of beginning the *Convivio* precisely where he left off the *Vita Nuova*, he writes the first ode of the former on the conflict between his memory of Beatrice and his attraction to the new lady, the *donna gentile*, and gently resolves this conflict in favor of the latter. Thus he leaves the memory of death completely behind him and proceeds to celebrate life on earth. After this resolution of the conflict between the living and the dead, he maintains a delicate balance between the various pairs of contrasting elements, for instance, the inner and the outer, the carnal and the spiritual, the literal and the allegorical, the life of action and that of contemplation, etc. Thus the *Convivio* is permeated by the Dionysian logic of concord and continuity in contrast to the *Vita Nuova*, which is suffused with the Augustinian sense of conflict and struggle.

The *Convivio* was written in the tradition of Bernard Sylvester's *De mundi universitate* and Alan of Lille's *De planctu naturae*, in which cosmology and psychology, theology and anthropology, politics and ethics, the internal and the external world, are fused into one systematic whole. As Thomas G. Bergin suggests, the immediate model for Dante's *Convivio* may very well have been Brunetto Latini's *Trésor* and *Tesoretto*, whose encyclopaedic scope surely reflects the style of Bernard Sylvester and Alan of Lille.[52] The rampant Dionysian sensibility in the *Convivio* does not even allow the sharp Augustinian distinction between the authority of supernatural revelation and that of natural reason. This point can be illustrated by Dante's proof for the immortality of the soul in tractate 2, chapter 9.

He first musters all the arguments that natural reason can provide on its own in support of the soul's immortality, and then concludes the proof by capping it by the divine assurance: "And further we are assured of it by the most truthful teaching of Christ."[53] Bergin is rather puzzled at this manner of argument and says, "It is strange at first sight that Dante should reserve 'the teaching of Christ,' surely the only telling argument for a Christian, for his last 'proof.' "[54] Gilson considers the possibility of regarding Dante's argument as an Averroistic influence, but eventually rejects this, primarily because Dante's proof of personal immortality is in obvious conflict with the Averroists' rejection of it.[55]

The whole puzzle will at once cease to be puzzling as soon as Dante's proof is placed in the Dionysian context. In Dionysian universalism, there is only one truth for all; the authority of natural reason is continuous with the authority of revelation. Every truth is open to discovery by human reason, but this may appear to leave no important role for the authority of revelation to play. In the Dionysian world, the authority of revelation can still play one or two roles. First, there are many people who have inadequate training and insufficient time to discover the truth on their own. For them, the truths of divine revelation can be a substitute for the truths of human discovery. The truths of revelation can also be of some use even to the people who can discover truth on their own; they can find confirmation of their discoveries by witnessing their concordance with the truths of revelation.

What is important to notice in Dante's proof is not its substance but its manner. Gilson is clearly too distracted by its substance to diagnose its manner. Dante's manner of proof may also be regarded as Boethian, since it is precisely this mode of argument that Boethius uses to prove the truths of the Christian faith in his *Consolation of Philosophy*. Since Dante adopts the allegorical convention of Lady Philosophy from *The Consolation of Philosophy*, his acceptance of the

Boethian style of argument cannot take us by surprise. Dante's mode of argument may also be considered as Anselmian, because it eminently fulfills Anselm's ideal of showing necessary reasons for all the Christian dogmas. I have no objection to any of these labels, as long as they are understood to convey Dionysian universalism. But the label of Latin Averroism would be quite incorrect for Dante's mode of argument because its doctrine of the double authority admits the possibility of conflict between the two authorities and because this possibility is incompatible with Dionysian universalism.

But there is one serious trouble with the *Convivio*. In the course of its composition, the allegorical scheme becomes thinner and thinner and finally evaporates in the fourth tractate. This is quite understandable. In the Dionysian mirror of things, the allegorical scheme is to use the perceptible world for the reflection of the supersensible reality. In the case of the *Convivio*, however, Dante is interested in the perceptible world in its own right. Since Dante can confront the perceptible world without any allegorical mediation, he really leaves no proper role for allegory to play in the *Convivio*. Hence his allegorical exposition is bound to give way to literal exposition.

The Dionysianism of the *Convivio* is highly immanent whereas the allegory of things has been developed for transcendent Dionysianism. For the same reason, the allegorical mode of exposition in the *Romance of the Rose* also deteriorates to a literal exposition. Even from the beginning, the *Convivio* is far more firmly committed to literal sensibility than to allegorical sensibility. The general format Dante adopts for the composition of the *Convivio* is to confine allegory to the ode at the beginning of each tractate and then to write a series of commentaries on the meaning of that ode. The commentaries themselves must have the literal sense alone, since they are the devices for explaining the allegorical senses of the odes as well as their literal senses, and since they are not meant to be another set of allegories for explaining the odes. That is, whatever allegory may be contained in the odes is meant to be translated into literal sense in their commentaries.

Hence we can point out the central difference between the transcendent and the immanent allegories of things. The raison d'être for transcendent allegory is the inaccessibility of transcendent reality to the literal sense—that is, allegory is employed precisely because literal sense cannot capture it. In contrast to this, the raison d'être for immanent allegory is its eventual elimination by literal account.

In fact, the degree of success in this elimination is the degree of success in its communication; the success of Dante's commentaries becomes complete only when they can translate, without remainder or residual, the allegory of the odes into literal sense. Hence the same allegorical residual which serves as a mark of success in the transcendent allegory functions as a mark of failure in the immanent allegory. The transcendent allegory is a device of intimation; the immanent allegory is a device of explanation.

This distinction between the immanent and the transcendent allegories appears to correspond roughly to C. S. Lewis's distinction between allegory proper and sacramentalism or symbolism.[56] In the case of allegory proper, Lewis says, one starts out with an immaterial fact and then invents visibilia to express it. In the case of sacramentalism, on the other hand, one proceeds in the opposite way, that is, one begins with visibilia and tries to see the reflection of some transcendent reality in them. The immaterial fact one starts out with in the former case is an immanent entity like our passions. Hence allegory proper is for a tangible explication of some immanent and yet intangible fact; sacramentalism or symbolism is for the visible manifestation of some invisible transcendent reality.

It is not only allegory but also verse that suffers from Dante's immanent Dionysianism, since his sense of verse has been developed during his early schooling in transcendent Dionysianism. The use of verse in the *Convivio* is limited to the composition of the odes, and prose becomes the medium for the composition of their commentaries which constitute the bulk of the *Convivio*. So the use of verse as well as the device of allegory in the *Convivio* turns out to be an unreflective and gratuitous carry-over from Dante's transcendent to his immanent period. Perhaps realizing this, he drops both in his composition of *De monarchia*. Thus he obtains a concordance between his form and content, his message and media, by using the immanent materials for the exposition of the immanent theme.

There is one more sign of Dante's maturity in *De monarchia*; he shifts his emphasis from the plane of contemplation to that of action. If the *Convivio* is viewed as a program of contemplation, *De monarchia* is a program of action.* The program of contemplation generally

---

*This point may be contested by some on the ground that Dante exalts moral philosophy as the highest of all sciences in the *Convivio*. But this exaltation of moral philosophy is only a part of Dante's attempt to see a systematic relation of all sciences, and as such his attempt is quite similar to St. Bonaventure's systematization of all human arts and sciences

presupposes that order and truth prevail in the world since no one would be happy to contemplate a predominantly disorderly world. Now suppose that disorder and untruth rather than order and truth prevail in the world. Then order and truth must first be instilled into the world as the essential prerequisite for contemplation.

In the *Convivio* Dante is already quite conscious of disorder and untruth in the earthly domain; the only domain of unambiguous order for him is the celestial world of stars. Thus, for a satisfactory execution of his program of contemplation, he knows that he has to partly close his eyes to the earthly realm and concentrate his attention on the astral sphere. But by this time he is too much of an immanentist to do this in comfort. So he appears to be compelled to abandon his program of contemplation and advocate his program of action. He acts very much in the spirit of Karl Marx, who revolts against the contemplation-oriented German idealism by saying that the real business of philosophy is not to understand the world but to change it. In *De monarchia*, as it were, Dante is moving away from the Dionysian idealism to its realism.

The Dionysian idealists were the Porretani, the followers of Gilbert of La Porrée, who tried to find order and beauty in the lowest sphere of the Creation. This romantic idea that order and beauty pervade even the material sphere comes to be shattered for Dante by the political reality of his time. So Dante is a realist in many different senses; he is the first realistic Porretanus. Whereas the idealistic Porretani have been intent on finding the unity and order installed by God the Great Artisan in the world, the realistic Porretani recognize the urgent need to introduce unity and order in imitation of the Great Artisan (cf. *De monarchia*, bk. 1, chaps. 5–9). Thus the old idea of the imitation of God, or *imago dei*, is extended from the sphere of contemplation to that of action and from the life of suffering to that of doing. Hence Dante shifts the medieval attention from God the Great Artisan to man the imitating artisan, and thereby prepares for the birth of the Renaissance idea of politics as a supreme human art.

There still remains an evident difference between his program of

---

in *De reductione artium ad theologiam*, in which moral philosophy is also exalted higher than metaphysics. Both of these attempts are made within the framework of contemplation or understanding rather than that of action and practice. Whether or not one recognizes the primacy of action over contemplation does not in itself determine whether or not one shall have a program of action. For one can still have a program of action even if one still subscribes to the primacy of contemplation over action. Conversely, one may have no program of action even if one acknowledges the primacy of action over contemplation.

action and that of the Renaissance. Whereas the latter tends to be divorced from the divine program, Dante's cannot allow the separation of the human program from the divine program without gravely compromising his universalism. But his universalism is one thing he cannot sacrifice for anything else; in fact, his universalism in its immanent version comes to its maturation in *De monarchia*. The realization of this immanentistic universalism would amount to the advent of the Age of the Holy Spirit prophesied by such Dionysian radicals as Rupert of Deutz and Joachim of Floris.

As the universal human community, Dante's *imperium* is not simply a political institution in its ordinary sense. In the first place, it is meant to bind all mankind in one communal nexus. Then, perhaps even more striking, it is meant to be the ultimate arena in which all the potentials of every individual are to be fulfilled. The only political conception that comes close to it is the contemporary notion of the total state. But unlike the totalitarian state, Dante's *imperium* is in complete harmony with God's Providence, and its ultimate function is the fullest realization of the individual. In this spirit of the universal community, Dante develops his conception of universal history and assigns a prominent role to the Roman tradition. He believes that the very notion of the universal community is a unique legacy of the Roman tradition (*De monarchia*, bk. 2, chap. 5).

Dino Bigongiari says that Dante derives his universalism from the old cosmopolitanism of the Stoics.[57] Although it may be almost impossible to establish the direct continuity between the Stoics and Dante, it is obvious that the universalistic tendency of the Stoics is in tune with Dionysian universalism. Some have thought it better to give the label of Averroism to Dante's universalism rather than that of Stoicism.[58] Again, the labels for *De monarchia* do not count any more than for the *Convivio*; all we have to be aware of is Dante's Dionysian universalism, which can easily accommodate Stoicism as well as Averroism.

Dante lives up to the artistic idea of introducing order and beauty not only as a political thinker but also as a poet. He implements this poetic program of action in his cultivation of the vernacular tongue. He conceives the contrast between Latin and the vernacular as analogous to the contrast between the eternal intelligible world and the transitory corporeal world (*Convivio*, 1. 5). Latin is a sovereign, noble language immune from decay; the vernacular is a subservient, lowly language constantly subject to decay.

He is fully appreciative of the order and beauty that is enduringly established in the sovereign Latin. As a Porretanus, however, he is intent upon introducing order and beauty into the lowly, transitory vulgar tongue. Dante writes all his poetic works in the vernacular and uses Latin only for such discursive treatises as *De monarchia* and *De vulgari eloquentia.* Thus the progressive growth of Dante's Dionysian immanentism is to take down order and beauty lower and lower into the perceptible world, but this immanentism comes to be shattered with his bitter political disillusion and despair. With this shattering experience, he takes the transcendental turn and composes his greatest work, *La Divina Commedia.*

Dante's transcendental turn may be conceived as a double pivot rather than a single one. It could be understood as a single pivot, if Dante moved on to the composition of the *Commedia* after the *Convivio* and *De monarchia.* It would be understood as a double pivot if he commenced the *Commedia* between the *Convivio* and *De monarchia.* This is a difficult question to settle because the composition date of *De monarchia* is still being disputed. In the case of the double pivot, Dante would have taken his first transcendental turn after his disappointment with the *Convivio.* Sometime after he began writing the *Commedia*, he must have realized his error in not having tried the plane of action and seen the need to go back to the immanent phase of his Dionysian career. In that event, *De monarchia* would have been composed during his second immanentist period, which ended in a far graver disillusion than his first one. This may have eventually extinguished the brief rekindling of his old hope for and faith in this world, and have forced him to make the final pivot for his transcendental turn.

Whichever way his transcendental turn may be conceived, at least one thing is clear, that is, there is no need for him to reject anything of his immanent period in making this turn. He can and does retain everything. All he has to do is to change his perspective and view every perceptible object as a mirror of the transcendent reality rather than in its own right. Thus he regains allegory in its transcendent mode and comes back to Beatrice (his conversion). But the Beatrice he regains is not the Beatrice of *La Vita Nuova*, who is shrouded partly in the Augustinian and partly in the Dionysian sensibility. The Beatrice of the *Commedia* takes on a fully Dionysian gown.

The model for the composition of the *Commedia* is Bernard Sylvester's *De mundi universitate* rather than Augustine's *Confessions*, Bonaventure's *Itinerarium* rather than Augustine's *De trinitate*. Dante invokes the authority of Dionysius the Areopagite in justifying his distinction of the angelic orders (*Par.* 28. 130–39). He tells us that Gregory, who had departed from the authority of Dionysius, recognized his error on his arrival in Heaven, and that only Dionysius had it right all along because he got it straight from Paul, the only one who had firsthand knowledge of the celestial sphere. The really important point that lies behind these humorous remarks is the Dionysian idea that cosmology is integrally tied up with theology.

What makes Dante's ascent so breath-taking is his capacity to retain the awareness of the nether world always so close at hand and also to keep alive the immediate sense of the immense distance from it. This perpetual sense of breath-taking suspension in the immense space of plenitude is of course prepared by his descent to the bottom of Hell, but his descent into the Inferno has in turn been prepared by his descent into the secular world during the period of his Dionysian immanentism. For his suffering and despair in the Inferno is the reliving of his suffering and despair in this world. Thus the Beatrice of the *Commedia* takes on the fully Dionysian dimension of grandeur and majesty, which is barely visible only in a germinal form in the Beatrice of *La Vita Nuova*. To be sure, there are a few streaks of celestial imagery in the *Vita Nuova*, but they are usually submerged beneath the Augustinian self-confessional agony.

So the transformation of the Beatrice of *La Vita Nuova* into the Beatrice of *La Divina Commedia* is like the transformation of a small harpsichord into a grand pianoforte. The former's monotonous range is expanded into the latter's immense range of complex contrast. To use one more musical metaphor, Beatrice of *La Vita Nuova* is the solo voice that constitutes its monophony. On the other hand, Beatrice of the *Commedia* becomes only one of the three voices that constitute its polyphony.

The Dionysian universalism developed in the *Convivio* and *De monarchia* is retained intact in the *Commedia*. Mindful of this universalism, we need not be shocked to find Siger of Brabant included in the circles of the heavenly theologians any more than to meet, in the throng of the just rulers, Ripheus the Trojan, who lived before the Incarnation. Dante explains the presence of the latter through his doctrine of invisible sanctification, that is, the power of grace working internally and invisibly in the soul of Ripheus and bringing about his salvation although he was born too early to have the benefit of baptism, the visible manifestation of grace (*Par.* 20. 118–23).

Dante's explanation of the presence of Siger of Brabant is a little less clear: "This is the eternal light of Siger who, lecturing in the street of the Straw, syllogized invidious [*invidiosi*] truths" (*Par.* 10. 136–38). He means to say that Siger of Brabant became invidious or offensive for producing some truths through the power of natural reason alone ("syllogized"/"syllogism" is taken as the central organon of natural reason in the scholastic tradition), that is Siger's truths of natural reason turned out to be invidious to the orthodoxy which thrives on Augustinian particularism.* Gilson's label of Latin Averroism is again not quite to Dante's point. Indeed, Siger of Brabant may very well have been a Latin Averroist, but it is not this partisan label that assures him a place in Dante's Heaven. What counts is his discovery of truths of natural reason, and Dante's universalism entails their unity with the truths of revelation. It is this unity of all truths that brings Siger into the same circle of theologians with Albertus Magnus, Dionysius, and Boethius, all of whom have championed the unity of truths one way or another (cf. *Par.* 10. 97 ff.).

Dionysian universalism also becomes prominent in the logic of continuity that governs Dante's journey. If Dante's journey were to be constructed on an Augustinian model, Virgil would take him to a juncture of two paths, perhaps a broad passage down to Hell and a narrow one up to Purgatory and Paradise, and tell him, "Here is the momentous choice and it is yours to make." Or he might first take him down to Hell and come back to the same crossroad, and then take him up to the other path. Incidentally, this metaphor of the two divergent paths is what Augustine uses to describe Petrarch's fall in the third dialogue of the *Secretum.* But Dante's is one continuous passage from Hell through Purgatory up to Heaven. His descent is an integral part of his ascent; his perdition is an integral part of his

---

*There has been some dispute about the translation of the word *invidiosi*. Some have thought that the correct translation of this word should be "enviable" rather than "invidious." In that event, Dante would be saying that the truths discovered through Siger of Brabant's syllogistic arguments provoked admiration among his friends and followers. It is further possible that *invidiosi* in Dante's usage may have meant both "invidious" and "enviable." Whichever translation of *invidiosi* is adopted, it makes little difference for our understanding of Dante's central point, namely, that in the Heaven of the Sun, Siger of Brabant stands as the theologian of natural reason.

salvation. For this reason, I have adopted the distinction between the natural and the spiritual order in place of the Thomistic distinction between the natural and the supernatural orders in explaining Dante's cosmos.[59] In contrast to the obvious discontinuity between the natural and the supernatural orders, I have stressed the continuity between the natural and the spiritual orders in the *Commedia*.

I am likely to be told that the presence of Hell, the locus of eternal damnation, mars the integrity of Dante's universalism. In spite of the apparent validity of this observation, I am not quite convinced of its ultimate truth. For a truly universalistic cosmos has to have a place for everything, darkness as well as light, vice as well as virtue, perdition as well as salvation, etc. All it has to guard against is the Manichean dualism, and Dante seems to accomplish that quite well.

To stress Dante's Dionysian universalism is not to exclude the Augustinian tradition from the *Commedia;* such an exclusion would be precisely against the spirit of Dante's universalism.* The particularism of the Augustinian tradition is all appropriated into Dante's universalistic cosmos, and a vivid example of this is his appropriation of Augustinian personalism. Since Augustinians stress the inwardness of the soul, they have been the great champions of personalism. This Augustinian personalism is manifested in Dante's relationships with his three guides. Since these represent the Three Persons of the Trinity, their constant help for Dante, from the inception of his journey to its consummation, poignantly portrays the Augustinian personalism in the Christian's encounter with his Creator.

To take Dante's three guides as personification allegories would annul this personalistic dimension of the *Commedia* on the allegorical plane. Virgil as Natural Reason and Beatrice as Revelation would be too impersonal to establish and maintain truly personal relations with Dante the pilgrim on the plane of spiritual sense. It is not only these three guides but also all the other personages in the *Commedia*

---

*One of the striking features of the *Commedia* is the modest role it assigns to Augustine. Augustine is not one of the blessed who meet or instruct Dante during his ascent to the Empyrean. Dante sees him only in the Celestial Rose, when St. Bernard points him out in his explanation of its seating arrangement. Even there, Augustine is seated below John the Baptist, Francis, and Benedict (cf. *Par.* 32. 31–35). In Dante's celestial kingdom, Augustine is a saint of the fourth rank. This inconspicuous ranking Dante gives Augustine in his *Commedia*, which can be taken as an open affront to his immense authority as the chief spokesman of the Church in the Latin West, is convincing evidence that Augustinianism has been assimilated into the *Commedia* only as one of the minor currents of its universalistic ethos.

who are meant to convey the Augustinian personalism. But this personalism is presented not as an episode of the inward reflection but as an integral feature of the cosmic itinerary.

Dante's three guides represent not only his appropriation of Augustine's *De trinitate* but also his transformation of *De civitate dei*. Augustine's *De civitate dei* is meant to be a record of the continuous strife between the Christians and the pagans, and between the spiritual and the carnal. This continuous strife embodies the Augustinian spirit of particularistic exclusion, but Dante assimilates it into his Dionysian spirit of universalistic inclusion by adopting Virgil as a figure of the Son and Beatrice as a figure of the Holy Spirit. In the Augustinian sensibility, the Roman Empire has been firmly established as the most vivid manifestation of the pagan spirit and woman as the most tangible expression of carnality. Dante's Virgil and Beatrice stand for these two domains of Augustinian exclusion and condemnation. In this conquest of Augustine's particularism, Dante is only exploiting the universalistic transformation of *De civitate dei* which had already been accomplished at the hands of Hugh of Saint-Victor, Rupert of Deutz, Anselm of Havelberg, Joachim of Floris, et al.

Petrarch's Descent to the Literal Plane

I have gone into all these historical details to gain a proper context for appreciating Petrarch's experience on Mount Ventoux. Petrarch's vexation in his inward self is his revulsion against Dante's Dionysian sensibility; he feels naturally justified in confirming this revulsion with the prestige of Augustine. In a typically Augustinian personalistic manner, he responds to Augustine's remark on the superiority of the inward soul to the external world. Since he opened the *Confessions* at random and his eyes fell upon no other passage, he feels as though the spirit of the saint had personally guided his hands and eyes in their random motion. He says, "What I had there read I believed to be addressed to me and no other."[60] He further justifies this personalistic mode of appropriating the chance experience by showing its similarity to that of St. Augustine himself and St. Anthony. Also in this personalistic manner, evidently, Petrarch looks upon the fact that he has brought along a copy of the *Confessions* with him, and even the fact that that copy has come into his possession as a gift from Dionigi da Borgo San Sepolcro, an Augus-

tinian friar and his confessor. So he decides to recount the entire experience in a letter to the friar.

Petrarch's personalistic mode of response is in obvious contrast to
the normal way of reading a book. A book is not usually written as a
letter from one person to another; it is more or less addressed to an
impersonal audience. Hence, it is very hard to respond to such a
more or less public object as a book in such a personalistic manner as
Petrarch's. In the case of his experience, we may have to concede at
least one point, namely, he really fell upon an appropriate passage.
But even this point is not quite so compelling as to justify his personalistic response. The truth of the matter is that there are hundreds
of other passages in the *Confessions* that could equally well have
served Petrarch's purpose, since this book is a sustained record of
Augustine's interior voice. Anybody opening it even at random has
a good chance of landing on one of these numerous passages. But
what counts is not what he finds there but how he responds to it,
and his personalistic mode of response is, of course, an integral
feature of the Augustinian sensibility.

As Bergin observes, "Much has been made of the ascent of Mt.
Ventoux as a dramatic illustration of the poet's 'modernity,' and I
believe with reason."[61] As I have already suggested, Petrarch's idea
of climbing a high mountain is derived from the Dantesque sensibility
which is in turn drawing its inspiration from the well-established
practice among the Franciscans. When Bonaventure was called
forth from his magisterial post to assume the general command of
the Franciscan Order, he withdrew into solitude on Mount Alverno
and tried to relive the mystical experience of the founding father.
Mountain climbing had become such a revered way of the Franciscan
anagogia that Bonaventure came to regard it as the best preparation
for assuming the leadership of the Franciscan Order. It is from this
preparation on the holy Mount of the Order that he came forth with
the central theme of his masterpiece, *The Journey of the Mind to God*.
In the Prologue, Bonaventure explains this point:

> At the example of our most blessed father Francis, I, too, was
> seeking peace with a longing spirit—I, a sinner unworthy in all
> ways, who yet had become the seventh Father General of the
> Brothers after the passing away of this most blessed father. At a
> time close to the thirty-third anniversary of the blessed man's

departure, it came about by divine prompting that I walked up
Mount Alverno, longing to find some peace of soul at that place
of peace. While I was there, meditating on the different ways of
the mind's ascent to God, there came to me among other
thoughts the memory of the miracle which had occurred in this
very place to blessed Francis himself: the vision of a six-winged
Seraph in the likeness of the Crucified. In my meditation, it was
at once clear to me that this vision represented not only the con-
templative rapture of our father, but also the road by which this
rapture is attained. [*Itinerarium*, prol. 2][62]

In climbing Mount Alverno, Bonaventure is not initiating a new
practice but, rather, is following an old custom that goes back to their
founding father. As children of the Dionysian sensibility, the Franciscans took the meditative life of a monk out of the cloisters into the
open world and felt perfectly natural in employing the experience of
climbing a high mountain as an effective impetus for the Dionysian
anagogia. Thus with them the high mountain peak has become the
launching pad for the flight of the soul to God. Petrarch is eagerly
following the Franciscan tradition in his ascent of Mount Ventoux,
but he cannot stay with it beyond its summit.

Whereas Bonaventure's ascent of Mount Alverno naturally leads
into his meditation on the celestial world at the top, Petrarch's ascent
turns into an abrupt descent there. Finally poised on the Franciscan
launching pad of the Dionysian *anagogia*, to Petrarch's dismay, his
soul swoops down to the terrestrial plain instead of taking off in
celestial flight. But the resourceful Petrarch is not to be defeated by
this Dionysian embarrassment; he decides to accept it gratefully as an
exposé of the Dionysian pretense on the unity of soteriology and
cosmology and as a demonstration of the Augustinian insight into the
incommensurability of interiority and exteriority.

The segregation of interiority from exteriority had been the monastic way of preserving and cultivating the interior life of meditation
before the ascendancy of the Dionysian ethos. For example, it has
been said that Bernard of Clairvaux, who always traveled in a cowl,
seldom paid full attention to the natural world. But the Benedictine
motive was quite different from Petrarch's. Whereas the Benedictines
felt the need of separating their interior world from the exterior world
because they considered the latter too repulsive and offensive,

Petrarch's need is dictated by the beauty and splendor of the external world, which turns out to be too enchanting and disturbing.

So the modernity of Petrarch's experience resides not in his attempt to climb a high mountain but in his inability to contain the entire experience in the Dionysian allegorical sensibility, which in turn reflects his intense captivation with the literal significance of the ascent rather than its allegorical significance. Instead of taking the ascent allegorically, Petrarch eventually takes it literally. In the case of Dante's climb, whether his mountain is real or fictional is not terribly significant. This alone is sufficient to show the relative insignificance of literal sense for him. In the case of Petrarch's experience, however, the literal sense is never meant to take second place to the allegorical sense. He can never be satisfied with an allegorical unity of the inner and the outer because he needs to have their literal unity for his full satisfaction.

Petrarch's demand for the literal unity of interiority and exteriority reflects the Augustinian identity thesis of carnal and spiritual senses. With Augustine, however, the identity or unity in question was claimed only for one miraculous moment of history, the Incarnation; Petrarch wants to extend it to every moment of history as a matter of general rule rather than of exception. This Petrarchan extension had already been foretold by the Dionysian immanentists such as Rupert of Deutz and Joachim of Floris, in their prophecy of the Age of the Spirit, in which the literal unity of carnal and spiritual senses (what had taken place only in the Head of the Mystical Body of Christ) was to be fully realized in the whole world (to be extended to its entire Body). Petrarch feels and acts as though this prophesied age had or should have already arrived. Thus Petrarchan literal sensibility is the immediate descendant of Dionysian immanentism, and as such is radically different from the literal sensibility of pagan antiquity. Whereas the latter excludes spiritual sense, the former is meant to contain it.

Petrarch is by no means the first to take this radical position of presuming that the Age of the Spirit has or should have already arrived, for this presumption had inspired the emergence of the mendicant orders. In the *Convivio, De vulgari eloquentia,* and *De monarchia,* as we have seen, Dante had striven to maintain the same immanentistic spirit as the friars of these new orders. But he was forced to retreat into the old position of the Dionysian transcendentism by his disillusion with this world; he came to learn to expect only the allegorical, and never the literal, unity of carnal and spiritual senses in the mundane world. It is this lesson of the disillusioned but mature Dante that is embodied in the *Divina Commedia*.

The *Commedia* can be read as Dante's appropriation of the immanentistic Dionysian doctrine of the three ages: the Inferno as the appropriation of the Age of the Father, the Purgatorio as that of the Age of the Son, and the Terrestrial Paradise as that of the Age of the Holy Spirit. In this *historical* interpretation of the *Commedia*, Virgil represents the Father, Statius the Son, and Beatrice the Spirit. Dante's descent to the Inferno corresponds to the story of the Fall in Genesis. Since this part of his journey is guided by Virgil alone, it stands for the Age of the Father alone. Dante's arrival at Purgatorio corresponds to the Exodus; the penitents sing the Psalm of *In exitu israel de aegypto* during their voyage to the shore of Purgatorio (*Purg.* 2. 46). His ascent of the Mount of Purgatory to its middle corresponds to the era of the Old Testament after the Fall, and the emergence of tSatius on the Fourth Terrace stands for the transition from the era of the Old to that of the New Testament. Hence Dante's ascent of Purgatorio represents the Age of the Son with the Father. The coming of Beatrice to the Terrestrial Paradise portrays the advent of the Age of the Spirit; Beatrice's Procession signifies the unfolding of this final age. Since Beatrice comes with the Griffin, Dante's sojourn in the Terrestrial Paradise represents the Age of the Spirit with the Son.*

Since all these events take place on earth, they can be read *historically* in the vein of Dionysian immanentism. But Dante's ascent of Paradiso cannot be given this sort of *historical* reading because it is situated in the transtemporal, heavenly sphere. By absorbing the *historical* events of the first two canticles into the transtemporal schema of ascent of the last canticle, Dante transforms the immanentistic Dionysian doctrine of the three ages into the traditional form of the transcendentistic, Dionysian *anagogia*. This is why the *Commedia* can be called Dante's transcendentistic retreat from Dionysian immanentism.

Petrarch cannot take the Dantesque retreat back to the allegorical consolation of Dionysian transcendentism because he is too much a

*As some Dante scholars have pointed out, Dante's prophecy of Veltro and *DXV* is clear textual evidence of Joachim's influence on Dante, because it is obviously Dante's adaption of Joachim's prophecy of the *DUX*, the leader of the final age. See, for technical details, R. E. Kaske's informative article "Dante's *DXV*," in John Freccero, ed., *Dante*, pp. 122–40.

child of Dionysian immanentism. Nor can he rejoice in the literal
unity of carnal and spiritual senses because he cannot find it any more
readily than Dante could. So he feels their disunity in the very discordance of his own inner and outer worlds; the only thing he can do
is to justify this discordance with the authority of St. Augustine.

Since Petrarch can no longer employ the towering mountain peaks
for the Dionysian *anagogia*, he transforms them into symbols of his
interior world:

> From thought to thought, from mountain peak to mountain,
> Love leads me on; for I can never still
> My trouble on the world's well-beaten ways.
> . . . .
> In high mountains, in the woods I find
> A little solace; every haunt of man
> Is to my mood a mortal enemy.
> . . . .
> Now it's my whole desire and all my pleasure
> Up to the highest mountain-pass to climb
> To dizzy and unshadowed solitude.[63]
>
> [*Rime*, no. 129]

The length and height of the mountains become the Petrarchan
projection of the depth and gravity of the inner solitude. In spite of
this symbolic projection, the Dantesque allegorical fusion of interiority and exteriority has been torn apart by the Petrarchan literal
sensibility, and this rupture becomes Petrarch's "sickness unto
death," the sickness of the modern man. It is this sickness that
Petrarch brings down from Mount Ventoux.

Part 2

The Form of Life in Literal Sensibility

3

The Petrarchan Dilemma

In his valiant fight to protect Augustinian inwardness against the raging Dionysian ethos, Petrarch assembles what may be called the Petrarchan platoon of the champions of interiority which, besides Augustine, includes Socrates, Plato, Seneca, and Cicero. In the last of these, however, he finds one ghastly blemish, namely, Cicero's political dispute with Anthony. So Petrarch resorts to one of his favorite practices of writing fictitious letters to his spiritual friends of antiquity (*Epistolae familiares*, bk. 24, epistle 3). Petrarch is especially disturbed about the fact that this political entanglement of Cicero's occurred during his mature old age, and laments, "Where were the peace and quiet that befitted your years, your profession, your station in life?"[1]

As far as Cicero himself was concerned, I suppose, his political entanglement was an act of duty and self-sacrifice dictated by the Roman republican spirit, and his complete withdrawal from public into private life would have been a flagrant violation of Roman Stoicism. Insensitive to this Roman spirit, Petrarch could not help understanding Cicero's motives in his own terms and thus taking his justification as no more than a flimsy excuse for his vanity. The Cicero he truly cherishes is the Cicero of the *Tusculan Disputations*, which replay the main themes of Plato's dialogues, the *Apology* and the *Phaedo*, accounts of Socrates' preparation for his impending death.[2]

The uniquely Petrarchan practice of addressing letters to people long since dead, like Cicero, and claiming them as his intimate friends is a little bizarre outside of the Petrarchan world of interiority. In this practice, Petrarch's personalism almost turns into subjectivism, the most extreme form of personalism. Subjectivism is not content simply to stress the superior importance of inwardness over the external world; it will even disregard the existence of external entities. For example, it matters little to Petrarch's subjective world whether Cicero and Augustine are still living or are already dead; the only thing that counts in that world is what they represent to Petrarch's inward self.

As a self-appointed champion of inwardness, Petrarch wages his campaign against the supporters of the external world. So he condemns the medieval scholasticism, the Dionysian theology par excellence; ridicules the Aristotelians, the practitioners of natural science; and castigates the doctors of medicine, the ministers to the body. Then he flaunts his own ignorance in the eyes of learned people, in his *De sui ipsius et multorum ignorantia* (On his own Ignorance and That of Many Others), one of three works that Petrarch himself called his "invectives."[3]

This "invective" was provoked by a contemptuous observation on the part of four learned Aristotelians in Venice to the effect that Petrarch was a good man but uncultured or without learning. Petrarch vengefully retorts that the cultured knowledge these learned gentlemen take pride in is knowledge of the external world, which is concerned with such trivial questions as "how many hairs there are in the lion's mane; how many feathers in the hawk's tail, etc."[4] Consequently, their proud knowledge only reflects ignorance of their true selves. In contrast to this, his own ignorance is that of trivial, external matters, which he believes to be the Socratic ignorance, which in turn reflects his Socratic devotion to self-knowledge ("Know thyself"). So Petrarch says he is quite happy to be labeled a good man without learning.

The tone of this "invective" clearly contradicts Petrarch's claim that he was truly happy to be a good but unlearned man. Why did he, then, feel such intense anger at their contemptuous remark? The simple truth of the matter is that one of his great ambitions was to be an exceptionally learned man. After all, as the first humanist he spent an incredible amount of time and energy on the Roman classics and manuscripts, which surely belong to the province of external knowledge. And yet he still hated to be called a scholar because of his aversion to a pedantic preoccupation with external affairs.[5] So he was really caught between love and hatred of knowledge of the external world.

This ambivalence also shows up in Petrarch's ascent of Mount Ventoux. If he had been solely concerned with the internal world, he would have been so indifferent to the external one as not even to think of climbing that mountain. Once on the top, he became so captivated with the beautiful scene below that he almost went into a trance. One eloquent testimony to his obsession with externals is his extraordinary sensitivity to the Latin style. One of the reasons for his aversion to scholasticism is his disgust with its sloppy Latin; his admiration of Cicero is as much due to Cicero's elegant Latin as his Stoicism. So Petrarch's interest in externals was as intense as his concern for inwardness.

In his critical knowledge of himself, Petrarch fully understood that his problem arose from being caught between the demands of these two worlds. He further equated the external world with the material or perceivable, and the internal world with the spiritual or intelligible. Fully aware of the gravity of his problem, he called it a malady or sickness and tried to diagnose it in his *Secretum meum*. Of course, this is the sickness that he had brought down from Mount Ventoux with him.

Petrarch's Self-Analysis in the *Secretum meum*

The *Secretum meum* is given the form of a dialogue between Petrarch and his mentor Augustine over a period of three days under the auspices of Lady Truth. One is bound to be irritated if one approaches it as a philosophical disputation between two contestants, for it is meant to be a clinical conversation between a physician and his patient. In the proem, Lady Truth brings St. Augustine to Petrarch as the physician for his sickly soul. Although Petrarch has long been stricken with a dangerous illness and is now very close to death, the lady tells Augustine, he is not even aware of the gravity of his malady. Since Augustine himself has endured the same malady, she goes on to ask him to take pity on his devoted disciple Petrarch and to bring some relief to his suffering.

So the aim of the three-day dialogue is the search, not for some philosophical truth, but for the remedy for Petrarch's sickness.[6] In fact, Petrarch himself can recite by rote all the Stoic maxims that are supposed to cure his sickly soul, but they are totally useless to him. Petrarch's problem lies not in understanding objective truths but in assessing his subjective conditions, and Augustine is summoned to help him in this regard. Hence the *Secretum* is a dialogue of self-examination.

The cause for the ignorance of subjective conditions cannot take the same form as the cause for the ignorance of objective conditions.

The lack of acquaintance which is often the latter of the two causes cannot be the cause for the former; there is no way for the self to remain unacquainted with itself. Hence a lack of self-knowledge must be attributed, not to a lack of self-acquaintance, but to one's own delusion or self-deception. One of Augustine's important functions in the *Secretum* is to expose Petrarch's delusions and to lead him out of his own self-deception (pp. 16 and 182). Of course, this emphasis on self-deception and self-knowledge reflects Petrarch's personalism.

Petrarch's personalism also governs the mode of argument in the *Secretum*. In trying to persuade Petrarch, Augustine does not rely on the external authority of the Church but always appeals to the internal authority of natural reason, which constitutes human nature itself. Because of this, he quotes frequently from Greek and Roman authors but only occasionally from the Bible. Even these infrequent Biblical quotations come in only as a way of confirming the arguments of natural reason. Hence the mode of argument in the *Secretum* may be said to resemble Dante's in his *Convivio* and *De monarchia*, but this apparent resemblance hides a fundamental difference. Whereas Dante appeals to natural reason as an objective authority in his search for universal truths, Petrarch cannot be content with such an objective authority since he is in search of those truths that can give him personal conviction. Hence his appeal to natural reason becomes an appeal to his interior authority.

In the first book, which covers the dialogue of the first day, Augustine reminds Petrarch of the general maxims of the Stoic sages. The immortal soul usually forgets its divine origin while it is imprisoned in the mortal body; meditation on the mortality of the body and this world is the surest aid in scorning the seduction of this world and liberating the soul from the fetters of the body. Since the soul holds the power of enslaving itself to the body (by way of vice) and also that of liberating itself from the body (by way of virtue), Augustine recites the Stoic argument: the happiness and misery of the soul are always dictated by its own will.

In the course of this argument, Augustine makes it clear that Petrarch has been far from single-minded in living up to these Stoic maxims. But Petrarch says that is only one side of his vexatious dilemma; the other side of it is his equal incapacity to be single-minded in enjoying life in this world because he cannot completely repudiate other-worldly concern. He laments:

Yet am I more miserable than they, for they, whatever may be their latter end, enjoy at least the pleasures of the present time; but as for me, I know not either what my end will be, and I taste no pleasure that is not poisoned with these embittering thoughts. [p. 37]

To lose the capacity to enjoy both worlds is the distressing consequence of being caught between the two.

Book 2 (the second day) of the *Secretum* is Petrarch's version of the medieval examination of conscience. Augustine runs through the list of seven deadly sins and finds Petrarch free from the sins of envy, wrath, and gluttony but guilty of cupidity, ambition, lust, and *accidia* or melancholy. Petrarch insists on his being free from cupidity (he was only providing for his old age) and ambition (he has withdrawn from the courtly world into his world of seclusion).

Augustine says that Petrarch's self-defense only reflects his self-deception. For Petrarch has withdrawn into seclusion and devoted himself to poetry in order to gain the worldly fame and glory which he cannot attain in the political world because he cannot cope with the courtly maneuvers of that world. Augustine goes on to remind Petrarch that his ravenous acquisition of worldly possessions has far exceeded the moderate aim of providing for his old age. Instead, Petrarch has gone on "dreaming of riches and power such as neither emperors nor kings have ever fully enjoyed" (p. 71). In fact, Augustine continues, Petrarch has been seeking the power of complete independence, that is, to be independent of everyone else in the whole world. Of course, this is the sovereign power which medieval Christians believed to be available only to God; even to dream of attaining such power was considered a pernicious sin.

Petrarch's desire for sovereign power is also reflected in his hatred of fortune. Augustine says, "You are vexed with Fortune." Petrarch replies, "And am I not right to hate her? Proud, violent, blind, she makes a mock of mankind" (p. 88). Augustine now says that this bitter complaint against fortune is rather unjustified since Petrarch has been abundantly blessed by her. Petrarch's reply shows that his bitter attitude stems from his hatred of dependence on fortune rather than her stingy provision for him. He says, "Up to now, as you see, I have lived always in dependence on others; it is the bitterest cup of all" (p. 94). Augustine is quite astonished at this and replies:

So then in this great whirlpool of human affairs, amid so many vicissitudes, with the future all dark before you; in a word, placed as you are at the caprice of Fortune, you will be the only

one of so many millions of mankind who shall live a life exempt
from care! [p. 94]

Petrarch's desire to be his own sovereign lord extends even to his
attitude toward his body and his environment. Although his body
has been a fairly obedient slave, he still complains, he resents being
subjected to its perpetual demands, "implicating me in its sufferings,
loading me with its burdens, asking me to sleep when my soul is
awake, and subjecting me to other human necessities which it would
be tedious to go through" (p. 96). For the same reason, he also detests filthy urban environments. He appears to regard even his body
and his environment as the tentacles of fortune for the subjection of
his helpless soul to her caprice.

It is again to his vexation with fortune that Petrarch attributes his
accidia. This is the dreadful assault of depression, melancholy, or despair. Whereas the other passions attack him in bouts, Petrarch
complains, the assault of this passion is perpetual and incessant. He
shudders at the very name of this malady. He cannot even think of
fighting it because he cannot meet it in single combat. He is besieged
by a host of its troops: "Picture to yourself some one beset with countless enemies, with no hope of escape or of pity, with no comfort
anywhere, with every one and everything against him" (p. 86). His
melancholy or depression has now turned into paranoia.

Petrarch's passionate desire to be a sovereign self is one of the most
significant marks of modernity that sets him apart from the men of
antiquity and medieval Christianity. Both Stoic sages and medieval
Christians were troubled by the fickleness of fortune, but they tried
to cope with it by disregarding or quietly accepting it. Petrarch
cannot bring himself to follow this passive mode of resolving the
conflict. In place of this subservient response, he insists on adopting
an active mode of resolution by securing for himself lordly independence of the caprice of fortune. It is this Petrarchan obsession that
rendered Renaissance man, perhaps, more conscious of the Wheel of
Fortune than anything else.

Accidia, or spiritual depression, was by no means new to the
Renaissance man; it is known to be one of the persistent problems
that medieval Christians had to cope with. But there is a remarkable
difference between the medieval and the Renaissance varieties of
accidia. Whereas the medieval was a rather quiet variety associated
with the usual connotation of the word *melancholia*, the Petrarchan

variety is definitely a turbulent one. And it is this turbulent variety that is integrally linked with paranoia.

Medieval despair was a quiet sense of depression usually stemming from disappointment with the poor gifts of fortune. Petrarchan despair becomes a passionate feeling that stems from the frustration of the ambition to establish the lordship of his sovereign self. Since this demonic ambition can be achieved only by controlling and manipulating others, its failure is bound to result in the conviction that, contrary to one's ambition, one has been controlled and manipulated by others. Hence the despair of the Renaissance man and his paranoia are likely to be two features of one and the same malady. As such, they are the inevitable symptoms of the Petrarchan obsession to be free of the caprice of fortune and establish the lordship of his sovereign self.

Augustine regards lust as the gravest of all Petrarch's sins, "that which turns you most aside from the thought of things divine" (p. 77). It is to the examination of this sin that Augustine devotes the dialogue of the third day (book 3). At its outset he tells Petrarch that he is bound by two strong chains and that he is so dazzled by their glitter as to mistake these fetters for treasures. Petrarch is eager to be told what they are, and Augustine tells him that they are "love and glory." This takes Petrarch by surprise because he has all along taken for granted the nobility of these two passions.

Since Petrarch is attached to these two "noble passions" with a single-minded devotion, he refuses to divest himself of them by simply accepting the authority of some ancient maxims. He believes that such uncritical behavior would be a serious mistake: "But what makes us go wrong is that we bind ourselves obstinately to old opinions, and will not easily part from them" (p. 111). When Augustine appeals to the unity of truth and its objectivity ("But truth itself is one and always the same"), Petrarch is even willing to reject *it*, if it contradicts his personal conviction. In this fanatic commitment to personalism, Petrarch is about to out-Augustine Augustine himself. Augustine is quite distressed at this maddening tendency of Petrarch's personalism:

> I should certainly maintain that to take for truth some ancient falsehood, and to take as falsehood some newly-discovered truth, as though all authority for truth were a matter of time, is the very climax of madness. [p. 111]

Since Petrarch is so convinced of the nobility of love and glory, he challenges Augustine to prove that they are truly evils before proposing any remedies for them. Augustine accedes to this request and tells him that his love of Laura, a mortal woman, is the subjection of his immortal soul to the filthy chains of the mortal earth. Augustine further points out that Petrarch has imposed this subjection upon himself with a religious fervor for the past sixteen years. Petrarch tries to defend his love by openly admitting that he owes all his virtues and glories to Laura and that she has inspired and sustained all of his toils without number.

Certainly, this appears to be an admission of guilt rather than its excuse. Augustine tells him that Laura has been the cause of his ruin because she has completely turned him away from the Creator. In confirmation of this point, Augustine draws his attention to the coincidence that his attraction to Laura took place about the same time as his repudiation of his religious concern. Petrarch was always conscious of having fallen in love with Laura on Good Friday, that is, the day of Christ's death on the cross (see *Rime*, nos. 3 and 211).

Petrarch tries to justify his love for Laura on the ground that it has led him to love God, but Augustine exposes this claim as another case of Petrarch's self-deception. Augustine shows him that he has, in fact, inverted the true order. Whereas our love of creatures should reflect and be subservient to our love of the Creator, Petrarch's love of God only reflects and is subservient to his love of Laura. This inversion is, of course, an act of idolatry in its Christian definition, and Petrarch was keenly conscious of the idolatrous character of his love throughout his life.

Petrarch also tries to defend his love on the ground that he loves Laura's soul rather than her body. Whereupon Augustine asks him if he would still love her soul if it were encased in an ugly body. Petrarch frankly admits his inability to feel such a love; as Francesco de Sanctis says, the feeling for lovely form is second nature to him.[7] The reason Petrarch gives for his inability is quite interesting: one cannot discern the beauty of a soul unless it is manifest in visible form. This demand for the visible manifestation of the invisible is, again, one of the unique hallmarks Petrarch brings to the Renaissance sensibility.

Any ancient Platonist would have taken for granted that the beauty of the intelligible realm can never be fully manifest in the chaotic material world, and Augustine himself would never have questioned this point. But with the arrival of the Porretani and their immanent Platonism, the discrepancy between the intelligible and the perceptible realms has been replaced by their intimate union. Whereas the ancient Platonists expected only an intellectual intuition of intelligible entities, the new Platonists like Petrarch are now demanding a sensible intuition of those entities. Furthermore, whatever *cannot* be shown in such a visible perception is inconsequential to Petrarchan personalism.

This is a new requirement for relevance and significance that Petrarch introduces into the Renaissance, and it is in perfect accord with his personalism. It is this new demand of Petrarchan personalism that appears to have inspired the development of perspectivism in Renaissance painting. In this Renaissance perspectivism, what counts is not what the things are in themselves but what they appear to be to the perceiver. That is, the center of perception is shifted from the perceived to the perceiver.

Petrarch makes his final attempt to defend his love by appealing to the power of Laura's virtue and constancy. She has not only kept her virtue in spite of his frequent entreaties, but has also taken him by the hand as though he were blind and set him right in the way of virtue whenever he has gone astray. Augustine's reply to this defense appears to be innocuous: "In a word, your life became wholly dependent on hers" (p. 134). But it is this harmless remark that finally breaks down Petrarch's defense. He gives in by saying, "I must own myself beaten; for it appears all you have said is taken from the very heart of the book of experience."

This final admission of Petrarch clearly shows how much importance he attaches to his desire to be sovereign and independent. Up to this point, he has defended his love of Laura as though there could be nothing more precious. But as soon as he realizes that his love has been jeopardizing his own autonomy, he feels as though all the power of his defensive argument were taken from him. It is this fanatic desire for sovereign independence that has constituted "the very heart of the book of experience" for Petrarch, and it is this argument from the book of experience, not from the book of classical maxims, that pierces the Petrarchan personalistic heart.

Augustine's understanding of Petrarch's love for Laura almost verges on the psychoanalysis of subconscious desires. He tells Petrarch that he has developed an obsessive passion for the laurels of empire and poetry probably because their name resembles Laura. A contemporary psychoanalyst would say that Petrarch's obsession with fame and glory in the world of politics and poetry was a transference of his love for Laura. Discovering that the laurel of empire was beyond his reach, Augustine goes on to say, Petrarch has devoted himself to attaining the laurel of poetry. In the language of psychoanalysis, Petrarch's craving for poetic glory was a surrogate or substitute for his craving for political glory. Augustine points out to Petrarch that his driving ambition toward glory and fame has plunged him into the frenzied toil of writing the history of Rome and his epic, the *Africa*.

Augustine tells Petrarch that he has completely reversed the order of virtue and glory. Augustine says, "You know that glory is in a sense the shadow of virtue" (p. 182). Instead of seeking virtue for its own sake, Petrarch has been obsessed with the pursuit of glory as his real end. Augustine tells Petrarch that this obsession with glory and fame not only distracts him from the care of his soul but also contradicts his contempt for the vulgar crowd. Augustine shows him that the essence of glory lies in public reputation which passes from mouth to mouth. He goes on to say:

> It is, then, but a breath, a changing wind; and, what will disgust you more, it is the breath of a crowd. I know to whom I am speaking. I have observed that no man more than you abhors the manners and behavior of the common herd. [p. 167]

Augustine reveals to Petrarch his subconscious motive for the pursuit of fame: the false immortality of fame has been his surrogate for the true immortality of the soul. In the *Symposium*, Plato defines love as our longing for immortality. Since Petrarch is seeking his love in this mortal world, the only immortality he can expect is that of fame and glory because only these can survive his death. So it is his love for Laura that ultimately drives him into his perpetual struggle for glory and fame in this world.

R. R. Bolgar has rightly called Petrarch the high priest of the Renaissance cult of fame. He further identifies this cult as a necessary by-product of the cult of virtue: "So, glory is at once the proof of natural excellence or *virtus* and the reward required to bring this excellence to perfection."[8] This may very well have been the case with the Roman sage, but not with Petrarch. Petrarch himself admits that the cult of fame with him is a necessary adjunct to his cult of immortality, which in turn stems from his cult of love.

Augustine reminds Petrarch of the brevity of human fame and glory. Since their essence resides in the transitory breath of the common herd, says Augustine, fame and glory are not much more durable than fragile human life itself. So anyone seeking the false immortality of fame and glory is bound to meet what Petrarch in his *Africa* calls man's second death. Fame and glory may last a little longer, if they are kept alive in books and other written records. But even these written records cannot ultimately escape the common fate of decay and extinction inherent in things of this mortal world. Hence those who can survive the second death have to suffer what Petrarch calls the third death.

Augustine counsels Petrarch to regain control of himself by ridding himself of this blinding obsession with the erroneous pursuit of illusory immortality. He tells Petrarch that the completion of his epic will not do any good either for his soul or for the glory of his epic hero, Scipio. Augustine urges him to abandon all his work on Roman history and the *Africa* at once, and to devote himself to the care of his soul alone. And he backs up his exhortation with the Ciceronian maxim that the life of a wise man is all one preparation for death.

Augustine's exhortation proves completely inefficacious against Petrarch's irrevocable stand on this world. He is convinced that life in this world cannot be used only as a preparation for life in the other world. He is determined to live in this world for its own sake in spite of its mortality. He tells Augustine that he will worry about eternal things when he goes to the eternal world. Even if he wanted to abandon earthly concerns, Petrarch tells Augustine, he does not have the power to do so. Augustine tells him that nothing can be done about it because it is the matter of one's will, or rather existential choice. So Augustine is forced to terminate his effort to persuade and says, "Well, so it must be, if it cannot be otherwise" (p. 192). This is the parting of the ways for Petrarch and his Augustine.

So it appears at the end of the *Secretum* that Petrarch resolutely abandons Augustine's steep and narrow path and wholeheartedly embraces his own straight and broad one. Such a resolute choice would surely resolve Petrarch's problem and would not be a fault except in the medieval Christian sense. All he has to do from now on is to forget the other world and devote himself to life in this world, then there would be no more Petrarchan problem left in Petrarch. But unfortunately, this simple way out of his dilemma is completely beyond his power. In truth, Petrarch can never detach himself from the world of eternity any more readily than he can from this world. What he really longs for and insists on having is this world in the mode of eternity, or conversely, the other world in the mode of mundane immediacy.

It has been well-established Platonic practice to conceive of the two worlds as having mutually contradictory attributes. This world is mutable and transitory, while the other world is immutable and eternal. The other world is orderly and beautiful, while this world is chaotic and ugly. Because of the incompatibility of these contradictory attributes, medieval Christians had resigned themselves to expecting only an allegorical representation of the eternal in the temporal sphere. This allegorical mood was dictated by the Platonic dictum that time is only the moving image of eternity.

Petrarch cannot be content with this medieval allegorical resolution of the two worlds. He is too much of a literalist; he goes even beyond Augustine in espousing Augustinian literalism. As I pointed out in the last chapter, the central thrust of Augustinian Biblical exegesis is to find spiritual sense embodied in literal sense. As far as Augustine is concerned, however, this union of the two senses is claimed only for one privileged moment in human history, the Incarnation. But Petrarch, the new Augustinian, insists on extending this privileged union to every moment in history. Thus he seeks to have the temporal in the mode of the eternal or the latter in the mode of the former. This neo-Augustinian demand entails the Petrarchan attempt to invest the temporal with the attributes of the eternal, or vice versa, an attempt that may be called the "Petrarchan investiture."

Instead of uniting the two incompatible domains into one, the Petrarchan investiture is bound to result in the dilemma of getting caught between the two, or "[having] one foot on earth and one in heaven."[9] It is this inner conflict that Petrarch regards as the ultimate source of all his miseries. The recognition of this inner conflict is the most important insight he gains from his three-day dialogue with Augustine in the *Secretum*. As some critics have said, it may very well be the case that Petrarch's *Secretum* was occasioned by his double frustration in love and ambition.[10] In the *Secretum* itself, however, Petrarch does not even think of attributing his miseries to external causes. Since his conflict is understood as being exclusively internal, the alternative title for *Secretum meum* in some manuscripts, *De secreto conflictu curarum mearum* (On the Inner Conflict of my Concerns), is not only justifiable but also quite revealing.

Morris Bishop observes that in the *Secretum* Petrarch divides himself into the two figures of Petrarch-Augustinus and Petrarch-Franciscus, and that he does this in the hope of reuniting them in a more confident whole or spiritual purge.[11] Indeed, Petrarch does divide himself in two, but the hope of reunification never materializes. That the two figures cannot be rejoined is dictated by Petrarch's adoption of Augustinian dyadic logic. The disputation of the *Secretum* is limited to two protagonists, neither of whom is prepared to give way to the other. The only third person is Lady Truth, but she has no intention of intervening as a mediator.

The two Petrarchs should be understood as the respective representatives of the old and the new Augustinianism. Petrarch-Augustinus represents Augustine's own Augustinianism, which resolutely rejects this world for the sake of the other; Petrarch-Franciscus represents Petrarch's own Augustinianism, which finds it impossible to forsake this world for the other. Petrarch-Augustinus is the old Augustine who recognizes the unity of literal and spiritual senses only in one Christian miracle, the Incarnation; Petrarch-Franciscus is the new Augustine who insists on extending this unity to the entire universe.

The transition from old to new Augustinianism has been achieved through the Dionysian sensibility; especially the Victorines of the twelfth century played a crucial role in this transformation of the Augustinian sensibility. Dionysian universalism is surely one way of extending the miraculous unity of literal and spiritual senses to the entire universe, but this unity remains only allegorical for the Dionysian transcendentists. The Dionysian immanentists, however, claimed the unity of the two senses on the literal or historical level. As we have seen in the previous chapter, Rupert of Deutz and Joachim of Floris claim the eventual advent of the Age of the Spirit, in which the sanctification of the entire world will be fulfilled in the cosmic unity of the two senses.

Petrarch goes one step further than even these Dionysian radicals. Whereas they had talked of the Age of the Spirit largely in the future tense, whether distant or imminent future, Petrarch feels and acts as though the Age of the Spirit had—or should have—already come upon the earth. It is this assumption or pretense that lies behind the Petrarchan investiture. Thus, the Petrarchan or new Augustinian sensibility is the immediate descendent of Dionysian immanentism. This is why Petrarch-Augustinus (the old Augustine) is time and again irritated and distressed by Petrarch-Franciscus (the new Augustine); as a matter of fact, the demands and feelings of the latter are quite alien and outrageous to the former. What is truly Augustinian in the Petrarchan sensibility is its emphasis on inwardness; and we have, in the previous chapter, seen a similar phenomenon occurring with the Victorines of the twelfth century.

The *Secretum*, which may appear to record the dispute between old and new Augustinianism, really presents the Petrarchan version of the continuous conflict between Augustinianism and Dionysianism. In chapter 2 we have seen that this conflict had been at the heart of the thematic dialectic of the Western ethos since the condemnation of John Scotus Erigena, and that various attempts had been made toward its resolution. In the *Secretum*, Petrarch fully examines the nature of this continuing conflict, especially the strife of Augustinianism against Dionysian immanentism, and demonstrates the impossibility of achieving a satisfactory resolution of it.

The interminable dispute between Petrarch-Augustinus and Petrarch-Franciscus shows the irreconcilability of the thematic conflict in question without destroying the integrity of its components. The only sensible course of action appears to be the spiritual purge of eliminating one of its protagonists. Theodore E. Mommsen says that Petrarch is fascinated by the metaphor of the parting ways and that he admires Hercules for his courageous choice (*in bivio*).[12] Petrarch observes that Hercules attained a wholesome life-plan by his resolute choice at the parting of the two ways. For the sake of the integrity of his own existence, Petrarch sees the urgent need to make his own resolute choice. But he also knows that such a choice is beyond his power precisely because the two parting ways constitute the two inseparable poles of the Petrarchan soul. It is this recognition of the impossibility of choosing between the two poles of his own soul, coupled with his conviction of their irreconcilability, that provides the Petrarchan dilemma with its unique sense of poignancy.

I have gone into quite a detailed exploration of the *Secretum* because of my suspicion that it may prove to be the secret key (if there is one) to understanding Petrarch and his works. In fact, as Thomas G. Bergin documents, the assessment of this little work among Petrarch scholars has been far from unanimous.[13] Some have regarded it as a "precious document," while others have been rather annoyed by "its pretentiousness." If it is to be the secret key to comprehending the complex nature of Petrarch and his works, it is bound to be not only precious but pretentious. I may go a little further and exaggerate its importance by claiming that it may be the essential key to understanding the most prevalent predicament of modern man. I shall partly illustrate this claim with a couple of outstanding cases, those of Martin Luther and Sören Kierkegaard.

The Petrarchan Sickness in the Modern West

Norman O. Brown has called our attention to the enormous significance of Luther's literalism for the development of modern European sensibility. Brown says, "Luther's word is *Eindeutigkeit*: The 'single, simple, solid and stable meaning' of scripture: *unum simplicem solidum et constantem sensus.*"[14] It is with this motto of *Eindeutigkeit* that Luther became the father of Protestant literalism, which sometimes takes the form of fundamentalism.

Luther's literalism stemmed from his attempt to recapture the Augustinian principle of Biblical exegesis that spiritual sense be contained in literal sense. Hence his literalism eventuates in the impossible dream of uniting the eternal and the temporal, or the spiritual and the carnal. This dream is vividly manifest in his doctrine of the Eucharist. Evidently, he felt that the traditional dogma of transubstantiation was too feeble and too remote to capture the Augustinian spirit of immediate union. So in its place he advocated his doctrine of real and physical presence—that is, the Lord is literally and physically present in the Eucharist.*

---

*Luther's doctrine of the Eucharist is generally known as consubstantiation as opposed to the Catholic doctrine of transubstantiation. The latter holds that the consecration of the Eucharist transforms the *substance* of the bread and wine into the *substance* of the flesh and blood of Christ, while their accidents remain unchanged. The former holds that in the Eucharist the substances both of Christ's flesh and blood and of the bread and wine are present in union with each other. The difference between these two doctrines lies in different conceptions of *substance*. In Catholic doctrine, 'substance' means metaphysical substance, the unperceivable substratum of a material object. In Lutheran doctrine, 'substance' means the physical substance, which consists of the accidents of the metaphysical substance.

The doctrine of consubstantiation amounts to claiming the *physical presence* ("in, with, and under the earthly elements") of the Lord in the Eucharist, while the doctrine of transubstantiation claims his *metaphysical presence*. The former is a more immediate presence than the latter because it is visible and tangible while the latter is invisible and intangible. Distressed at this Lutheran notion of physical presence, John Calvin blamed the Lutherans for effacing the absolute distinction between flesh and spirit, and formulated his doctrine of real but spiritual presence in opposition to the Lutheran doctrine of real and physical presence.

In spite of this longing for the intimate union of the eternal and the temporal, Luther is at the same time disgusted with Renaissance immanentism and its tendency to confuse the two. So he spares no effort in insisting upon the incompatibility of the inner and the outer, the spiritual and the carnal. Furthermore, he appoints himself champion of the interior spirit in his fight against the external authority of the Catholic Church.

Like Petrarch's, Luther's is the internal problem of getting caught between the temporal and the eternal and not being able to reject either of them. His notorious antagonism toward his father and the Church may very well have been a projection of this internal conflict. In the *Secretum*, as we have seen, Petrarch compared his own inner struggle to a relentless battle or siege, and showed symptoms of a paranoid complex. If this is also the case with Luther, the usual Freudian accounting for his aggression would be the reversal of the true order. Whereas the Freudians would tend to view Luther's inner conflict as a result of his internalizing his external conflict with his father, his external conflict with his father is more likely to have been a consequence of his externalizing his own inner conflict.

In *Philosophical Fragments*, Kierkegaard restates Luther's problem in the language of paradox. He regards it as the central paradox of Christianity that the Eternal came into existence in a historical moment.[15] He claims that this event poses an existential paradox for every serious Christian—namely, that his eternal happiness is based on a historical occasion. Because of this paradox, he says, Christianity is an outrageous folly or absurdity (*quia absurdum*) that is bound to offend any reasonable man.

In *The Sickness unto Death*, Kierkegaard takes the Lutheran agony out of its original religious context and gives it a universal formulation. He defines despair as a uniquely human sickness arising from the internal discrepancy felt between incompatible components, the temporal and the eternal, the finite and the infinite.[16] These are the categories that Petrarch himself uses in analyzing his own malady. Since these incommensurate components can never be brought into harmonious reconciliation, Kierkegaard claims, this sickness cannot be terminated except by death. Hence he calls it "the sickness unto death."

Kierkegaard recognizes only one way to heal this sickness of spirit, namely, the religious act of "grounding oneself transparently in the Creator." But Petrarch cannot bring himself to accept this religious resolution of his problem; in Kierkegaard's language, he is compelled to take the defiant stance of trying to be himself by detaching himself from the "Power which posited it."[17] Kierkegaard recognizes the affinity of this despair of defiance with Stoic fortitude; Petrarch feels perpetually fascinated with Stoic fortitude as manifested by Seneca and Cicero.

This sickness unto death was so widespread that Kierkegaard was convinced of its universality. He regarded it as the inevitable destiny of being human. Despair per se in one form or another may be found in any human community, but the despair which stems from the disrelation of the temporal and the eternal is a legacy of the Petrarchan tradition. Thus Petrarch's sickness turns out to be the prototype for the modern European sickness, and for this alone he deserves to be called the first modern man. It is, furthermore, quite likely that he was keenly aware of setting up this sickly pattern when he said "That I became a lesson [*essempio*] to the rest" or "And I became a fable [*favola*] to mankind" (see *Rime* nos. 1 and 23). Let us now try our secret key to unlock some of Petrarch's own complex behavior and works.

Petrarch exalts rhetoric as the highest form of all philosophy. This exaltation would be an offense and scandal to any classical philosopher, who would not admit rhetoric even as a lowest branch of philosophy proper. Rhetoric is an art of persuasion, whereas philosophy is a science of demonstration. At best rhetoric may be regarded as a poor substitute for philosophy. But Petrarch knew very well that the existential dilemma he was confronted with could not be settled by any metaphysical argumentation. For this reason, the science of metaphysics proved to be of little use to him. Since only the art of persuasion could give him some help in his existential choice, he had every reason to exalt rhetoric over metaphysics.

In his eyes, Cicero the master rhetorician stands well above Aristotle the master metaphysician. Even Plato appears to be worthy of his respect mainly as the source of Ciceronian rhetoric. Thomas G. Bergin says, "Dante wants us to *see* with him and Petrarch wants us to *feel* with him."[18] Dante has the metaphysician's eye; Petrarch has the rhetorician's heart. Cosmology and ethics, the question of fact and the question of value, which are fused in the Dantesque sensibility, are sundered in the Petrarchan world. This rupture that intensifies Petrarchan personalism becomes a permanent legacy to modern man.

Petrarch, who can settle his mind neither in heaven nor on earth, becomes a true spiritual exile. The notion of spiritual exile is a legacy from medieval Christianity: pious Christians were taught to look upon their earthly sojourn as an exile from their true home in heaven. But this medieval sense of exile was fundamentally a temporary one because of the pious hope and longing to reach the permanent home in heaven. In contrast to this, Petrarch's sense of exile becomes a permanent one because he has abandoned this hope and longing. As Bergin says, Petrarch becomes a truly displaced person, feeling at home nowhere, not even in his native Italy.[19] Bergin goes on to point out that even his language is that of a displaced person, "one who speaks his native tongue correctly and carefully but not quite colloquially." In short, Petrarch is an alienated man, and his alienation is rooted in his perpetual suspension between the heavenly and the earthly kingdoms.

Paradox and the Petrarchan Sensibility

In the first eclogue, Petrarch tries to reproduce the internal conflict of his *Secretum*. This pastoral poem is cast in the form of a dialogue between Monicus and Silvius, and is meant to highlight the contrast between the cloistered life his brother Gherardo has chosen as a Carthusian monk and the secular life he himself has chosen as a worldly poet. In the opening lines of the poem, Silvius describes the contrast:

> Monicus, hidden away alone in your quiet cavern,
> You have been free to ignore the cares of the flock and the
>   pastures;
> I must continue to range over thorny hills and through
>   thickets.[20]
>
> [Eclogue 1. 1–3]

In reply, Monicus says that all of Silvius's problems are of his own making: "Silvius, why do you grumble? The true cause of all of your troubles / Lies in yourself and no other"[21] (Eclogue 1. 6–7).

Monicus, who has chosen the Augustinian way of renunciation, is supposed to have only one eye. In contrast to this, Silvius presumably has two eyes. If Silvius were to drive the other-worldly concern completely out of his mind, he would also have only one eye. So his retention of two eyes should be understood as a symbol of his struggle to possess both worlds. In fact, Silvius describes his trouble as a perpetual attempt to "go back and forth" between the loftiest summit and the depths of the valleys (Eclogue 1. 32–42). It is this sense of perpetual oscillation that clearly distinguishes Petrarch from Dante. In sharp contrast to Petrarch's, Dante's sense of space is thoroughly unidirectional; that is, he is always moving forward and never retraces his steps, whether it be from the *Convivio* to *De monarchia,* or from Hell through Purgatory to Heaven.

Monicus and Silvius go on to describe their respective favorite poets. Monicus loves David; Silvius admires Homer and Virgil. Monicus says that his David sings of the One, his power and glory (Eclogue 1. 91 ff.). In Silvius's view, however, David is just like Monicus, that is, his single-minded devotion to the One comes from his shutting himself up in the little cavern of Jerusalem (Eclogue 1. 72 ff.). In contrast to this, Silvius claims, his Homer and Virgil sing of the spirits ruling over the three kingdoms of Heaven, Ocean, and Tartarus (Eclogue 1. 74 ff.). In short, his poets have to keep both eyes open.

When Silvius describes the hero of his own epic, which is to be modeled after the works of Homer and Virgil, he takes pains to endow him with both heavenly and earthly attributes:

> . . . Fame tells of a youthful hero,
> Favored by heaven and born of the race of the gods and
>   now filling
> Meadows and fields of the African shore with report of his
>   exploits.
>
> [Eclogue 1. 102–04][22]

Since Silvius is determined to be a two-eyed poet, he is destined to part ways with his one-eyed brother Monicus. So the pastoral dialogue ends with Monicus's sad farewell to Silvius.

Thus the imagery of one and two, or rather one *or* two, pervades the entire eclogue. To begin with, it is concerned with the destiny that "has shaped different lots for twin brothers, / Born of one mother" (Eclogue 1. 4–5).[23] Perhaps for the sake of a perfect numerical contrast, the one-eyed Monicus loves one poet (David) while the two-eyed Silvius loves two (Homer and Virgil). The one-and-two imagery becomes so intricate in the dialogue between the two brothers that the one-eyed Monicus eventually gets confused about the priority of one to two or that of two to one, and says:

> Happily you may have heard of the mountain where two
>   mighty rivers
> Spring from one source alone, or where there pours forth from
>   twin fountains
> One sacred stream which from them draws its source and its
>   name and its waters?[24]
>
> [Eclogue 1. 62–64]

Of these two, Silvius prefers the latter—that is, the one stream that
flows from two sources. Of course, this imagery captures Silvius's ideal
of being a two-eyed poet who can bring heavenly and earthly affairs
together into one epic.

That this pastoral poem is cast in the form of a dialogue is itself
one of its unique features. As Bergin points out, Petrarch writes not
only his first eclogue but his entire *Bucolicum carmen* in the form of
conversations between shepherds.[25] Aldo S. Bernardo has patiently
demonstrated how the dialogue form is one of the persistent charac-
teristics of Petrarch's composition.[26] As Bernardo shows, the form of
dramatic dialogue not only dominates the *Secretum* but becomes
prominent in the *Africa* and the *Triumphs*. What truly surprises him is
the frequent appearance of dialogues and monologues even in
Petrarch's *Epistolae metricae*.[27] In most cases, however, these dialogues
and monologues are simply the projection of Petrarch's inner speech,
which accompanies the perpetual conflict and tension in his heart.
Hence there is no substantial difference between his monologues
and dialogues; their common essence is the form of dialogical argumentation. In the dialogues, the argumentation takes place between
two persons; in the monologues, it takes place between the two poles
of one person. In either case, the form of dialogical argumentation is
an eminently suitable way of objectifying Petrarch's subjective tension and torment.

Petrarch's oscillation between the heavenly and the earthly poles
of his existence appears to be reflected in the perpetual fluctuation of
his moods. Robert M. Durling has called our attention to this fluctuation in his fine study of Petrarch's *Rime*.[28] He regards the *Rime*
as a cumulative record of Petrarch's shifting moods. He is fascinated
with the continuous mutation of Petrarch's mood from moment to
moment and says, "His state varies abruptly from the extreme of
hopelessness to manic joy."[29] Here are two sonnets that illustrate this
abrupt change:

> Go, burning sighs, into that frozen heart;
> Shatter the ice that now with pity vies,
> And if a mortal prayer can reach the skies,
> Let death or mercy end at last this smart.
>
> Go, loving thoughts, and speak aloud and show
> What hides where her fair glance is not extended:

If her contempt or my star is offended
We shall be out of hope and out of woe.

You certainly can say, though not quite well,
That our condition is as dark as hell,
While her own is serene, peaceful and fair.

Go, you are safe, because Love comes with us;
And wicked fortune may decline and pass,
If the signs of my sun predict the air.[30]

[*Rime*, no. 153]

As Petrarch anticipates, his mood changes in a short while from
despondency to ecstacy:

I saw on earth angelic manners show;
Heavenly beauties, in the world, alone,
So that recalling them is joy and woe,
For it seems shadow, smoke or dream that shone.

And I saw those two lights with tears abound,
That thousand times were envied by the sun:
And I heard between sighs some words resound
That make hills move and rivers stop to run.

Love, wisdom, valour, pity and distress
Made in weeping a sweeter symphony
Than any to be heard here in this world;

The sky was so entranced by the harmony,
That no leaf on the branch was being curled:
The air and wind were filled with such sweetness.[31]

[*Rime*, no. 156]

Petrarch regards his changing mood as a fluctuation between life
and death; he feels he is always suspended "halfway between living
and dead" (*Rime*, no. 23). Durling says, "One of the basic structural
principles in the *Canzoniere* is the juxtaposition of such conflicting—
and chronologically sequential—states."[32] Petrarch does not always
confine one sonnet or canzone to one mood: the juxtaposition of his
conflicting moods gives birth to the Petrarchan oxymoron, whose
essence Leonard Forster tries to distill in one phrase, "the icy fire."[33]
Forster selects the following sonnet to illustrate the working of the
Petrarchan oxymoron:

Can it be love that fills my heart and brain?
If love, dear God, what is its quality?
If it is good, why does it torture me?
If evil, why this sweetness in my pain?

If I burn gladly, why do I complain?
If I hate burning, why do I never flee?
O life-in-death, O lovely agony,
How can you rule me so, if I'm not fain?

And if I'm willing, why do I suffer so?—
By such contrary winds I'm blown in terror
In a frail and rudderless bark on open seas,

Ballasted all with ignorance and error.
Even my own desire I do not know;
I burn in winter and in high summer freeze.[34]

[*Rime*, no. 132]

Although only two lines of overtly oxymoronic statement occur in this sonnet ("O life-in death, O lovely agony" and "I burn in winter and in high summer freeze"), the sense of Petrarchan paradox implicity pervades the entire poem. As Forster says, Petrarch relies on the conditional, interrogative pattern of "if-why" in the construction of this poem.[35] This "if-why" pattern not only conveys the sense of Petrarchan paradox, but also reflects the dialogical mood of the self-examining heart.

Petrarch's may be called the paradoxical sensibility. This is not to say that the literary device of paradox is his invention or his monopoly; paradox is indeed one of the oldest of human inventions. What is noteworthy about the Petrarchan paradox is its ubiquity. Since paradox normally consists in the seemingly impossible conjunction of two or more incompatible predicates, it is usually reserved for the description of exceptional cases of abnormality or supernormality. With Petrarch, however, paradox becomes an integral feature of his normality. In her *Paradoxia Epidemica: The Renaissance Tradition of Paradox*, Rosalie L. Colie has shown how paradox becomes an epidemic in Renaissance literature.[36] Although she counts Petrarch among the prominent masters of this Renaissance epidemic art, she does not give him the credit for being its fountainhead. I may be exaggerating a bit. Petrarch's position as the source of the Renaissance *paradoxia epidemica* appears to be as solid as his position as the founding father of Renaissance humanism.

With the New Critics, paradox and ambiguity have been well established as the two focal points of literary criticism and interpretation. These critics are firmly convinced that the highest level of reading a piece of literature is to understand all its paradoxes and ambiguities. This conviction in turn reflects their assumption that the meaning of a poem or a novel can never be clear and straightforward but is bound to be paradoxical and ambiguous. The same point can be restated in terms of a poet or a novelist: a writer, at least a great one, should be presumed to be a person of conflicting views on everything. In either formulation, Petrarch clearly emerges as the prototype for the canon of the New Criticism.

The New Critics came to settle on these assumptions and presuppositions because they developed their canon within the context of modern European literature, which is indeed a harem of paradoxes and ambiguities. But the provinciality of their approach becomes obvious as soon as it is extended beyond the province of the modern European tradition. For example, one of the impassable obstacles that confronts its application to medieval literature is medieval didacticism; it is so intractable that it almost becomes offensive to the paradoxical sensibility of the New Criticism.

Since didactic works in general are meant to convey some straightforward teachings, they cannot leave much room for paradox and ambiguity. Hence the New Critics have been rather hard on any didactic tendency. This is their dogma: true works of literature should be free of didactic simplicity. Herbert Muller has reminded Cleanth Brooks, one of the ardent opponents of the didactic heresy, that this tenet of the New Criticism must pay the heavy price of condemning even the Bible, Milton, and Dante.[37] In his effort to meet this charge and exempt Dante from condemnation as didactic, Brooks sets out to find some streaks of paradox and ambiguity in the *Commedia*. But all he can find to his purpose is Dante's relegation of one or two popes to the Inferno. On this scant evidence, Brooks wants to exempt Dante from the didactic heresy: "Indeed, I should say that Dante was willing to expose his preachment to something very like 'ironical contemplation.' "[38]

Dante places a couple of popes in his Hell not for any "ironic contemplation" but for their outright damnation. He wants to convey the simple orthodox teaching that every unrepentant sinner is subject to condemnation whether he has occupied an exalted or a humble station in life. There is nothing paradoxical or ambiguous about it.

As a matter of fact, the entire *Commedia* is permeated with the spirit of clarity and coherence rather than one of paradox and ambiguity. In contrast to Petrarch, Dante reserves paradox for the extraordinary function of stating the two dogmas of Christian mystery, the Incarnation and the Trinity. Although he is fully aware of the paradoxical character of these two dogmas, he never shows any sign of ambiguity in his acceptance of them. In the case of Petrarch, even the acceptance of simple facts is usually loaded with ambiguity. This is why his sonnets and odes are often riddled with a series of interrogative sentences.

In the *Commedia*, then, paradox comes into the human sphere only by virtue of the infusion of divinity, whose paradoxical nature is given in the dogmas of the Incarnation and the Trinity. A good example of this is the first line in St. Bernard's prayer to the Queen of Heaven on Dante's behalf: "Virgin mother, daughter of thy son" (*Par.* 33. 1). This line consists of two oxymora that are inconceivable in purely human terms. But the first of them (her being a virgin and a mother at the same time) manifests the mystery of the Incarnation; the second (her being the daughter of her own son) reflects the mystery of the Trinity. In contrast to this infusion of paradox into the human from the divine sphere in Dante, with Petrarch man himself becomes the source of paradox. Thus the Petrarchan man is a new Sphinx.

Petrarch makes two sustained attempts to resolve the riddle of this new Sphinx: one in the *Triumphs* and the other in the *Africa*. Since the Petrarchan tension consists in being trapped between the temporal and the eternal, its resolution can take two forms. Petrarch can either start out with the temporal and invest it with the eternal attributes, or bring the heavenly down to earth for temporal or historical concretion. One is the way of ascent; the other is the way of descent. Petrarch takes the way of ascent in the *Triumphs* and the way of descent in the *Africa*.

The *Triumphs*

The *Triumphs* is Petrarch's vision of six processions of Love, Chastity, Death, Fame, Time, and Eternity. The central theme of these six *Triumphs* is the immortality of the mortal, that is, how to secure the immortality of earthly existence. Throughout the *Rime*, the mutability and mortality of earthly love is one of the most obsessive and recurrent themes. In the *Triumphs*, Petrarch tries to overcome this mortality by transforming the mutation of temporal existence into a succession of transmutations.

The Triumph of Love presents the mortality of earthly love and passion, which is overcome by the Triumph of Chastity; in other words, the mortality of human passions is overcome by subjecting them to human virtue. Human virtues are also mortal, although they may be a little more durable than human passions. So the Triumph of Chastity is superseded by the Triumph of Death, which is in turn superseded by the Triumph of Fame. The power of fame perpetuates the earthly existence beyond its natural death. But this second human existence cannot avoid its second death, the oblivion of time. The Triumph of Fame is superseded by the Triumph of Time, which is in turn overcome by the Triumph of Eternity. Only eternity can assure the final immortality of the earthly.

Thus the six processions in the *Triumphs* turn out to be Petrarch's long detour on the way to realizing that real immortality can be secured only in the eternal kingdom. Of course, this is an obvious conclusion to anyone who knows that only the eternal can truly endure, or rather that "eternity" and "immortality" are only two different labels for one and the same thing. As far as Petrarch is concerned, he makes this detour simply because he is intent upon securing immortality for the temporal existence in its own right, that is, without paying the price of surrendering it as a vassalage to the Kingdom of Heaven. Hence, even in the Triumph of Eternity he cannot bring himself to a wholehearted acceptance of the heavenly world for its own sake.

In the last Triumph, Petrarch clearly expresses his deep-seated reservation about the heavenly kingdom in many different ways. To begin with, he says that, unlike the first five Triumphs, the last one is not a procession at all:

> Five of these Triumphs on the earth below
> We have beheld, and at the end, the sixth,
> God willing, we shall see in heaven above.[39]

Whereas the first five Triumphs are described in the past tense, the last Triumph is cast in the future tense. The former is supposedly Petrarch's witness report; the latter is no more than an expression of pious hope. Petrarch refuses to take his processions to the heavenly kingdom for the resolution of the theme of earthly immortality.

Instead he is intent on remaining on earth; he concludes the six Triumphs in Rome, the earthly city par excellence.

The eternal kingdom Petrarch projects in the last Triumph is no more than an idealization of the earthly kingdom:

> So ran my thought; and as I pondered it
> More and more deeply, I at last beheld
> A world made new and changeless and eternal.
>
> I saw the sun, the heavens, and the stars
> And land and sea unmade, and made again
> More beauteous and more joyous than before.[40]

What Petrarch sees in his vision of eternity is neither the angels nor their Creator, but the sun and stars, the land and sea of the visible world. Furthermore, he takes pains to tell us that his vision is no more than a creation of his own imagination.

Although the living Laura is presented as the central figure only of the Triumph of Chastity, the six Triumphs may be regarded as the successive transmutations of this Laura. As Bergin points out, there are many Lauras: Laura-Sophonisba, Laura-Daphne, and Laura-Beatrice.[41] Laura-Sophonisba is the lady of sensuous beauty; Laura-Daphne is the symbol of fame; Laura-Beatrice is the symbol of eternity. To this list, we may add Larua-Diana, the symbol of chastity or virtue. The first two Triumphs are for the transmutation of Laura-Sophonisba into Laura-Diana; the middle two, for that of Laura-Diana into Laura-Daphne; the last two, for that of Laura-Daphne into Laura-Beatrice.

In truth, Laura is a many-faced lady; the *Triumphs* is a successive display of her various faces. Laura maintains her immortality through her elusiveness: "Showing to me her shadow, veil or gear,/From time to time, never her face entire" (*Rime*, no. 119).[42] Thus she becomes the object of the endless Petrarchan pursuit; she is the cruel Diana who refuses to respond to Petrarch's love. In the Triumph of Death, Petrarch gains a chance to find out what Laura's true feeling toward him during her life was. In spite of her cruel appearance, she now tells him, she always loved him dearly:

> Sighing, she answered: "Never was my heart
> From thee divided, nor shall ever be.
> Thy flame I tempered with my countenance
>
> Because there was no other way than this
> To save us both . . .[43]

Laura's perpetual elusiveness is the only way to ensure the immortality of her beauty and his love. Since the earthly ideal is rooted in earthly desire, Petrarch knows, its fulfillment is simultaneously its extinction. Hence, his repeated failure to catch up with Laura turns out to be his assurance of keeping her in his permanent possession. This is the Petrarchan way of possessing the temporal in the mode of eternity, or of establishing the infinite sovereignty of his finite self over mutability.

Since Laura has to take on so many different faces, as many critics have pointed out, she tends to be much more a fabrication of Petrarch's imagination and fantasy than a creature of the real world.[44] As Bergin says, this product of fantasy chiefly portrays Petrarch's subjective feelings rather than Laura's responses to them.[45] Although Petrarch gives a far more concrete description of Laura's sensuous beauty than Dante does of Beatrice's, he also gives far fewer historical details of his love affair than Dante. In fact, Petrarch was faced with the charge of having fabricated Laura and tried to clear himself of this accusation in one of his letters (*Epistolae familiares*, 11. 9). Although the historical existence of Laura seems to be beyond dispute, she appears to be no more than a convenient means for displaying the many splendors of Petrarch's fecund imagination.

Perhaps in due recognition of the fictitious character of Laura's transmutability, Petrarch conceives his *Triumphs* in the medieval tradition of the dream-vision. For this reason, Petrarch is likely to have thought that he was treading in the footsteps of Dante. His *Triumphs* are written in the terza rima of the *Commedia*; the processions are reminiscent of Beatrice's Procession on the top of Mount Purgatory, which in turn harks back to the medieval ecclesiastical processions. Hidden behind these and a few other points of apparent similarity, however, lies a marked difference in the content of the two visions.

Whereas Dante's vision is intended to be objective, Petrarch's turns out to be subjective. Everything Dante sees on his journey is meant to be an allegorical reflection of the transcendent reality; everything Petrarch sees in the *Triumphs* is no more than a series of successive projections of his own imagination. This difference in the contents of the two poets' respective visions can best be illustrated by comparing the role of Beatrice with that of Laura. Beatrice's ultimate function is to guide and lead Dante's vision to its final end. When she arrives with Dante in the Empyrean, she gracefully yields her place to St. Bernard and resumes her role as one of the regular members of the celestial community. She is only an allegorical veil that has to be lifted at the moment of Dante's beatific vision.

In contrast to this, Laura is not an allegorical veil to be removed to reveal the transcendent reality of the eternal kingdom. As a matter of fact, Petrarch never attains a beatific vision. The object of that vision appears to him only as a participle in a subjunctive clause (*ch'i' veggia ivi presente il sommo bene*—"If I may there behold the Highest Good"—*Triumphus aeternitatis*, l. 37). Laura is the ultimate screen for the final projection of Petrarch's imagination in its eternal mode. "In the full flower of youth they shall possess/Immortal beauty and eternal fame" (*Triumphus aeternitatis*, lines 133–34). She is not only the way to but the end of Petrarch's vision.

By contrasting the subjectivity of Petrarch's vision with the objectivity of Dante's, I do not intend to say that Dante's is a true vision of reality while Petrarch's is not. Both visions are poetic and fictional. The subjectivity and objectivity in question are meant to belong to the domain of the poets' intentions rather than to that of reality itself. Dante's intention of giving his vision an objective reference is rooted in his Christian faith; Petrarch's claim to give his vision only a subjective reference reflects his loss of that faith.

Since his gaining of Laura has been his loss of Christ, Petrarch knows that his view of eternity through Laura cannot be given an objective reference to the transcendent reality. So he describes the Triumph of Eternity, not as a vision of a procession in the past tense, but as an expression of his pious hope in the future tense. Dante, on the other hand, shows his beatific vision even in the past tense. Whatever is said in the past tense is usually a matter of objective fact, whereas many things said in the future tense are no more than subjective longings.

Whereas Dante's vision is a product of the subordinate imagination, Petrarch's is a product of the sovereign imagination. The function of the former is to retain and report what is real; that of the latter is to create and sustain what may not be real at all. Dante's imagination is subservient to the voice of reality; Petrarch's is sovereign in ruling over the domain of its own creation.

The subjectivity of Petrarch's vision marks the divergence of his *Triumphs* from the medieval tradition of dream-vision, which has been assumed to be a special access to hidden, objective reality. For example, Dante's vision is his privileged access to the transcendent reality, which fulfills his aspirations. Whereas Dante's vision is an objective fulfillment, Petrarch's remains a subjective aspiration. Hence Petrarch is faced with one problem that has never been known to Dante, that is, how to give his vision objective reality and fulfillment lest it remain an idle fantasy. This is his task of concretion.

The *Africa*

Petrarch undertakes this task of concretion in his epic the *Africa*, in which he brings his man of action, Publius Cornelius Scipio Africanus Major, down from the domain of heavenly vision to that of earthly action. Hence historical reality or truth constitutes the foundation of this epic. The *Africa* is meant to be a poetic rendition of a historical incident in strict adherence to authentic historical records, especially Livy's. For this reason, as Thomas G. Bergin says, this epic is an integral feature of Petrarch's *historical works*.[46]

The *Africa* opens with Scipio's dream, the *somnium scipionis*, which goes back to Cicero's *Republic*. In the last book of his *Republic*, Plato raises the question of whether or not the virtuous and the vicious lives on this earth will be rewarded and punished in the other world in accordance with their respective merits and demerits. Plato tries to answer this question through his Myth of Er, who comes back to this world after his death and describes the state of the other world. In imitation of this, Cicero writes the *somnium scipionis* in the last book of his own *Republic*. In this dream, Scipio Africanus Minor goes up to heaven and sees his adoptive grandfather, Scipio Africanus Major.

The moral of the dream is to give the Roman version of the Platonic moral in the Myth of Er. In this dream, Scipio the Elder tells Scipio the Younger that the blessed life in heaven is given only as a reward to those who have lived virtuously on the earth. The virtuous life according to Cicero is quite different from both the virtuous life in Platonic thinking and the saintly life in the Christian teaching. In Platonic thought, the virtuous life par excellence is the life of a philosopher, whose public service to his country is only secondary to his life of inner wisdom. In Christian teaching, the virtuous life is renunciation of this world for the sake of the other world. In the Ciceronian conception, the main accent of virtuous life falls upon public duty, or rather meritorious service to one's country. Hence the prominent people who are paraded in the Ciceronian heaven are not hermetic saints or sages but men of distinction in public service, namely, the eminent political and military leaders of Roman history.

Although most of Cicero's *Republic* has been lost, the *somnium scipionis* has survived intact through Macrobius's commentary. The main thrust of this commentary is to shift the emphasis from this world to the other world. As C. S. Lewis explains, Macrobius makes this shift by taking advantage of one parenthetical remark: "Nothing—nothing anyway that goes on earth (*quod quidem in terris fiat*)— is more pleasing to God than those councils and communities of men bound together by law which we call commonwealths."[47] Macrobius reinstates the virtues of a secluded sage and a religious hermit by packing them into this saving clause, and further elevates them higher than the Ciceronian virtues of public service.

In this Macrobian transformation, the *somnium scipionis* became conducive to theother-worldly ethos of Christianity and was looked upon as the most influential model for many works in the genre of medieval dream-vision. For example, Scipio's ascent is one of the models for Dante's ascent in his *Commedia*. Especially, there are two episodes in Dante's Paradise that clearly reflect the influence of Scipio's dream, namely, Dante's meeting of his illustrious great-grandfather Cacciaguida in the Heaven of Mars, and his bird's-eye view of the puny earth from the Heaven of the Fixed Stars.

Since Petrarch is to use this dream as an occasion of descent rather than ascent, he has to purge it of the Macrobian distortion. But the restoration of the *somnium scipionis* to its original form seems to be insufficient for his need; he introduces quite a few changes of his own into Cicero's original version. Most of these center around his drastic decision to make Scipio the Elder the dreamer in his epic rather than Scipio the Younger. Thus, in his version of the dream, Scipio Africanus Major goes up to heaven, meets his father and uncle, and hears the prophecy of his destiny in his African campaign against Carthage.

This drastic change appears to be dictated by the new role Petrarch wants to give the dream in his epic, which is quite different from its role in Cicero's *Republic*. In the latter work the *somnium scipionis* is presented retrospectively; the dream is not only the concluding section of Cicero's *Republic*, but comes to Scipio the Younger during the evening following Massinissa's laudatory account of Scipio the Elder's glorious deeds to his grandson. Cicero uses Scipio the Elder as an eminent example of the virtuous life that has already been achieved.

What Petrarch needs in his scheme of descent is a hero whose accomplishment is ahead of him rather than behind him. It is in this prospective mood that he opens his epic with the *somnium scipionis*. If he were to adhere to Cicero's original version, he would have had to bring Scipio the Younger down to earth as his epic hero rather than Scipio the Elder. But the former does not quite have the glamour and magic that the latter has gained by vanquishing Hannibal at the Battle of Zama. So Petrarch appears to be compelled to replace Scipio the Younger with Scipio the Elder as the dreamer in his version of the *somnium scipionis*.

In the meeting of Scipio the Elder with his father and uncle, Petrarch accentuates the imminent sense of accomplishment and fulfillment. His father and uncle, both of whom had been killed in the Spanish campaign against Carthaginian forces, urge Scipio the Elder to avenge their untimely death and fulfill their unfinished mission (bk. 1, lines 453 ff.). It is with this sense of future accomplishment and fulfillment on earth that we may account for the two notable omissions which Aldo Bernardo has alertly noted.[48] These are Petrarch's exclusion of the doctrine of immortality and the explanation of the structure of the heavens in Cicero's original version of the dream. There is no point in explaining the structure of the heavens to Petrarch's earthbound hero; such an explanation would only become a distraction from his dedication to the earthly mission. Petrarch does not really exclude, but rather replaces, the Ciceronian doctrine of immortality with his own—that is, immortality should be conceived of not as an innate state of the soul but as a goal to be attained by surviving the first, second, and third deaths (see bk. 2, ll. 413 ff.). This is the idea Petrarch carries over from his *Triumphs*.

Petrarch devotes the first two books of the *Africa* to Scipio's dream; at the end of the second book he brings Scipio down to lead the Romans against the Carthaginians. The confrontation of these two forces consumes the bulk of his epic, namely, book 3 through book 7, leaving the last two books for the conclusion, which dovetails with its opening in the first two books. The confrontation in question is the culmination of the historical struggle between Rome and Carthage for the conquest and control of the entire Mediterranean world. The operation of Augustinian dyadic logic becomes most prominent in Petrarch's portrayal of this struggle between the two cities.

In the *Africa*, Rome and Carthage are conceived according to the Augustinian-Manichean scheme. Rome is the city of heavenly virtue; Carthage is the city of hellish vice. Giuseppe Toffanin says, "The *Africa* becomes the real *Divine Comedy*."[49] However, Toffanin does not explain exactly what he means to convey by this rather cryptic assertion. If Dante could bring down the heavenly host from his Paradiso, summon up the infernal army from his Inferno, and let them meet on the earth, he would create a struggle quite similar to Scipio's African campaign in Petrarch's epic. While Scipio is compared to the Sun, the source of all good, Hannibal is depicted as the infernal serpent, the root of all evil (see 4. 253 ff., 417; 7. 750 ff.; 8. 220 ff.). Scipio expects to return to heaven after his death; Sophonisba descends to Tartarus after her suicide.

Petrarch contrives the battle between the two cities in three successive stages. The first stage is the juxtaposition of Roman history with that of Carthage and Africa in books 3 and 4. The second stage is the fight between Syphax and Massinissa, two Numidian kings who are caught between Rome and Carthage, and their respective representatives, Scipio and Sophonisba. Petrarch devotes book 5 to this battle. These two stages eventually lead up to the final stage in books 6 and 7, where Scipio meets and vanquishes Hannibal at the Battle of Zama.

In the first stage of this confrontation, Laelius is dispatched as Scipio's emissary to Libya to restore the alliance with King Syphax. On his arrival there, Laelius is struck with the gorgeous palace of Syphax, which is represented as a vivid embodiment of African luxury and cupidity (3. 90 ff.). After traversing the vast, glittering hall, Laelius conveys Scipio's simple message of friendship to King Syphax. In the course of a banquet in honor of the messenger, a minstrel sings the history of Africa (3. 378 ff.). The central theme of this historical narration is the Herculean labor that has established an empire of wealth and power by conquering the savage world. What is remarkable in this account of African history is that the two vices of cupidity and ambition, which Augustine had called two of Petrarch's grave sins in the second book of his *Secretum*, now appear as the two chief driving forces behind Carthage's expansionism.

In response to the recitation of African history, Laelius gives a long resumé of Roman history (3. 459 ff.). In contrast to the constant theme of toil and care occurring throughout African history, liberty is the central theme of Roman history (3. 522; 4. 15). Also, the theme of heavenly grace in the latter is contrasted to that of Herculean labor in the former. One is presented as the race of divine origin and grace; the other, as the race of earthly origin and effort. The Scipios best exemplify the Roman embodiment of heavenly origin and virtue (4. 100 ff.). In contrast to the African history of self-seeking cupidity, Roman history is a record of simple self-sacrifice and dedication.

Sophonisba is the central figure in the second stage of the confrontation between Rome and Carthage. She is Hasdrubal's daughter, whose beauty cannot be rivaled even by that of a goddess (5. 64). Carthage had induced Syphax to forsake his alliance with Rome by marrying him to Sophonisba; she is the embodiment of lust, one of the serious sins which Petrarch admits as being among his own in the *Secretum*. By installing her as the queen of Syphax's palace, which has already been presented as the symbol of cupidity in book 3 of the *Africa*, Petrarch appears to indicate lust as the common root both of concupiscence and of cupidity. The original title of the *Triumph of Love* is *Triumphus cupidinis*; the words *cupido* and *cupiditas* both derive from the common root *cupere* (desire).

Petrarch's personalism becomes most prominent in the Sophonisba episode; he omits the entire battle between Massinissa's and Syphax's forces from his epic. This battle is already behind us when we find Massinissa walking into the conquered palace of Syphax, where he instantly falls helpless victim to the vanquished queen (5. 1 ff.). From then on he becomes the prize for the tug-of-war between Sophonisba and Scipio, that is, the war between *voluptas* and *virtus*; and what is intriguing about this war are the Machiavellian tactics of cunning and scheming that permeate it.

Even before Sophonisba opens her mouth and presents her eloquent plea for mercy, Massinissa melts like a piece of wax in fire (5. 72 ff.). In her petition, she appeals to his masculine instinct to protect a helpless victim. In order to make her case more compelling, she describes herself as a widowed captive, although her husband is still alive (see 5. 80). She further appeals to Massinissa's sense of decency by telling him that all she wants is to avoid the yoke of the haughty Romans and be allowed to have her own honorable kind of death (5. 87 ff.). From her position as prisoner of war, she adroitly exercises her Machiavellian ingenuity to manipulate and captivate Massinissa's emotion. This sort of emotional engineering is by no means new to Sophonisba. Her marriage to Syphax had been a sly maneuver of political expediency; her sensuous beauty had proven deadly in shifting his allegiance from Rome to Carthage. Her present stratagem with Massinissa is only a continuation of her renowned career in power politics.

Even when Massinissa becomes Sophonisba's victim, he cannot forget the towering figure of his master Scipio, although he is far away. So he is caught between two powerful personalities. Petrarch describes his torment in one of his favorite metaphors of tension and conflict, Scylla and Charybdis (5. 156). Massinissa is willing to go further than granting Sophonisba's simple request; he wants to have her for his queen. In this scheme he has his turn to become a little Machiavellian; he decides to marry her then and there and present his marriage as a *fait accompli* to Scipio (5. 201 ff.). He hopes that this plot will enable him to keep Sophonisba instead of sending her away as a prisoner to Rome. So he quickly contracts a marriage that is denounced as an act of adultery by the populace, who knows that Syphax is still alive.

Scipio responds to Massinissa's impetuous behavior with all the available resources at his command. First, he gives Massinissa a long sermon (5. 386 ff.). He appeals to his sense of virtue by telling him that only virtue can withstand the assault of the temptation of pleasure, which is a far more fearful enemy to cope with than any field army. Unlike the latter, pleasure can penetrate the armed gates of the mighty and the secret chambers of the inner man. Scipio tells Massinissa that the conquest of his own inner rebellion will be a far greater victory than his conquest of Syphax. Scipio concludes his sermon by reminding him of Roman might and right: by right, Sophonisba as a prisoner belongs to the mighty Roman people and cannot be left in Massinissa's possession.

During the sermon, Massinissa melts away like snow in a warm wind, just as he did in the presence of Sophonisba (5. 440 ff.). But he again becomes a helpless victim of his lust as soon as he is away from Scipio's severity and rigidity, and even thinks of running away with Sophonisba. He abandons this desperate scheme only because he knows of no place to escape to: "Roman power all escape / Precludes, and Scipio is feared in furthest earth" (5. 602 ff.).[50] Keenly conscious of his total dependence on Scipio, he finally accepts the fate of surrendering Sophonisba to Scipio with Jobean resignation: "Life he brought / And life he took away" (5. 564 ff.).[51] Massinissa at least keeps his promise that Sophonisba shall avoid the Roman yoke; he sends her poison and allows her to end her own life.

The outcome of the tug-of-war between Scipio and Sophonisba is not a clear-cut victory of virtue in its own right over vice. Scipio manages to win back Massinissa from Sophonisba not because he embodies all virtue but, rather, because he happens to wield all the power of Rome. The battle could have gone the other way if Sophonisba had enjoyed the same might as Scipio instead of being a powerless captive. So the *virtus* that wins over *voluptas* is not Roman but Machiavellian *virtus*, that is, the power of control and manipulation. In this display of Machiavellian *virtus* Scipio proves to be the master of all.

Prudence is perhaps the most prominent of all Scipio's virtues; he tries to foresee all possible contingencies and prepare adequately for them. While his days are filled with action, his nights are devoted to the planning of countless strategies (5. 490 ff.; also 7. 152 ff.). In book 3 of his *Rerum memorandarum*, as Aldo Bernardo reports, Petrarch recognizes two alternative ways of possessing the virtue of prudence: the way of *solertia* (artfulness, ingenuity, sagacity) and *calliditas* (cunning, skill), or the way of *sapientia* (wisdom).[52] Petrarch takes delight in showing how Scipio abundantly possessed both *solertia* and *calliditas*. Thus Scipio's prudence turns out to be the requisite virtue for action rather than for contemplation, which is presumably *sapientia* in the Petrarchan scheme. Scipio is a consummate master of forethought, a new Prometheus (which etymologically means "fore-thought").

The prudent Scipio is not content simply to release Massinissa from Sophonisba's talons; he also tries to revive his sagging morale by giving him a new sense of life. He anticipates the danger of Massinissa's suicide and administers to his sickly patient like a doctor (6. 81 ff.). Scipio showers upon Massinissa Roman awards and gifts in recognition of his victorious campaign against Syphax, and encourages him with the promise of greater rewards for his future contributions (6. 147 ff.). Scipio does not hesitate to appeal to Massinissa's territorial ambition; the former instills and intensifies in the latter the hope of expanding his kingdom under Roman auspices. None of these Scipionic tactics is a deed of virtue for its own sake, but rather a Machiavellian scheme for control and manipulation. No doubt, Scipio employs these schemes toward a virtuous end; for that matter, Machiavelli himself never advocated the use of his artful measures for an evil end.

Of course, Carthage is expected to employ the devious measures

of deceit and cunning for an evil end. Through a fraudulent offer
for a negotiated settlement, she tries to gain the time needed for
recalling Hannibal and Mago to meet Scipio. On receiving the order
of recall, Hannibal writhes with hatred and bitterly complains of
the jealousy and plots (*invidia atque dolus*) of his own people, which
are now forcing him to retreat from Latium (6. 440). He says that
he can never be compelled to retreat by the Roman forces, whom
he has so long trampled upon. It is not the mighty Scipio but the
perfidious Hanno who is imposing the ignominious deed upon him
(6. 441 ff.). Before finally sailing with his forces for Carthage, Hannibal vents his anger and hatred by slaughtering children and old
folk who have taken refuge in a Roman shrine (6. 476 ff.). This
Hannibal episode is meant to be seen in juxtaposition with the Massinissa episode. While Scipio employs his artful schemes to promote
friendship even with the Numidian savages and to earn their loyalty,
the suspected stratagems are the source of mutual hatred and internal
dissension among the Carthaginians (namely, Hannibal and Hanno).

With the recall of Hannibal from Italy, we move into the third
stage of the confrontation between Rome and Carthage. At the
news of his return, the Roman troops become terror-stricken because they are still living with a vivid memory of their repeated defeats under his cruel might (7. 31 ff.). But their terror and anxiety
melt away at the mere sight of Scipio's glorious face. This episode
demonstrates the immense power the two military leaders exercise
over their men; the myriads of troops under their command are no
more than puppets in the mighty struggle between the two titans.
Scipio is referred to as the greatest of the great (*maximus in magno
Scipio*); Hannibal is credited with incredible, superhuman feats
(cf. 3. 276; 7. 552 ff.).

On returning to the African shore, Hannibal sends out spies to
scout the Roman forces (7. 95 ff.). When Scipio captures these spies,
he provides them with a guided tour of the Roman camps and urges
them to report faithfully what they have seen. Petrarch may have
intended this episode to covey the message that Scipio responds to
the devious Carthaginian maneuver with a straightforward move.
But this incident turns out to be a double-edged sword, for Scipio
would surely not have employed this tactic of open display unless he
were convinced of its efficacy. As a matter of fact, the spies return to
their camps, completely stupefied by the audacity of Scipio's forth-

right act and overwhelmed by what they have seen at the Roman camps (7. 106 ff.). A dramatic display of power and self-confidence for a stunning psychological impact is always one of the treasured weapons in the Machiavellian arsenal.

Before the Battle of Zama, Scipio meets Hannibal face to face in a peace conference (7. 152 ff.). Hannibal tries to persuade Scipio to accept his offer of a peaceful settlement instead of risking his fortune in an uncertain battle. He alludes persuasively to the irony of fickle fortune: the aged conquerer who has at some time beaten down all the Roman generals, including Scipio's own father, is now willing to yield to young Scipio (7. 218 ff.). He goes on to confess that his insatiable avarice has been the chief cause for his expansionism and that fortune forced him into serfdom through her initial smile upon his greedy ambition. The three highlights of Hannibal's talk are cupidity, ambition, and fortune, which in turn echo back to Petrarch's examination of conscience before Augustine in book 2 of the *Secretum*.

Scipio counters Hannibal's notion of fortune with an affirmation of his belief in Providence (7. 368 ff.). Scipio means to have Hannibal understand that what appears to be the working of fickle fortune is actually the manifestation of the divine will. Hannibal and the Carthaginians cannot recognize the working of Providence because they do not believe in the deity of justice and might. They are infidels; they have no fear of God. In contrast to their godless arrogance, the piety of the Romans is rooted in their fidelity to the highest deity. Hannibal's argument, built on the unpredictable turn of fickle fortune, may make sense to infidels, but it appears to be no more than an expression of their impiety to the Romans who believe in Providence. Scipio is willing to meet his fate in open battle. The prospective battle, which is seen as a play of fortune by Hannibal, is believed by Scipio to be a manifestation of the divine will. One is the perspective of an infidel; the other is that of a believer. In fact, at this point the entire African campaign assumes the air of a Crusade, a war of the faithful against the heathens.

In order to influence the outcome of the impending battle, the two matrons of Rome and Carthage plead their respective causes before Jupiter (7. 506 ff.). Lady Carthage's plea is essentially a matter of bitter complaint against the gods: some cruel gods, she states, must be opposing her fortune. She is convinced that no mortals can obstruct her path because she is blessed with abundant gifts of nature and her dear son Hannibal operates with superhuman energy and ingenuity. She begs Jupiter to eliminate this unfair obstruction and intervention which she suspects on the part of some immortals. This plea is clearly in accord with the conception of fortune that Hannibal has tried to convey to Scipio, because such unfair intervention would not be a manifestation of Jupiter's will and as such would constitute a fortuitous event that could be attributed to fortune.

When Lady Rome presents her case before Jupiter, she first accuses Carthage and Hannibal of fraud and cruelty. She reminds Jupiter of Scipio's divine birth and godly spirit. In contrast to Lady Carthage's depiction of her Hannibal as a mortal rivaling the might of the immortals, Lady Rome pictures her Scipio as an immortal trying to cleanse the earth of mortals' fraud and deceit. Whereas Lady Carthage is intent on the success of territorial expansionism, Lady Rome asks only for the safety of liberty.

After hearing these two pleas, Jupiter is disturbed at the sorry state of the earth (7. 665 ff.). He attributes this decadence to the dwindling force of virtue and announces his intention to descend to earth in human form to restore its power. He gives only a veiled prophecy of the outcome of the impending battle, saying that the victor will have the honor of providing the earthly site for his own Incarnation. In spite of this cryptic prophecy, Jupiter clearly states his preference by saying that virtue is the only thing that pleases him and that he disdains the wealth and glory of the earth.

Jupiter's pronouncement clarifies Petrarch's conception of virtue: virtue is not meant to be a product of human toil like wealth and power because it is the very nature of the immortals. Even Hannibal cannot achieve it through ardent struggle and effort; one has to be born with it, like Scipio. The Petrarchan virtue is a gift of the gods, and this is what is meant by the Christian doctrine of grace. Thus Petrarch's conception of virtue is analogous to the Christian conception of grace.

Finally the Romans meet the Carthaginians at Zama. In spite of all the elaborate plans and thorough preparations made by the two superhuman generals for this great battle, one fortuitous accident determines its outcome. As usual, Hannibal has deployed his famous troop of war-trained elephants in front of his central force. In previous campaigns, this troop has repeatedly performed the marvelous function of breaking right through the middle of the enemy forces. At the opening of the Battle of Zama, the elephants become terrified by the tumultuous blasting of numerous Roman bugles, turn around, and charge right into the middle of their own forces. This event, which has been anticipated neither by Hannibal nor by Scipio, instantly opens a broad lane of attack for the Roman forces, and the Carthaginians find themselves in retreat and disintegration when the battle has hardly begun. Our poet cannot restrain his own shock and exclaims:

> O blind intelligence of men,
> Ignorant and deluded! The beasts so great a leader
> Stationed in the van with anxious care for safety,
> These same have brought disaster and first loss to his army![53]
>
> [7. 924–27]

This incident is a dramatic illustration of the Fortune vs. Providence debate; it can be regarded as an act of fickle fortune by Hannibal and as an expression of divine will by Scipio. Both of them are depicted as masters of careful planning and precaution throughout the Battle of Zama, but the victory goes to the one whose prudence thrives with the connivance of heaven and earth.

Scipio's role is not limited to that of a tactician; he amply displays his valor as a warrior. He seeks out and engages Hannibal in single combat; they exchange the thunderbolts of war. Disheartened at the irretrievable outcome of the battle, Hannibal finally decides to escape from the bloody scene. This is the conclusion of the Battle of Zama. The Battle of Zama in turn concludes the three-stage conflict between Rome and Carthage, or rather between Scipio and Hannibal.

Petrarch appears to have spent much painful effort in the elaborate construction of these three stages. The first stage is conceived as a one-phase confrontation; the second as a two-phase confrontation; the third as a three-phase confrontation.

The first stage consists of the meeting between Laelius and Syphax. Since they are meeting as the Roman and Carthaginian representatives, their confrontation may be regarded as a meeting through proxies. The second stage is the confrontation of Scipio and Sophonisba through a common intermediary, Massinissa. Since Massinissa has two successive meetings (first with Sophonisba and then with Scipio), the second stage consists of two phases. Although this stage still presents no direct meeting between the two main protagonists, the meeting is a little more direct than the meeting in the first stage. In the confrontation of the first stage, only the intermediaries become involved while the protagonists stay in the background. In the confrontation of the second stage, however, the protagonists themselves become involved, although their involvement does not yet bring them into a direct encounter.

Only the third stage provides a direct confrontation, not only between Scipio and Hannibal, but also between the Roman and the Carthaginian forces. The first phase of this direct confrontation is the meeting of Scipio and Hannibal at the peace table; the second phase is the meeting of the two matrons of Rome and Carthage in front of Jupiter's throne. The former is the confrontation of the two protagonists; the latter represents the confrontation of the two cities. These two confrontations are brought together in the Battle of Zama, which constitutes the third phase of the third stage. There the Romans slaughter the Carthaginians and Scipio overpowers Hannibal. In addition to this double-barreled confrontation, this final phase also consummates the previous meetings of the intermediaries by making the Numidians and other foreign troops integral parts of the battle.

With this multiphased confrontation behind him, Petrarch moves into his favorite theme of fame and glory in book 8. Scipio is liberal in his profuse admiration of Hannibal's genius, his mastery of arms, and his incredible endurance (8. 117 ff.). Scipio says that the only deficiencies in Hannibal are his lack of truth and piety. In a generous disagreement with Hannibal's estimate of himself as the third greatest military genius after Alexander and Pyrrhus, Scipio classifies him as by far the greatest one in history. This provokes Massinissa's adulation of Scipio as a "magnificent detractor of your own / And glorious admirer of the deeds of others" (8. 145 ff). The simpleminded Massinissa does not seem to see that Scipio's generous praise of Hannibal is the surest way to insure his own glory and fame.

If Hannibal is far greater even than Alexander and Pyrrhus, then his conqueror must obviously be the greatest in the history of mankind. To detract from one's opponent is the quickest way to downgrade one's own prestige; to exalt the powers of one's opponent is the soundest way to consolidate one's own glory. Lest this point be lost to the simpletons, Petrarch elaborates on it further in a rather ingenuous episode. A soldier who has overheard Scipio's eulogy of Hannibal gets a chance to ask Laelius what place Scipio is reserving for himself in his order of ranking the great military leaders. Laelius replies

to him with a metaphor: the sun is never mentioned in the ranking of
the brightest stars, but this omission does not reflect an oversight
(8. 220 ff.). On the contrary, he explains to the soldier, it only
reveals the obvious and incontestable superiority of the sun over the
brightest stars. Of course, Scipio is the sun in his own mind as well
as in others'.

Scipio's true glory is juxtaposed with the ugly deeds of those
Romans seeking false glory. On receiving the news of the Roman
victory at Zama, Claudius, the former consul, hastens to Africa in
order to reap the honor and glory that rightly belong to Scipio (8.
482 ff.). But the greedy Claudius runs into a horrendous storm during
his voyage to Carthage and creates a comic scene with his fearful
quaking (8. 521). In this headlong rush for glory and honor, the
present consul, Cornelius Lentulus, has a little more pernicious
scheme than that of Claudius. Lentulus intrigues to take over Scipio's
high command and establish his fame by securing for himself the
honor of concluding the Libyan war (8. 558 ff.). But the magnani-
mous Scipio is not distressed at all by these ugly outbursts of his
fellow Romans' envy and ambition. For he knows that true glory
consists not in the dubious acclaim of the herd but in virtue's naked
splendor.

After accepting the surrender of Carthage and burning her militant
fleet, Scipio sails for Rome. On finding the poet Ennius wrapped in
deep meditation on his ship, Scipio asks him to break his silence for
the benefit of others. In response to this request, Ennius says that he
has been contemplating Scipio's peerless deeds and accomplishments
(9. 24 ff.). This reply appears to reveal Petrarch's idea of contemplation.

In the old Platonic tradition down to Dante, the distinction
between action and contemplation corresponded to the distinction
between the temporal and the eternal spheres. Our needs in the
temporal world are taken care of by active life, the ultimate end of
which is to free our soul of mundane concerns so it may meditate
on the eternal world. The life of contemplation is accomplished by
the meditative flight of the soul to the heavenly sphere, leaving
behind all earthly matters. Hence there has always been a sharp
disjunction between action and contemplation.

In contrast to this traditional separation, Petrarch appears to conceive the relation of action and contemplation in one continuous
scheme; that is, the life of contemplation consists of meditating upon

the accomplishments of the active life. If so, contemplation does not require the flight of the soul from earth to heaven since it is simply an extension of the active life on earth. Of course, this is the inevitable consequence of the Petrarchan sensibility, which always insists on seeing the unity of literal and spiritual sense, and of the temporal and the eternal. Scipio is a symbol of this Petrarchan unity since he is the hero whose mission is to fulfill eternal ideals on earth. The Petrarchan sensibility cannot allow the disjunction of heaven and earth, which is a prerequisite for the separation of contemplation from action.

One of the central reasons for Petrarch's admiration of Scipio as an epic hero is Scipio's dual character. Whereas most famous men of action tend to be extroverts who leave little room for inner meditation, Scipio is a man of deeply meditative moods. Strangely, however, Petrarch has very little to say about the precise nature of Scipio's meditative life. As one of the precious examples of that life, Petrarch cites Scipio's habit of meditating in the temple of Jupiter on the Capitoline (4. 115 ff.). During these moments of meditation, Jupiter seems to give Scipio some special inspiration and instruction on important practical affairs. Thus, Scipio's meditation appears to be an integral part of his active life rather than a contemplation of the truths of eternity, whether it comes before or after his practical deed. If so, this is a drastically new idea of contemplation that Petrarch introduces to the Renaissance.

This new view of contemplation also dictates a new role for the poetic imagination. Petrarch has Ennius explain this point to Scipio: the vocation of the poetic imagination does not lie in the apparent license to invent fictions (9. 90 ff.). Truth is the only foundation for poetic creation, Ennius continues, although the poet may shroud the truth with the veil of fiction. By "truth" he means the truth of human history rather than that of eternal heaven. The function of the poetic imagination, then, is to transmute the virtuous deeds of history-making heroes into eternal paradigms so that these virtuous deeds can stand as the source of perpetual inspiration (9. 97 ff.). As it were, the poetic imagination creates its own Platonic heaven of eternal objects for contemplation.

This creation of a new Platonic heaven by the poetic imagination comes as a complete reversal of traditional Platonism. Whereas the function of imagination in the old Platonism was to bring down the *images* of eternity to the temporal domain, its new function is to generate the former from the latter. The old function is an act of descent; the new function is an act of ascent. This new function can also be described as the transformation of history into philosophy, since it changes the contingent events of history into eternal paradigms of philosophical truth. The place of the poet is accordingly elevated far higher than that of a historian or philosopher; as a matter of fact, these two are now given subservient roles under the new Petrarchan master builder, the poet.

Thus, in the Petrarchan scheme, the faculty of imagination sheds its old subordinate role of imitation and takes on a new awesome role of creation. In this new role it deserves the title of "sovereign imagination," just as it does in the *Triumphs*. We have already seen, then, how the heaven of eternity comes into being as a transformation of temporal affairs by the poetic imagination. In order to symbolize this new sovereignty, Petrarch has Ennius crowned with laurels along with Scipio on the Capitoline (9. 400 ff.).

Since the poet transmutes contingent events of history into the eternal heaven, he creates poetic immortality. The poet Ennius informs Scipio of his concern that Scipio's immortal deeds may not have the fate of being immortalized by proper heralds (9. 50). Later on Ennius tells Scipio of his prophetic vision of Petrarch's immortal epic singing his glory (9. 216 ff.). Thus Petrarch adopts the strange device of concluding his historical epic with a unmistakable note of self-reference.

This note of self-reference has been there all along throughout the *Africa*. As Bergin points out, the intrusion of the personal is rather disproportionate in the opening dedicatory passage of the first book.[54] The theme of personal reference is never abandoned but, rather, becomes submerged when Petrarch's epic moves into historical narration. As we have already seen, the vices that motivate the Carthaginians are precisely the same vices that Augustine exposes as Petrarch's grave sins in the *Secretum*. Obviously, Sophonisba is a projection of his own Laura as an embodiment of sensuous beauty; Scipio is the ideal for his own passionate aspiration. The *Africa* is ultimately an epic of his own soul, perhaps a little more poignantly, even, than the *Commedia* is of Dante's soul. Petrarch's epic can indeed be read as the *Psychomachia* ("our mind is a battlefield") of his tormented soul of the *Secretum*. Thus the theme of personalism in the *Africa* is as insistent as it is in his *Triumphs*.

To read Petrarch's epic as the *Psychomachia* of his tormented soul is perhaps the only way to overcome what Bergin calls its defects of perfection.[55] Its heroes and heroines are too perfect to be true. Scipio is a personification of all virtues; Hannibal is that of all vices. Both of them are so perfect that neither of them is capable of any internal conflict. By internal conflict, I mean not only the conflict within Scipio's soul alone but also the conflict of his own interests with the destiny of his community. In Virgil's *Aeneid*, for example, the conflict between the hero's concerns as a person and his obligation as the tribal leader, as manifested in the Dido episode, excites our sympathy and gives the epic great dignity and vitality. We can experience this sort of sympathy and sense of dignity in the *Africa* only by reading it on an allegorical level.

Scipionic Individualism

Let us now look at the *Africa* as a resolution of the Petrarchan conflict and dilemma outlined in the *Secretum*. Some Petrarch scholars have regarded this epic as Petrarch's attempt to bring the Roman and Christian virtues into a harmonious unity.[56] Although the Petrarchan conflict of the *Secretum* is not exactly that of Roman virtues with Christian dictates, we must first understand the nature of this reconciliation of the two traditions—if it is indeed a reconciliation.

The Scipio of the *Africa* may not stand very well as an embodiment of Roman virtue. To begin with, he is too young. Because the Roman virtues were believed to be the achievement of long education and cultivation, an old Roman sage or hero is the natural medium for their mature embodiment. Since a young man has not had time enough for such an arduous achievement, Petrarch endows his Scipio with all his virtues as a divine gift. This is clearly a doctrine of grace that better suits a Jewish patriarch or a Christian saint than a Roman sage. Thus the Scipio of the *Africa* turns out to be Petrarch's transference of Judeo-Christian values to Roman territory.

Petrarch is very conscious of Scipio's achievement of his heroic deeds at a relatively early age and points out his resemblance to Christ in this regard. As Aldo Bernardo says, he also takes joy in drawing our attention to many other points of resemblance between Scipio and Christ.[57] In short, Scipio and Christ are Petrarch's twin pillars of the secular and the religious ideals.

That Scipio is Petrarch's secular Christ is the most fundamental theme pervading his description of Scipio. He constantly reminds us of Scipio's divine origin. Scipio is a special favorite of Jupiter; he is abundantly endowed with divine gifts. He is the Redeemer (*Servator*) of his nation (9. 375). In spite of this redemptive role, he is finally driven into exile by the envy of his own people, although he does not meet the cruel fate of crucifixion. He is the best possible replica of the mighty Jupiter; his description as *maximus in magno Scipio* surely resonates with the epithet of the Jupiter of the Capitoline, *Iuppiter Optimus Maximus*. In short, the Scipio of the *Africa* almost amounts to being the Petrarchan Jupiter Incarnate.

Incarnation may be a little too strong a word to describe the relation of Scipio to Jupiter in view of Jupiter's own announcement of his future incarnation. In that event, Scipio may best be regarded as the most eminent figure for the future incarnate Jupiter, and in that capacity he appears to be the Roman Moses. Scipio's mission is to secure Roman liberty against the Carthaginian threat; Moses' is to deliver the Jews from Egyptian bondage. While the Mosaic Jews flee Africa, the Scipionic Romans sail toward it. Dante chose the example of the Exodus to explain the fourfold meaning of his epic in his letter to Can Grande; the *Africa* appears to be Petrarch's reversal or transference of the Exodus. My friend Robert Hollander may be right in assuming that Petrarch had the perverse compulsion to reverse everything Dante had done.

Petrarch's transference of Christian values to the Roman arena culminates in his imposition of the dogma of the Incarnation on Jupiter. When Jupiter is confronted with the pleas of Rome and Carthage just before the Battle of Zama, as we have seen, he feels much distressed at the strife-ridden world and decides to be reborn in human form in order to replenish the dwindling force of virtue on earth (7. 710 ff.). This is surely conceived in an analogy to the Incarnation of the Christian God, whose purpose is to bring grace to overcome the flood of original sin on earth. Petrarch merely translates the mystery of the Incarnation from the Christian language of grace into the Roman language of virtue, and then transfers it from Yahweh to Jupiter. This transference endows Jupiter with a few other un-Roman attributes besides the Incarnation. For example, Petrarch depicts Jupiter as the god of vengeance and Scipio's mission as a campaign of revenge. But the theme of vengeance is rather anomalous to the Roman concept of Jupiter the Mightiest. A vengeful Jupiter is more like the God of Abraham and Moses ("Vengeance is mine") than that of Aeneas and Augustus.

The historical Scipio was a convenient vehicle for Petrarch's transference because he was already too individualistic to fit comfortably into the Roman tradition. As H. H. Scullard says, Scipio Africanus Major lived at a time of great cultural change in Roman history, when Greek ideas were flooding into Rome and reshaping her basic values.[58] Sensing the superiority of Greek to Roman culture, Scipio championed the cause of improving Roman tradition by accepting the Greek legacies. The traditionalists were appalled and offended, and brought the charge of philhellenism against him. In Roman eyes, he was just too much of a Greek individualist to be a decent Roman.

The essence of Roman *pietas* as manifested in Virgil's Aeneas is to subordinate the individual to the community. Directly counter to this Roman grain, Scipio cultivated a great personality cult around himself. He was really ushering in the spirit of individualism, which would eventually transform republican Rome into imperial Rome through the personal ambitions of Julius Caesar and Augustus. Scipio was finally forced into exile, not only by the envious rabble as Petrarch claims, but by such conscientious guardians of the Roman tradition as Cato the Censor. As Scullard tells us, it was not tradition-bound Roman historians but alien Greek writers, especially Polybius, who built up the almost mystical and magical legend around Scipio.[59] Even the Roman eulogies of Scipio have been influenced by these Greek writers. For example, Livy's adulatory account of Scipio's African campaign largely follows the tone of Polybius's writings; Ennius's panegyric of Scipio is one of the first Roman literary products nurtured under the influence of Greek ideas. Since Scipio's individualism is so close to Renaissance individualism, Petrarch can readily impose on him the virtues of Petrarchan individualism, which is the secular form of the individualism of the Christian saints and martyrs.

As Aldo Bernardo points out, the two longest entries in Petrarch's *De viribus illustribus* are his biographies of Scipio and Julius Caesar.[60] According to the individualistic tendency, Caesar may have been a little more un-Roman than Scipio, since he tried to subjugate the Roman Republic to his will. Because of this un-Roman attempt, Caesar had to meet a little crueler fate than Scipio's. In his resolute stand against Caesar, Brutus was as fiercely motivated by Roman patriotism as Cato the Censor had been in his firm denunciation of Scipio. Petrarch's intention in his historical works is presumably to restore the Roman values in their original form, but it is the un-Roman virtues of certain Romans that perpetually fascinate him.

Because of their un-Roman virtue of individualism, Caesar and Scipio gained immense popularity during the Renaissance. Petrarch is not the only Renaissance poet who had the ambition to write a Scipionic epic; Zanobi da Strada was seized by the same aspiration but renounced it in deference to Petrarch's tremendous prestige. The debate between Guarino da Verona and Poggio Bracciolini on the relative greatness of Caesar and Scipio may be taken as a good indication of the overwhelming influence these two titans had in shaping the Renaissance conception of man. Caesar and Scipio were the models for generating such fascinating figures as Lorenzo the Magnificent and Cesare Borgia. In short, the Scipio of the *Africa* is the Renaissance man, or rather his prototype.

This prototype is derived through the Petrarchan imitation of God. The imitation of Christ had been the central idea governing the life of all pious Christians throughout the Middle Ages. Since Christ is God, imitation of him is imitation of God. But the medieval imitation is not of God in power and glory but in weakness and suffering. What Petrarch wants is the imitation of God in all his glory and power, and we shall call this the Petrarchan imitation of God in order to distinguish it from the medieval imitation.

This Petrarchan imitation had already been partly achieved by the Christian monks of the twelfth and thirteenth centuries. For example, St. Bernard of Clairvaux, who undoubtedly intended to imitate Christ in weakness and suffering, sought and gained immense power and influence, which ranged over such a vast scope as the agricultural project of reclaiming wilderness, the military enterprise of instigating a Crusade, and the political intrigue of making and unmaking popes. In combining a highly active life with intense contemplation, St. Bernard is a Christian prototype for the Petrarchan secular heroism as portrayed in his Scipio. Hildebrand, who can be considered as an ecclesiastical counterpart of the monastic Bernard, had already achieved a Christian verson of Caesarean heroism in his momentous organizational reform of the Church as Gregory VII. With the emergence of the mendicant orders in the thirteenth century, the monks came out of their cloisters into the world and assumed even greater power and glory than the Bernards or Hildebrands.

Since these monks still retained the old ideal of imitating Christ in weakness and suffering while exercising immense power and authority, they came to combine inextricably the old and new modes of imitating God. Perhaps the most dramatic example of this dual imitation is the life of St. Francis, whose humility was attested by his stigmata, and whose power was manifested in the emergence of his order as the most powerful arm of the Church. In the *Commedia*, Dante also portrays both modes of imitation. The Purgatorio shows the imitation of God in weakness and suffering; the Inferno and Paradiso show the imitation of God in power and glory. Of course, the difference between the Inferno and Paradiso lies in the acceptance or rejection of grace. The imitation of God in the Inferno fails to attain true power and glory because it is attempted without grace, while in Paradiso it attains true power and glory because it is performed in grace.

The transition from Purgatorio to Paradiso is the transition from the imitation of God in humility to the imitation of God in glory. This transition is one of the central points that the radical Dionysians of the twelfth century had in mind when they spoke of the transition from the Age of the Son to the Age of the Spirit. We have already seen that Petrarch is an immediate descendent of these radicals. Scipio of the *Africa* is the saint and hero of the Petrarchan version of the Age of the Spirit. In short, the Petrarchan imitation of God is the secular version of the medieval imitation of him in glory and splendor.

When Petrarch claims to have the wide-open world rather than the "little Jerusalem" for his epic, he may appear to profess a more thoroughgoing universalism than Dante's. As it turns out, however, what Petrarch espouses in the *Africa* is his Roman version of Augustinian particularism. In his epic, he simply replaces the old Jews and the new Christians with the Romans as the chosen people. With Jupiter's special favor, he proclaims, the Romans are destined to conquer and control the entire world. Petrarch's own ambitious enterprise in Roman history is conceived as the holy mission of producing a Roman Bible for the people of Petrarchan election (cf. 9. 257 ff.). This Petrarchan particularism is most venomously expressed through the tone of vengefulness that pervades the *Africa*.

We have already seen how Augustinian logic, the logic of opposition, is adopted as the formal schema for the composition of the *Africa*. Now we can see that Petrarch's particularism is the substantive content of this epic, which dovetails with its formal structure. Thus, the resolution of the Petrarchan conflict in the *Africa* is dictated by Augustinian logic; it is a resolution by elimination instead of reconciliation. In the course of the African campaign, Scipio never shows interest in a peaceful reconciliation of the two cities. To one of the Carthaginian peace parties, he adamantly declares, "I am come as a conquerer and avenger, and not as a bringer of peace" (6. 345–46). So the Scipionic victory turns out to be a resolution that exacts the price of banishing Sophonisba to Tartarus and vanquishing Hannibal.

This heavy price for the Scipionic victory makes the Petrarchan resolution quite unsatisfactory. The Augustinian dyadic logic, which has functioned as the logic of renunciation throughout the Middle Ages, is now operating as the new logic of Petrarchan renunciation. What casts an even greater gloom than the price of renunciation is the fact that the Scipionic victory also fails to assure the foundation of internal harmony in Rome. Scipio's victory is greeted with the ravenous envy and greed of his fellow Romans; a lonely exile awaits him as his ultimate reward. With Augustinian world-weariness, no wonder Scipio longs to return to the other world (cf. 8. 630). So the final outcome of the great epic war can be epitomized by Sophonisba's banishment to Tartarus and Scipio's return to heaven—indeed a gloomy outcome and a disquieting resolution.

The Petrarchan Circle

The *Africa* appears to have been conceived as the dialectical counterpart to the *Triumphs*. The former is for Scipio; the latter is for Laura. One is a war epic; the other is a love lyric. The *Triumphs* begins with temporal beauty and transmutes it into a vision of eternity; the *Africa* opens with a vision of eternity and translates it into earthly action. The former is a poem of ascent; the latter is a poem of descent. The ascent is made through subjective aspiration; the descent is toward objective fulfillment. The *Triumphs*, which sprouts from earthly soil, is written in the vernacular, the transitory language of the earth; the *Africa*, which reaches down from the heavens, is written in Latin, the eternal language of heaven. This contrast between Latin and the vernacular as the respective languages of heaven and earth is Dante's, as we have seen in the previous chapter, and Petrarch may be exploiting this Dantesque contrast.

In these two works, Petrarch appropriates the two legacies of the courtly tradition, that is, love and war. These two themes have been intricately interwoven in the development of the courtly tradition. The relationship of love and war in the scale of knightly concerns is ever-changing, and so ambiguous that it becomes hard to determine which is the master and which the servant, or which is the end and which the means. Love and war are sometimes so intermingled that love becomes the love of war and war becomes the war of love.

Dante avoids this ambiguity by clearly establishing love as his sole theme in the *Commedia* and largely ignoring the theme of war. As a matter of fact, war as a theme has never been popular in the Italian tradition of the *dolce stil nuovo*, as is attested by Dante's admission that no Italian poet had yet achieved distinction as a poet of arms (*De vulgari eloquentia*, bk. 2, chap. 2). But Petrarch cannot ignore this neglected theme because of his own inner conflict, which can best be described as an eternal war (*guerra eterna*) (see *Rime*, no. 150; *Secretum*, bk. 2). So he gladly accepts both themes of love and war, and then tries to resolve their ambiguity by separating them into two of his major works, namely love for the *Triumphs* and war for the *Africa*.

There is no room for any open conflict in the *Triumphs* because love reigns over it supremely just as in the *Commedia*. Even the cruel Laura takes the trouble to return to Petrarch after her death to effect a harmonious reconciliation. But the *Africa* exults in the theme of universal conflict because it replaces the theme of love with that of war. The relation of *voluptas* and *virtus* that is contained in an orderly succession or supersession in the *Triumphs* erupts into open warfare in the *Africa*. The valorous knight of this epic is devoid of any deep feelings toward earthly beauty. Whereas the Laura of the *Triumphs* is a source of inspiration and edification, Sophonisba of the *Africa* is an instrument of degradation and perdition. Whereas the former is a lure toward heaven, the latter is a decoy for Tartarus. These opposite resolutions represent the two features of Petrarch's inherently ambiguous attitude toward the entire earthly existence.

The *Triumphs* and the *Africa* can be construed as two dialectical counterparts in the Petrarchan vicious circle. Scipio's dream, which occupies the first two books of the *Africa*, covers the same themes that are treated in the last two Triumphs. The confrontation of Rome and Carthage that constitutes the central five books of the epic is an intensified replay of the first two Triumphs. The last two books of the *Africa* are an elaboration of the theme of death and immortality on earth which is treated in the middle two Triumphs. The *Africa* ends with Scipio's triumphant procession on the Capitoline. It is this device of the triumphant procession of which the *Triumphs* are composed. However, the last Triumph is not really a procession but a vision, which in turn becomes the poetic device for the opening of the *Africa*. Thus the two works, one of which begins where the other leaves off, are like two serpents chasing each other's tail.

These two serpents constitute the two halves of the Petrarchan circle, which eloquently expresses the Petrarchan dilemma of being caught between two worlds—not only those of time and eternity, but also the medieval and the modern worlds. Petrarch belongs to both —and at the same time to neither—of the two worlds. Everything about him shows the systematic ambiguity of assuming both medieval and modern dimensions, depending on our perspective. For example, the *Triumphs*, which is written in the medieval vein of dream-vision allegory, is clearly an immanent allegory that can be translated into a literal account without allegorical residual. The *Africa*, which is written as a literal or historical epic, can also be read as an allegory, a Petrarchan *Psychomachia*. Petrarch has been called the first modern man of letters, but he is equally well qualified to stand as the last medieval man of letters.

Petrarch can be said always to be writing in two languages, because his literal account can be read on an allegorical plan while his allegorical story can be taken on a literal level. This inherent double perspective is a clear linguistic sign of his being a transitional figure. Within this double perspective, Petrarch's works take on a systematic ambiguity and paradox that are too pervasive and too extensive to be contained within a single phrase or sonnet. The paradox and ambiguity we find on such a small scale are merely symptomatic manifestations of Petrarch's pervasive tension and dilemma.

It is well-established practice in Petrarch scholarship to dissociate Petrarchism as a literary convention from his historical studies as a humanist. But this is a grave error. As we have seen, his historical works constitute the very foundation of his *Africa*, which we have called one half of the Petrarchan circle. So Petrarch's contributions to the disciplines of both poetry and history should be regarded as essential features of one and the same circle.

The two serpents of the Petrarchan circle represent not only the systematic ambiguity of the Petrarchan dilemma but also that of his attempt to resolve it. Scipio, who comes down to the earth, always looks up toward heaven; the vision of eternity that is gained through his ascent to heaven reflects nothing but earthly beauty. The

Petrarchan longing for heaven may be no more than an expression of Augustinian world-weariness; the Petrarchan love of this world may be no more than a reaction to the medieval frustration of meditative longing for the other world. Thus attraction and aversion are inseparably intertwined in the Petrarchan attitude toward both worlds.

Since Petrarch can neither abandon either of the two worlds nor settle in either of them, he perpetually oscillates between the two. His ascent of Mount Ventoux dictates his descent, which in turn compels his reascent. It is this cycle of ascent and descent, reascent and redescent that he appears to describe as his perpetual motion between the loftiest summit and the deepest valley in the first eclogue (lines 31–40). It is quite plausible to say that the *Triumphs* was composed during his ascent while the *Africa* was written in his descent. As a record of the dialogue at Monicus's cavern, the first eclogue should be presumed to be a work of Petrarchan ascent. This work concludes with Petrarch's prospect of descent for the Scipionic epic on the African shore.

Since neither Petrarch's ascent nor his descent attains a decisive closure, both his *Triumphs* and his *Africa* are destined to remain incomplete works. The incompleteness of the *Africa* is an obvious textual fact, but even the completeness of the *Triumphs* is far from clear as some critics have argued. The truth of the matter is that both works are meant to stand incomplete by their very nature, because neither of them is capable of being brought to a conclusive termination. Thus, not only the Petrarchan conflict but its resolution turns out to be a vicious circle. It is this Petrarchan vicious circle that the new Sphinx poses as the enigma to test Renaissance ingenuity.

4

The Boccaccian Tour de Force

Boccaccio in the Allegorical Tradition

In the *Amorosa visione*, Boccaccio deliberately accepts the medieval convention of the dream-vision allegory. A lady appears in his dream and guides him to a stately castle, where he is shown two gates, a narrow one leading to eternal peace, and a wide one leading to the joys and sorrows of earthly existence. The dreamer chooses the wide gate, which opens on a great hall whose walls are covered with frescoes. This hall of murals is divided into two galleries. The four walls of the first gallery show the Triumphs of Wisdom (the Seven Arts or Sciences), Fame (or Glory), Wealth, and Love; the second gallery is completely devoted to the Triumphs of Fortune. Having gone through these two galleries, Boccaccio and his guide walk out into a beautiful garden, where a company of ladies are singing and dancing.

In this garden of delight, Boccaccio meets and falls in love with Maria, who has descended from heaven for his salvation. At first he is rather intimidated by her lofty nobility, but with her understanding and encouragement he becomes her loyal servitor. His lady guide discreetly leaves him alone with Maria among the flowers. When he is about to make love to her, however, Boccaccio the dreamer awakens from his dream. The guide, then, tells him that he can see her again at the top of the narrow stairs, but the poem ends just as he is about to ascend the narrow passageway.

There are obvious points of resemblance between this vision of Boccaccio's and Petrarch's in his *Triumphs*; as a matter of fact, the latter work is believed to have been modeled on the former. But the points of difference may prove far more significant than the points of resemblance. Whereas Petrarch's is a vision of suspension between the two worlds, Boccaccio's is a vision of choice between them. Although

Petrarch's *Triumphs* assumes the form of ascent, as we have seen in the last chapter, it is not meant to be a renunciation of the earth in favor of heaven. Since this work is an expression of Petrarch's impossible longing to have the temporal world in the mode of eternity, or rather of his inability to accept earthly existence in its own right, it leaves him suspended between the two worlds in a state of perpetual indecision.

As we have seen in the last chapter, Petrarch admires Hercules for his courage in making a choice at the parting of the two ways (*in bivio*), and laments over his own lack of such courage. Whereas this device of the parting of the two ways never appears in Petrarch's *Triumphs*, it is with this choice that Boccaccio the poet opens his *Amorosa visione*. Boccaccio the dreamer, who just wants to look around first, may not have the resolute courage of Hercules, but this poetic device forces him into making a choice. Boccaccio the dreamer chooses the way of descent in contrast to the way of ascent in Petrarch's *Triumphs*.

Petrarch's object of ascent is to conquer the bitter gall of earthly existence, its mutability, which he tries to overcome by the allegorical device of having the Triumphs of mutability superseded by the Triumphs of durability. The supersession of the first by the second Triumph shows the overcoming of the fragility of passions by the durability of virtues; the supersession of the third by the fourth Triumph shows the conquest of mortality by the perpetuation of immortal fame; the supersession of the fifth by the last Triumph shows the redemption of the temporal in the heaven of eternity. But this Petrarchan resolution offers a poor bargain to anyone like Boccaccio who is determined to enjoy the vitality of the earthly existence.

In the Petrarchan Triumphs, life achieves the form of increasing durability only at the expense of progressively losing its vitality. The life of virtue may indeed be a little more durable than the life of passion, but that durability is secured by sacrificing the liveliness of the latter. The life in the Triumph of Fame, which attains a semblance of eternity, also retains only a semblance of its vitality; the immortality of fame is not really the conqueror of death but rather its child. The last Triumph, which completely transcends the mutability of time, can preserve life only in frozen pictures; it is no longer a procession in the living world of time but a vision of eternity which is changeless and lifeless.

Having no heart for a poor bargain like Petrarch's, Boccaccio shows a different order in the arrangement of his Triumphs. In his *Amorosa visione*, the Triumphs of durability are succeeded by those of mutability. The first gallery presents a vision of order and control in this world, while the second presents a vision of disorder and destruction. The four walls of the first gallery depict a world of relative durability that is attained through wisdom, power, wealth, and love; the second gallery is wholly devoted to the portrayal of the perpetual mutability of fortune, which destroys everything shown in the first gallery. By showing the second gallery after the first, Boccaccio means to convey the inevitable fate of earthly existence, or rather its inability to escape its own mutability. Of course, he can show this because he is willing to accept it.

Even within the first gallery, Boccaccio espouses a principle of life that is diametrically opposed to Petrarch's. Whereas the Triumph of Love comes first in Petrarch's vision, it is the last one in Boccaccio's. While Petrarch advocates mastery and control over the instinctual life, Boccaccio acknowledges its ultimate supremacy. In the *Amorosa visione*, all achievements in art, science, politics, and economics are subservient to the life of love. If Petrarch's principle is called voluntaristic Stoicism, Boccaccio's may be called erotic Epicureanism.

Francesco de Sanctis claims to detect a glaring discrepancy between Boccaccio's principle and Dante's. Whereas the ultimate good in the *Commedia* is science and contemplation, he says, science in Boccaccio's vision is only the beginning of the procession whose final goal is love.[1] But the ultimate end in the *Commedia* is not science but love. In fact, science per se does not play an important role in the *Commedia*. Although Dante the traveler gains a comprehensive knowledge of the entire universe during his journey, his knowledge cannot be attributed to any one of the arts or sciences because it is gained through direct experience. Furthermore, this direct knowledge of the universe is not pursued as the ultimate end of Dante's journey but only as the allegorical medium for preparing Dante for his vision of the transcendent reality.

Arts and sciences per se may be said to constitute the central theme of the *Convivio*, in which Dante tries to sum up all the accomplishments in the vast fields of the moral, physical, and metaphysical sciences. Consequently, contemplation of these scientific truths may also be regarded as Dante's ultimate end. In his composition of the Triumph of Wisdom (or Science), Boccaccio may have been influenced by Dante's *Convivio*. But contemplation assumes a radically different role in the *Commedia*. Whereas contemplation in the *Convivio* is an intellectual function for its own sake, in the *Commedia* it becomes subservient to the act of love. In the Christian view, the exaltation of intellectual contemplation as the highest end would be no less idolatrous than the exaltation of sensuous pleasure. For a pious Christian, contemplation is treasured because it is conceived of as a longing for God or as a loving union with him. In either event, contemplation is always subservient to the love of God.

Dante and Boccaccio agree on one fundamental point; that is, their ultimate end is love. Of course, the objects of their loves are different. If we borrow Augustine's distinction, Dante's love is *charitas* while Boccaccio's is *cupiditas* (*De trinitate*, bk. 9, chap. 8). The former is love of the Creator; the latter is love of creatures. Boccaccio's supremacy of secular love comes about by transferring to this world the Christian tradition of divine love. The Petrarchan notion of subjecting love and passion to the control of virtue is a Stoic legacy which is quite alien to the Christian tradition. When the medieval Christian monks adopted Stoic asceticism for the discipline of their souls, they regarded this discipline only as a means of restraining their earthly passions to enhance their love of God. In the *Commedia* Dante makes it emphatically clear that all Christian virtues are intended to promote the love of God.

Even Petrarch eventually comes around to accepting the supremacy of love in his *Triumphs*, in which love is the central theme not only of the first but also of the last Triumph. The Triumph of Eternity is no more than the transformation of the Triumph of Love into its eternal mode; all the intervening Triumphs are only the provisional means to this transformation. Hence the *Triumphs* are securely placed in the medieval Christian tradition not only in their allegorical form but also in their thematic content. Only in the *Africa* does Petrarch advocate the Stoic idea of conquering love with virtue, going against the grain of the Christian West. Whereas the Roman tradition stands on the ethics of virtue, Christianity is meant to be the religion of love.

It may be quite instructive to compare the *Africa* with the *Ninfale d'Ameto*, another intriguing allegorical work of Boccaccio. The seven nymphs who represent seven virtues tell the stories of their conquest, that is, how they have redeemed seven men who represent seven vices. In the *Ameto*, men are represented as being no better than

beasts; only through the power of these nymphs can they be converted to the life of culture and refinement. Boccaccio's allegorical
use of man and woman is diametrically opposed to that of Petrarch in
the *Africa*. In Petrarch's epic, heavenly virtue is represented by a man
(Scipio) and earthly vice by a woman (Sophonisba).

In this Petrarch is faithfully following Augustine, who regards only
man as a creature of heavenly rationality and woman as a creature of
bestial irrationality. Boccaccio, on the other hand, categorically
rejects this Augustinian male chauvinism. He is proud of writing *De
claris mulieribus*, the first biography of illustrious ladies in history,
which deliberately celebrates feminine glory, countering Petrarch's
praise of the masculine virtues in his *De viris illustribus*. Whereas
Petrarch sees Sophonisba as an incarnation of sensual cupidity in his
Africa, Boccaccio understands her as a great woman of heroic courage
who was not afraid to die to save her honor (see *De claris mulieribus*,
chap. 68).

In exalting woman over man, Boccaccio is reinstating the long
tradition that had come down from the troubadours through the
dolce stil nuovo to Dante, and which had been accepted even by the
Church in its adoration of the Queen of Heaven. The seven nymphs
in the *Ameto* identify themselves in Dante's words: "*Noi siamo qui ninfe,
e nel ciel siamo stelle*" ("Here we are nymphs and in heaven are stars"
—*Purg.* 31. 106). Whereas Scipio's mission is to demolish the force of
vice, the function of Boccaccio's nymphs is to convert and redeem it.
Scipio is a vengeful agent of Jupiter; the nymphs are the ministers of
love from Venus. While the former fights for virtue for its own sake,
the latter employ the various virtues as handmaidens in the service of
love.

The seven nymphs in Dante's Terrestrial Paradise are not warriors to be dispatched for a vengeful campaign against the infernal
forces, but servants who redeem sinful souls with the power of grace.
They tell Dante the pilgrim that their ordained mission is to lead him
to Beatrice's eyes (*Purg.* 31. 108–09). To be sure, Boccaccio's conception of redemption in the *Ameto* is like Dante's in the *Convivio* rather
than in the *Commedia*; the redemptive function of Boccaccio's seven
nymphs is to convert man's primitive savagery into an enlightened
and refined existence. Nonetheless, Boccaccio is faithfully following
in Dante's footsteps by advocating the redemptive function of the
virtues and their subjection to the sovereignty of love.

The sovereignty of love may sound a little blatant and blasphemous when, in the *Ameto*, Boccaccio presents Venus in the Dantesque aura of the Trinity:

> I' son luce del cielo unica e trina,
> principio e fine di ciascuna cosa
> de' qual me 'n fu nè fia nulla vicina.

> [I am the light of heaven, single and threefold,
> The beginning and end of all things,
> Of which nothing has been or is like me.]

Whereas Dante has presented the Trinity as the God of Love, Boccaccio is presenting the Goddess of Love as the Trinity. By reversing Dante's procedure, Boccaccio has indeed given secular form to the Dantesque God of Love, but even this transformation is not quite novel with Boccaccio. Dante himself has already attempted this transformation by dedicating every canzone of his *Convivio* to the Goddess of the Third Heaven. In fact, Boccaccio's view of the virtues in the *Ameto* is very much like Dante's view of civilized humanity (nobility) in the *Convivio*. Thus, Boccaccio's supremacy of love amounts to his repudiation of the Petrarchan revolution and his restoration of the Christian tradition.*

In all fairness to Petrarch, we must admit that he is not always enslaved by Augustinian male chauvinism. Petrarch adores Laura as well as Scipio; after all, he is a child of the *dolce stil nuovo* as well as of Augustinian Stoicism. But Laura is no less Petrarch's symbol for the supremacy of virtue than Scipio is. Hence, of all the various Lauras we have discussed in the previous chapter, Laura-Diana is the truly Petrarchan Laura. Since this Laura is, first of all, a symbol of virtue, she resembles Scipio in so many ways that some Petrarch scholars have been led to assume their interchangeability or equivalence.[2] As a symbol for the supremacy of virtue, this Petrarchan Diana always stands as a lady of chastity and cruelty, who forever eludes Petrarch's

---

*In talking of the Boccaccian responses or reactions to Petrarchan ideas or positions, I am treating them not as a matter of personal interaction or chronological sequence, but as a dialectical interplay of cultural themes or existential stances. Boccaccio wrote most of his works well before seeing the *Africa*, which Petrarch had refused to release except for one short passage. But the Petrarchan idea of the supremacy of virtue was a cultural theme familiar to Boccaccio and his contemporaries, because the ascetic lives of the late medieval Christians often took on the Stoic aura of virtue for virtue's sake when it was forgotten that the true function of the Christian virtues was to enrich the love of God. This Christian Stoicism eventually led to Puritanism.

loving grasp. Boccaccio's supremacy of love can be established by the subjugation of Diana to Venus. Perhaps for this reason, the catching and taming of Diana almost becomes an obsession with Boccaccio.

The first work Boccaccio produced in his illustrious literary career is a Diana story, *Caccia di Diana*. Of course, the object of Boccaccio's concern in his later career is not Diana the hunter but Diana the hunted. He develops this theme in another beautiful story of nymphs, the *Ninfale fiesolano*, in which he systematically reverses the symbolic roles of the nymphs and the shepherds in the *Ameto*. Whereas the shepherds represent primitive savagery and cruelty in the latter work, here they represent the beauty and innocence of natural existence uncontaminated by the dubious conventions of culture. The nymphs who are depicted as the merciful ministers of love in the *Ameto* are slaves of the cruel and merciless Diana in the *Ninfale*. Whereas the nymphs of the *Ameto* gather on the plains, the nymphs of the *Ninfale* assemble on the hills and mountains. The shepherd Ameto lives in the mountains and forests; Shepherd Africo lives on the plain. A nymph converts a shepherd from savagery to enlightenment in the *Ameto*; a shepherd liberates a nymph from the shackles of convention to the ecstasy of the natural life in the *Ninfale*.

The nymphs represent virtues in both stories, but these virtues perform radically different functions in the two. Whereas the nymphs of the *Ameto* represent the subservience of the virtues to love, those of the *Ninfale* stand for the supremacy of virtue over love. For Boccaccio, this supremacy appears to be the slavery to virtue; he seems to be as weary of this slavery to virtue as Dante is afraid of slavery to sin. Boccaccio depicts Diana's reign as a cruel tyranny and calls devotion to her a false faith (*falsa credenza*; *Ninfale*, stanza 6). Her tyranny surely reminds us of Scipio's rigidity and cruelty during his African campaign.

Mensola is one of the timid nymphs under Diana's sway, and Africo catches her with the aid of Venus. Hence Africo's conquest of Mensola symbolizes Venus's defeat of Diana, or rather the victory of love over virtue. To break down the protective walls of virtue is to expose the sheltered life to the storms of fortune, and the love of Africo and Mensola indeed produces tragic consequences. Here again Boccaccio shows his stout heart in accepting fortune in all her terror as an inevitable consequence of the supremacy of love.

In spite of their tragic fate, however, the love of Africo and Mensola bears lasting fruit, their son Pruneo, who becomes the founding

father of Fiesole and whose ten children sire the principal families of
Florence. All Diana can do in vengeful retaliation is to turn Mensola
into a river, but that is a fine ratification of Venus's victory over
Diana because the return to nature is precisely what is claimed
by the supremacy of love. Through his suicide, Africo becomes one
with another river that still bears his name. Thus, in the form
of two rivers of Fiesole, Africo and Mensola become symbols of the
vitality and fertility that sustain the life not only of Fiesole but of Florence.

In this story of the victory of love over virtue, Boccaccio completely
reverses the long Florentine tradition that the nobles of Florence
descended from the Romans while her commoners were the des-
cendents of immigrants from Fiesole. Even Dante has accepted this
tradition in the *Commedia*, where the corruption of Florence is diag-
nosed as the contamination of the old Roman stock by the beasts
from Fiesole (*Inf.* 15. 61–78). Dante's approval of Roman virtue is no
less emphatic than Petrarch's, but Boccaccio dares to go against both
of them in his rejection of Roman tradition. In the *Ninfale*, he depicts
the Romans as a band of cruel marauders who razed Fiesole to the
ground and then founded Florence in order to prevent the rebuilding
of Fiesole (*Ninfale*, sts. 454–55).

Africo's descendants survive Roman persecution and maintain
their dignity. They turn out to be the true children of love; they do
not retaliate against the Romans in a vengeful war. In a spirit of
reconciliation, they return to Florence, live together with the
Romans, and forget the old enmity. Thus, it is Africo's descendants
who transform Florence from a city of hatred and war into a city of
love and peace (*Ninfale*, st. 457). Since all these miracles stem from
the power of Venus, Boccaccio appeals to Love (*Amore*) at the
opening and the conclusion of his story. The Boccaccian supremacy
of love produces peace and harmony in vivid contrast to the vengeance and destruction produced by the Petrarchan supremacy of
virtue. But this supremacy of love can be established only by vanquishing Diana and Scipio, the Petrarchan conquerors.

Let us now return to the *Amorosa visione*. Since Boccaccio is willing
to liberate the life of love and instinct from the yoke of virtue, and to
let it live out its full career in the stormy sea of fortune, his vision in
the *Amorosa visione* moves in a direction precisely opposite to Petrarch's vision in the *Triumphs*. Whereas the latter moves toward
an ever greater durability and stability, the former moves toward an
ever greater mutability and vitality. Petrarch's processions in the

temporal domain are transformed into frozen pictures of eternity; Boccaccio's frescoes in the hall are succeeded by the joyous life in the garden. While the former is a movement from life to memory, the latter is a movement from memory to life.

Furthermore, life in the beautiful garden ends on a note of frustration, because the dreamer awakens from his dream at the very moment of his attempted fulfillment. This is in marked contrast with the medieval tradition of dream-vision, which seldom stops with promise alone but usually ends in fulfillment. For example, Dante's journey concludes with his beatific vision of the Trinity. Petrarch has already abandoned this medieval tradition by casting the Triumph of Eternity in the form of a pious hope rather than a fulfilled reality (a procession). Boccaccio takes one big step beyond Petrarch by replacing the Petrarchan note of hope with the Boccaccian note of frustration.

As we have seen in the last chapter, Petrarch's vision in his *Triumphs* progressively moves away from objective reality toward subjective fantasy, and this subjective orientation constitutes one important difference between Petrarch's ascent and Dante's in spite of their apparent resemblance. Because of its subjective orientation, we are prepared for the conclusion of the *Triumphs* on a note of unfulfilled aspiration. In contrast to Petrarch's vision, as we have just seen, Boccaccio's has been relentlessly moving toward an ever greater degree of reality and vitality, and this objective orientation marks one significant point of resemblance between his vision and Dante's, despite the apparent difference between the two kinds of objective reality involved. This objective orientation in Boccaccio's vision builds up in his readers the expectation of witnessing the fulfillment of the dreamer's aspiration, but Boccaccio the poet mercilessly defeats this expectation by waking the dreamer from his dream at the climactic moment.

Boccaccio's poetic aim in the *Amorosa visione* is to show that only the wakeful world of reality can be the proper domain for fulfillment and realization, while the world of dreams can offer only hope and promise. As we have seen, this point is also intimated in Petrarch's *Triumphs*, but Boccaccio brings forth the idea much more forcefully than Petrarch. Since the *Triumphs* fails to deliver objective fulfillment, as we have seen in the last chapter, Petrarch carries over the vision of eternity from the last Triumph to the first two books of the *Africa*, and then brings his epic hero from his dream world down to the world of mundane reality. Boccaccio is performing the same poetic task by waking the dreamer from his dream and bringing him into the world of objective reality. Unlike Petrarch, however, Boccaccio does not make the long detour of ascent and descent. Instead he takes a direct way, which has been prepared by the orientation of his vision toward an ever-greater degree of vitality and mobility.

Ernest H. Wilkins says that the *Amorosa visione* "constitutes only half of what Boccaccio originally intended to write."[3] If Boccaccio the dreamer were to go up the narrow passageway, he would give us the other half of Boccaccio's journey; the *Amorosa visione*, as it stands, ends with Boccaccio the traveler eager to ascend the narrow stairs.* But there is an irony between Boccaccio the traveler and Boccaccio the poet.† Boccaccio the traveler does not realize that the narrow staircase can be ascended only in a dream and not in wakefulness; he has forgotten that he has just gone through the broad gate not in wakefulness but only in dream. Boccaccio the traveler has not yet learned the Boccaccian poetic lesson that the ultimate end of his journey is to get him out of his dream world into the world of reality, and that only this step toward reality can fulfill what he has seen in his dream-vision.

It is not entirely the fault of Boccaccio the traveler that he has not learned this lesson, because the guide tells him to ascend the steep staircase if he wants to see the lady again. But here is an irony that Boccaccio the poet plays not only on the dreamer but also, perhaps, on his readers. The guide should have disappeared as soon as Boccaccio the traveler wakened from his dream, because the guide was introduced only as a part of his dream-vision. The guide has neither the right to her continued existence after the dream, nor justification for talking about the staircase, which should also have disappeared at the end of the dream. This bizarre episode resembles a picture walking out of its frame and becoming a real thing. This strange turn of events expresses Boccaccio's intent to break out of the world of dream-vision into the world of wakeful reality.

In the *Amorosa visione*, Boccaccio tries not only to end the medieval

---

*If Boccaccio were to have finished the other half of his vision, he would have had to induce himself to go back to sleep and resume his abruptly terminated dream. The resumption of a broken dream appears to be quite implausible. If the *Amorosa visione* had ended with the dreamer still in his dream, it could plausibly be claimed that the work is only half finished.

†On this point of irony, I have been instructed by a bright young Boccaccio scholar, Janet Smarr.

tradition of dream-vision but also to reduce its allegorical language to literal language. We have already witnessed a similar attempt in the *Triumphs*, which is written in the same language from its opening with an earthly procession to its conclusion with a heavenly vision. One of the amazing developments in the *Amorosa visione* is that Boccaccio's vision through the broad gate encompasses not only the human but also the divine world. The Triumph of Fame opens with the age of the immortals (Saturn and Jupiter) and giants and then covers all of human history. The Triumph of Love observes no greater distinction between the love of gods and goddesses and the love of men and women than the distinction between Greeks and Romans. In the beautiful garden, Boccaccio falls in love with Maria who has come down from heaven. In short, Boccaccio's journey through the broad gate represents his vision of the unity of the two worlds.

It is this Boccaccian unity that renders superfluous the allegorical use of our language. For the distinction between literal and allegorical usage has been dictated by the separation of the eternal or transcendent from the temporal or immanent world. Boccaccio can, in fact, see no difference between allegory on the one hand and fable or fiction on the other. In *Genealogia deorum gentilium*, he examines four kinds of fables or myths (bk. 14, chap. 9). The first kind is a complete fiction like Aesop's fables. The second kind is a mixture of truth and fiction; most poetic fictions (e.g. Ovid's *Metamorphoses*) belong to this group. The third kind is more like history than fiction; historical epics like Virgil's *Aeneid* belong to this group. The fourth kind is old wives' tales. Of these four groups, Boccaccio claims, only the last one has no truth value. The common function of fables in the first three categories is to present truth in a beautiful guise for edification and entertainment.

Boccaccio boldly asserts that every form of figuralism in the Bible can be assigned to one of these three truthful types of fable. There are fables as fictitious as Aesop's in the Bible, for example, the conference of the trees in the forest in choosing a king, in Judges 9: 8–15. The Old Testament is full of fables of the second kind. In this regard, Boccaccio says, the literary device used to describe the visions of Isaiah, Ezekiel, Daniel, and other sacred writers is the same as that of the secular poets. He believes that this second kind of fable is called "figures" by our theologians. The third kind of fable is used by Christ himself in his parables. Thus Boccaccio completely assimilates the allegorical tradition into the poetic fables of truth.

So the apparent allegory in his *Amorosa visione* turns out to be only a poetic fable; in this work Boccaccio accepts the medieval allegorical tradition only to reduce it to the literal plane. He manifests this reduction not only by leaving little mystery behind the narrow gate but also by adopting the plain and the garden for his poetic scenes in place of the mountain, which has stood as the most eminent symbol of *anagogia* throughout the medieval tradition of allegory. In the *Ameto*, Boccaccio makes the mountain the primitive habitat of an uncouth shepherd and places the festival of the nymphs on the plain. Ameto has to come down from his mountainous haunt to the plain before he can be initiated into the kingdom of virtue. In the *Ninfale*, Boccaccio makes the mountain Diana's tyrannous cloister and presents the plain as the symbol of freedom from all dubious conventions. Mensola can return to the state of nature by descending Diana's mountain to Africo's plain. In the *Amorosa visione*, Boccaccio the dreamer falls in love not on top of a mountain but in a garden.

Boccaccio in the Classical Tradition

In his *Teseida*, Boccaccio tries his hand at a martial epic. Theseus is the king of Athens, who conquers Thebes. Arcita and Palamone are two young Theban warriors who fall captive in this war and are imprisoned indefinitely in Athens. One day they fall in love with the beautiful Emilia, sister to Hippolytus, the Athenian queen, when they see her through the prison window. Through the accidental intercession of a friend, Arcita is released and goes back to Thebes. But he returns to Athens in disguise because he cannot endure the torment of love. While he is employed as Theseus' favorite servant, Palamone escapes. During his escape, he runs into Arcita and engages him in a duel. Theseus intervenes and arranges a tournament to settle their dispute over love: a year hence, Arcita and Palamone will return to Athens, each with one hundred knights under his command, for a grand tournament, whose victor shall have Emilia's hand.

For this occasion, Theseus prepares a grand stadium, which has three shrines separately dedicated to Mars, Venus, and Diana. Just before the tournament, Arcita goes to the shrine of Mars, Palamone to the shrine of Venus, and Emilia to the shrine of Diana; there they present their petitions to their favorite immortals. Arcita wins the tournament and the right to have Emilia, but is mortally wounded through an accident. While dying, he expresses his wish that Emilia be given to Palamone. In accordance with this wish, Theseus presides over the marriage of Palamone and Emilia.

The central theme of the *Teseida* is the disruption of feudal loyalty under the power of love. The relationship between Arcita and Palamone is one of the most sacred ties in the age of chivalry; they are not only related through blood but are also intimately linked with each other as brethren-in-arms who have taken the sacred oath of unlimited mutual aid. As such companions, they are supposed to have a common fate, sharing everything with each other in happiness or misery until their death. They form an inseparable pair like one of the pairs (peers) among Charlemagne's Twelve Peers, Roland and Oliver, Gerin and Gerier, Ives and Ivor, Othon and Berenger, and Anseis and Sanson. Hence their relationship is the most sacred, second only to that of a vassal to his lord in the feudal world.

The relationship between Arcita and Palamone takes on even greater poignancy because of their imprisonment in the enemy dungeon. Since they are the sole survivors of the Theban house, they have the sacred obligation of devoting themselves to the task of liberating Thebes from Theseus' rule. At the sight of Emilia, however, these two young warriors completely forget their special ties and their sacred obligation. Immediately they turn against each other and claim their respective rights to the beautiful girl. Thus is indeed the order of feudal loyalty instantaneously disrupted by the overwhelming power of love.

Arcita is freed and goes back to Thebes, but he can neither endure his freedom nor devote himself to the restoration of the Theban rule. Of his own will, he returns to the Athenian bondage. Palamone is no less helplessly vanquished by love; even after his escape from prison, he still remains completely possessed by his passion for Emilia. He seems to show no more concern for Thebes than Arcita does. When they meet by accident, they never think of reestablishing their old sacred ties, but fall upon each other in a fierce duel. Their fight is terminated temporarily by the intervention of Theseus; the man who is supposed to be their common enemy intervenes as their arbiter. It is again this common enemy who decrees and presides over the final tournament between the two young warriors. This tournament completes their transformation from knights of feudal loyalty into knights of love.

The outcome of the tournament is the victory of Venus over Mars and Diana. Arcita, who prays to Mars and wins the tournament, is prevented from possessing Emilia by an accident; Palamone, who prays to Venus, manages to have her, although he loses the tournament. Emilia, who prays to Diana, would like to preserve her chastity, but she finally consents to marry Palamone because of the plea of the dying Arcita and the advice of the reigning Theseus. The victory of Venus turns out to be a double one, that is, the conquest of the warrior of Mars and the maiden of Diana. Her conquest may be also described as the conversion of the warriors from war to love, and that of the maiden from chastity to fertility. Thus the supremacy of love is conclusively established by the *Teseida*.

The *Teseida* has been subject to a barrage of derogatory criticism. Francesco de Sanctis says that this sort of heroic literature was entirely foreign to Boccaccio's nature and talent.[4] Ernest H. Wilkins says that Boccaccio's motive for writing the *Teseida* was to win distinction as a poet of arms, whch Dante had said no Italian had yet achieved.[5] Although the *Teseida* as a martial epic may fall far short of excellence, it is extremely ingenious in establishing the supremacy of love over war. In the previous chapter, we saw how intimately the two themes of love and war have been entangled with each other in the courtly tradition, and how Petrarch tried to resolve their conflict by separating them into two related works. In the *Teseida*, I believe, Boccaccio is attempting his own resolution of this same conflict.

The dissolution of the sacred tie of feudal loyalty between Arcita and Palamone under the power of love does indeed appear to be disgraceful and destructive at first sight. In retrospect, however, we can see that the dissolution of that feudal relationship is a necessary condition for the eventual reconciliation of the two hostile cities. Suppose that Arcita and Palamone faithfully lived up to their feudal ideal. After their release and escape from the Athenian prison, they would have plotted another war against Athens and thereby perpetuated the hostility between the two cities.

Under her sovereign rule, Venus eventually brings about a harmonious reconciliation of all the parties. Even the dying Arcita manages to contribute his share toward this reconciliation by asking Emilia to marry Palamone, who in return builds a shrine to Arcita. Theseus also plays an indispensable role in this reconciliation by intervening and arbitrating in the fight between Arcita and Palamone. By sponsoring the marriage of Emilia to Palamone, Theseus is accepting his former foe as a member of his own family.

Above all, Theseus is performing these vital functions as the lord of the city of Athene; his contribution can be construed as the faithful subordination of Athene to Venus, or rather of wisdom to love. In his exhortation to Palamone and Emilia, Theseus calls his counsel of re-conciliation the wisdom of making a virtue out of necessity. This is a perfectly acceptable description of Athenian wisdom. It is this wisdom that makes the distinction between the two Venuses—or rather the two manifestations of Venus—the disruptive and the re-conciliatory. Through the intervention of Athenian wisdom, the dis-ruptive force of love is contained and diverted into a constructive channel. Thus wisdom becomes a supplementary force in establishing the supremacy of love over valor and chastity.

In the *Filostrato*, Boccaccio further elaborates on the supremacy of love. This time he presents his elaboration in the form of a romance rather than that of an epic. In the proem he explains the meaning of the title of his poem; *filostrato* means a man overcome and over-thrown by love. The man who is vanquished by love in the *Filostrato* is Troiolo, a princely warrior of Troy during the Trojan War.* Boccaccio has adopted and transformed this love story from Benoit's *Roman de Troie*, a romance devoted to the military encounters be-tween the Greeks and the Trojans. In Benoit's romance, as Nathan-iel E. Griffin tells us, the love story is presented as a diversion to break up the monotony of the successive encounters between the two military forces.[6] In Boccaccio's work, this peripheral event of the Trojan War is given the center of the stage while the war itself is relegated to the background. In doing this, of course, Boccaccio is exalting Venus over Mars.

Troiolo falls in love with Criseida, the daughter of Calchas, a Trojan priest who has defected to the Greeks. He experiences the consummation of his love through the help of his friend Pandaro, a cousin to Criseida. But Criseida has to go to the Greek camp and join her father, who has managed to have her included in the exchange of prisoners of war. She departs with a firm promise to return to Troiolo in ten days, but decides not to keep her promise when she falls in love with Diomede of the Greek camp. Thus Troiolo is forced to suffer the agony of love after its brief ecstasy.

*In Chaucer's adaptation of the *Teseida* in his Knight's Tale, Arcite assumes the alias of "Philostratus" when he returns to Athens in disguise. This indeed appears to indicate Chaucer's assumption that the *Teseida* and the *Filostrato* share the same central theme. The alias Arcita assumes in the *Teseida* is "Penteo"; this is the name of the Theban king who was torn to pieces by the Bacchantes in their frenzy. Since Arcita is a Theban prince who is metaphorically torn to pieces by his passion, the name of Penteo correctly describes his state of mind as *filostrato*.

The power of love in the *Filostrato* appears to be even more over-whelming than in the *Teseida*. Whereas the two warriors conquered by the power of love in the latter are prisoners in a dungeon, the one vanquished in the former is a lordly prince of Troy. In contrast to Emilia's exalted position as sister of the Athenian queen, Criseida occupies a relatively lowly position in comparison to Troiolo's princely rank, since she is a widowed daughter of Calchas. When she first hears of Troiolo's love for her, she readily assumes that Troiolo is only looking for some diversion and fears that she may be abused by his capricious passion (*Filostrato*, bk. 2, sts. 51 and 76). Only moments before he is stricken by love, Troiolo himself freely expresses his contempt for those who lose their liberty through their love of fickle women (1. 20–22). He goes on to tell us that this is a lesson he has learned from his own experience. It is this disdainful and lordly prince whom love strikes.

Love brings about a dramatic conversion in Troiolo; he is trans-formed from a fierce warrior into a submissive servant. He becomes an obedient slave not only to the Lord of Love but also to Lady Criseida. He is so possessed by love that he loses all his concern for the war with the Greeks (2. 3 and 33). He becomes a completely passive person, who can take no initiative in exploiting a favorable fortune or fighting against an adverse one. He can only fervently pray for the gift of love; he is only willing to do the will of his lady. He is all aflame with passion, but he has no will of his own. Without Pandaro's help, he could have done nothing to consummate his love. When the Greek proposal for the exchange of Antenor for Criseida is debated and accepted, he can find no way to influence the final decision of either his father or his lady. He truly becomes a *filostrato*.

Becoming the helpless slave of passion is the consequence of Boccac-cio's supremacy of love. Schleiermacher has claimed the sense of total dependence as being the essence of religion. Troiolo's sense of dependence is sufficiently great to verge on religious feeling; Boc-caccio extensively uses religious language to describe his behavior. To begin with, he is stricken by love in a temple. His prayers to the Lord of Love take on the form of pious religious petitions (see 1. 55; 4. 33). He adapts the Christian language of the Father and the Son to describe Venus and Cupid: "Praised be thy supreme power, fair Venus, and that of thy son Love" (2. 80). Finally, in his longest prayer to Venus, he portrays Venus as the almighty deity who has control over the entire universe, including Jove and Mars, as has been claimed in the *Teseida* and the *Amorosa visione* (3. 74–89).

Troiolo's state of total dependence is very much like that of a pious medieval Christian. The essence of Christian piety is humility, which is none other than the recognition of one's powerlessness, especially in the presence of almighty God. We have already seen that Boccaccio's Venus is his transformation of the God of spiritual love into the deity of carnal love. The total dependence and passivity on the part of Troiolo is a necessary consequence of this transformation. Troiolo is a pious man in the religion of love. If there is anything in him that does not quite measure up to the Christian model of piety and humility, it is his inability to suffer through the misfortunes of this world with Job's patience and to accept even the thorns in the flesh with Paul's gratitude.

In the *Fiammetta* Boccaccio once more tries out his theme of the supremacy of love, only this time the victim of love's overwhelming power is a woman rather than a man. The sense of religious aura in this case comes through even more insistently than in the *Filostrato*, because Boccaccio employs the living legacy of Christianity rather than the archaic remnant of pagan practice. Fiammetta is stricken with love in a Christian church on an Easter Sunday; this is a religious experience for her in every sense. She becomes as helpless a victim of her own passions as Troiolo. In both cases, the supremacy of love produces quite unsatisfactory consequences. Boccaccio himself expresses his dissatisfaction with these consequences by concluding both works with warnings against them. It is not so much the suffering of the victims as their lack of dignity that violates our sense of decency. We cannot but take offense at witnessing a valiant warrior being transformed into a petty slave to his emotions. A victim of love does not seem to fare any better than a slave of virtue. So Boccaccio has every reason to repudiate the supremacy of love as emphatically as the supremacy of virtue.

To be either a victim of love or a slave to virtue is becoming the Boccaccian dilemma, and Boccaccio seems to find the germ of its resolution in Criseida. As a dialectical counterpart to Troiolo's servitude, she enjoys her sovereign role. To be exact, she enjoys this role by sharing in the supremacy of love. Troiolo describes this sharing by saying that the Lord of Love takes his station in Criseida's eyes as a worthy locus of her power (1. 39). As Griffin points out, Boccaccio builds up Criseida's sovereignty by drawing largely from the tradition of the *dolce stil nuovo*.[7] The sovereign role of Criseida can also be regarded as Boccaccio's adaptation of Petrarch's Laura. In fact, the way Boccaccio transforms Benoit's Briseida from her lowly status into his Criseida of sovereign station is very much like the Petrarchan process of idealizing a lowly, earthly creature into an exalted, eternal beauty.

If Boccaccio had wanted to find a ready-made lady of nobility and dignity in Benoit's work, he could have easily found her in the person of Polyxena, a Trojan princess. Instead he deliberately chose a slave girl and changed her name and status. Whether the changing of her name from Briseida to Criseida was Boccaccio's own doing or his adoption of Armannino's is still open to debate among Boccaccio scholars.[8] In either event, the altered name appears to be part of his effort to transform the heroine. The disgraceful condition of Benoit's Briseida is so much like that of Briseis in the *Iliad* that A. Joly has assumed the former to have been modeled after the latter.[9]

At any rate, the changing of the name from Briseida to Criseida is likely to induce in our minds the association of her with Chryseis and Briseis, the Homeric pair at the center of the famous altercation between Agamemnon and Achilles (see *Iliad*, bk. 1). In the distribution of booty, Chryseis had been given to Agamemnon and Briseis to Achilles. Chryses, Chryseis' father, tries to ransom his daughter, but Agamemnon mercilessly turns down his entreaty. Thereupon Chryses, a priest of Apollo, prays to his god for vengeance, and Apollo responds by sending down many griefs on the Achaians. At the assembly of Greek chieftains, Achilles requests Calchas to interpret this misfortune and propose its remedy. Calchas replies that their misfortune is an expression of Apollo's anger, which can be appeased only by returning Chryseis in honor to her father. Thus forced to relinquish Chryseis, Agamemnon claims Briseis in compensation. In this Homeric episode, Briseis, who helplessly passes from one greedy hand to another, is a symbol of servitude and captivity. In contrast, Chryseis is a symbol of lordship and sovereignty because her release is dictated by the divine will of Apollo, who overrules even the will of the mightiest king among the Achaians.

In spite of Boccaccio's adaptation of the Petrarchan process of idealization, there is an important difference between Criseida and Laura in their sovereign roles. Criseida's sovereignty is rooted in the sphere of reality; Laura's is displayed in the sphere of ideality. Criseida's is exposed in the world of participation; Laura's is protected by the shield of chastity. Laura need not break any promise because she never makes one; Criseida has to cope with the unpleasant contingency of her own infidelity because she takes the trouble to form real ties with living people. Criseida always walks a precarious tightrope of compromise (that is, a continuing need to reconcile the conflicting demands of reality), while Laura is safely projected onto the transcendent screen of ideals. If there is a persistent sense of bitterness and irony in Boccaccio, this only shows that Boccaccio is prepared to bring the Petrarchan ideals down to the domain of reality and to face their grave consequences. This is the spirit of Boccaccian realism.

Perhaps in order to highlight the Boccaccian realism in Criseida's sovereignty in contrast to the Petrarchan idealism in Laura's, Boccaccio converts Briseida's virginity into Criseida's widowhood. It is this widowhood that prevents her from playing the role of a chaste maiden and at the same time gives freedom of action as a participant. She jealously guards the freedom and independence that she can enjoy only as a widow (2. 69). She dreads the prospect of losing this sovereign position by becoming the permanent possession of a husband (2. 73–74). She equally detests her role as the cruel guardian of her own chastity (2. 64–65). She knows that such a role would be incompatible with her desire to make the best of her brief youth (2. 71–72). In short, she wants to play her sovereign role in the domain of Venus, not in that of Diana.

This role is much more difficult to play in the domain of Venus. The virtue of moderation is harder to achieve than the virtue of abstinence. The Stoic ideal of suppressing the passions is often assumed to be better than the Epicurean ideal of their controlled enjoyment, not because the latter is less desirable than the former but because the former is more feasible than the latter. While the exaltation of Laura exacts the price of perpetual frustration, the sovereignty of Criseida is meant to assure the fulfillment of all desires under full control. Although Criseida often talks of her honor and dignity, she is never enslaved to her sense of chastity. The honor and dignity which are her real concerns consist of no more than a decent social reputation. She is keenly aware of the need to satisfy her desires (2. 127; 3. 50). In spite of her vigorous desires, however, she never allows herself to be overpowered by her tumultuous feelings as Troiolo does. Thus, her sovereignty resides in her self-mastery and self-control as much as in her mastery and control of Troiolo.

It is this unique sovereign role of Criseida that distinguishes the *Filostrato* from the *Teseida*. In the latter work Theseus plays the sovereign role, but this role falls upon him because of his official capacity as the king of Athens. Furthermore, he is not a participant in the love life of that epic. Criseida is a private person and exercises her sovereignty as a participant in the world of love. Perhaps to protect her sovereignty in participation, Boccaccio allows no one to intervene in an official capacity. The only person who is allowed to have a hand in the fate of love is Pandaro, who plays all his roles in a private capacity. Even he is not allowed to sway the course of events beyond their natural destiny. His role as a go-between is as subservient as that of a midwife.

Criseida's sovereign position is much more precarious than Theseus'. She is caught in the middle of the conflict between the Greeks and the Trojans, while Theseus enjoys undisputed rulership over Athens. Theseus' public sovereignty is for the protection of public order; Criseida's private sovereignty is for the promotion of private interests. The *Teseida* concludes on the note of reconciliation; the *Filostrato* ends on the note of separation. This obvious contrast between the two sovereigns is further manifested in the two roles assigned to fortune. Whereas fortune stays in the background in the *Teseida*, she makes her presence and power felt in the foreground throughout the *Filostrato*. Whereas fortune brings about the alienation of Criseida from Troiolo in the latter, she allows Theseus to intervene and reestablish order and harmony in the former. The sense of presiding over the workings of fortune is an essential feature of Theseus' public sovereignty, but this sense of control over fortune is completely missing in Creseida's private sovereignty.

From beginning to end, both Troiolo and Criseida are constantly aware of the ubiquitous presence of almighty fortune. When fortune smiles upon them, they joyfully express their gratitude for her generous gifts. When she turns against them, they vehemently pour upon her a series of invectives: "fickle fortune," "hostile fortune," "envious fortune," "grudging fortune," "treacherous fortune," "cruel fortune," etc. It is this mighty fortune who elicits the most dramatic difference between the sovereignty of Criseida and the servitude of Troiolo.

While Troiolo can only play the passive role of rejoicing in the favorable turn of fortune and suffering through its unfavorable turn, Criseida is intent on making an active response to its every turn. She knows that she cannot control the tides of fortune; she, however, feels that she had better make the best of them. Hence she adopts it as her cardinal rule to base all her decisions on a careful calculation of probable fortunes. That she retains this freedom of decision and exercises it judiciously is one of the essential marks of her sovereignty and makes an obvious contrast with Troiolo's total loss of the power of decision in his servitude. Criseida herself is rather distressed at the loss of self-mastery in Troiolo (4. 157).

As soon as she learns of Troiolo's love for her, she carefully calculates the advantages and disadvantages of her options (2. 69–78). Because of her youth and freedom as a childless widow, she feels that she has every reason to accept his love. At the same time, however, she is fully aware of the danger that his passion may not endure and that he may abandon her in shame and confusion. Even if his love turns out to be steadfast, she has to consider the possibility that her reputation may be seriously damaged by the exposure of their affair. She eventually decides to take the risk of love because she is no less eager to fulfill her desires than Troiolo and because she is determined to make the best of fortune and her youth. But she is intent on retaining the virtue of discretion and caution.

When Troiolo proposes his plan of elopement to prevent the surrendering of Criseida in exchange for Antenor, she coolly turns it down because that course of action would not only damage their reputation but would also eventually extinguish the ardor of Troiolo's love by giving him free possession of her whole self.

> And besides this, I desire thee to take thought to what happeneth in the case of almost everything. There is nothing so base that doth not, if it be guarded well, make itself ardently desired, and the more thou dost yearn to possess it, the sooner doth loathing spring in thy heart, if full power be granted thee to see it, and even more, to keep it.
>
> Our love which pleaseth thee so much, pleaseth thee because thou must act secretly and seldom come to this place. But if thou wilt have me freely, soon will be extinguished the glowing torch which now enkindleth thee—and me likewise. For if, as now, we wish our love to last, it must ever lie concealed. [4. 152–53][10]

Robert apRoberts takes this passage as Criseida's argument for preferring love *paramours* to marital love; that is, she would rather not elope with Troiolo because their marital love would not give them the same kind of intensity and delight as their present secret love.[11] If apRoberts's view is correct, Criseida would be no more than a slave to sensuality, who is simply repeating an old line from the tradition of courtly love.

Criseida indeed employs the language of sensuality in her effort to persuade Troiolo, but her argument fully reveals her concern with her own sovereignty. As it were, the language of power politics in love seeps through the language of sensual pleasure in her argument. She is really concerned about Troiolo's full power of seeing (*larga potestade di vederla*) and possessing her freely (*m'averai liberamente*). She knows that she would have to exchange her sovereignty over Troiolo for servitude to him, if she were to run away with him from Troy. Instead of accepting his plan, she proposes her own plan of going along with the prisoner exchange and then returning to Troy in ten days. She tells him that her plan of action is to follow the flow (*corso*) of fortune and that that is the way to tire out and eventually conquer it (4. 154).

When she proposes her plan to Troiolo, she shows plenty of confidence in her ability to execute it by firmly promising him that she will return without fail (*senza alcun fallo*) on the tenth day (4. 154). On hearing his skeptical response to this promise, she chides him for his lack of faith in her (4. 157). She goes on to tell him that she is clever enough to find the ways and means and to keep her promise (4. 159). As events take their course, it is clearly shown that her decision not to return is never dictated by the external barriers against her desire and will. This is one of the important points in which Chaucer's version diverges from Boccaccio's. In Chaucer's *Troilus and Criseyde*, Criseyde's final decision to stay in the Greek camp is partly influenced by the difficulty of her returning to Troy. In Boccaccio's *Filostrato*, however, Criseida retains her freedom of action to the end.

One of the arguments Diomede makes to win Criseida's love hinges on the probable outcome of the Trojan War (6. 16 ff.). He tells her that the defeat of Troy is near at hand and that this doom has been pronounced by her own father. When Troy falls, he assures her, no one in that city will be spared. For this reason alone, it would be foolish for her to cling to her Trojan love. She frankly admits to him that this is indeed a telling point:

> The times are cruel and you are in arms. Let the victory that thou dost expect, come. Then shall I know much better what to do. Perhaps then I shall be much more content with the

pleasures that now please me not, and thou mayest speak to me again. Perchance what thou sayest will be dearer to me then than it is now. One must regard time and season when one wisheth to capture another. [6. 31][12]

Criseida cannot, of course, reserve her power of choice between Troiolo and Diomede, or rather between the Trojans and the Greeks, until the conclusion of the war. By then it would be too late for her to exercise the option. Thus, her decision to remain with the Greeks appears to be chiefly influenced by her belief that Troy will soon be vanquished by the Greeks.

With the impending doom of Troy, she can remain faithful to Troiolo only by sacrificing her sovereignty and handing herself over as a victim of fortune. She can retain her sovereign position only by breaking her promise to Troiolo. So she is confronted with the dilemma of sacrificing either her fidelity or her sovereignty. This is the Boccaccian dilemma that is usually inevitable for anyone who plunges into the turbulent world of fortune. "Fickle (*mobile*) fortune" is only a synonym for "the mutable (*mutabile*) world," which is in turn a synonym for "the living world." Only death can assure immutability and constancy; only the renunciation of this living world, in the Stoic or Christian mode, can pave the assured way of fidelity in defiance of fortune. But Criseida is prepared to renounce neither this living world nor her sovereignty in it; she can ride the tides of fortune only by turning her back on poor Troiolo.

Criseida has often been derided as a slave to sensuality, but I believe that this is an erroneous judgment of her character. For example, Sanford B. Meech says that her sensuality leads to her infidelity.[13] But this is only an assumption that cannot be substantiated by the textual evidence of the *Filostrato*. In her decision not to return to Troy, Criseida is never overwhelmed by her passion for Diomede. There is nothing to indicate that her feelings for him are stronger than her attachment to Troiolo. Boccaccio carefully sums up the reasons for her decision:

> These things [Diomede's arguments as well as his appearance] cooled her in the warm thought she had of wishing only to return. These things turned her whole mind, which was intent upon seeing Troilus, and abated her desire, and a new hope put somewhat to flight her grievous torment. And it befell, moved by these reasons, she kept not her promises to Troilus. [6. 34][14]

Criseida's final decision is not dictated by turbulent emotions but is reached through cool deliberation. Her old attachment to Troiolo is abated not by her new infatuation with Diomede but by "a new hope [*nuova speranza*]." That is surely not a mark of her enslavement to sensuality but rather a clear sign of her capacity to lord it over all.

Her rejection of Troiolo is really her desertion of the doomed Troy; in this regard, the name "Troiolo" can aptly stand for Troy. When she made the promise to return to Troiolo, we have to admit, she could not have taken into consideration the circumstances which she came to see only after she was situated in the Greek camp. The new perspective that she gains there is one of the contingencies of fortune she has to live with from moment to moment, as contingent as the fact that she has been forced to leave Troy in the exchange of prisoners. She can maintain her sovereign position only by making the best of these contingencies as they arise, and this, perhaps, is what is meant by Theseus's counsel to make a virtue of necessity in the *Teseida*.

If we stress the sovereign role of Criseida, she resembles Petrarch's Scipio in many ways. In the previous chapter, we have seen that his outstanding virtue is called prudence, which consists of *solertia* (artfulness, ingenuity, sagacity) and *calliditas* (cunning, skill). Although Criseida may not have all these Scipionic virtues, she does have the requisite state of mind for exercising them properly. It is, indeed, the irony of the *Filostrato* that many different types of active virtues come to demand our attention while the passive hero occupies its center. For example, Pandaro is a man of active cunning; a hero or heroine of active sovereign ingenuity could be readily produced by combining his ingenuity with Criseida's sovereignty. This sort of combination is already intimated in the person of the daring, shrewd Diomede.

When this combination of Criseida's sovereignty and Pandaro's ingenuity is fully accomplished, it will produce the truly Boccaccian man or woman of the *Decameron*, a complete master of his or her own person and circumstances. This Boccaccian personality cannot be content with the fate of being victimized by love or tyrannized by virtue; his principle may be called the sovereignty of a person—or humanity—which clearly supersedes the supremacy not only of love but also of virtue. The sovereignty of humanity appears to resolve not only the Boccaccian dilemma in the supremacy of love but also the Petrarchan dilemma in the supremacy of virtue.

Boccaccio's Resolution of the Petrarchan Dilemma*

The ultimate essence of Scipionic virtue in the *Africa* is his total dedication to the destiny of Rome or her divine mission. This Scipionic dedication is so complete as to leave the hero no desire or passion of his own as a person; he does not even have his own will, because his will is in perfect accord with his public duty. By any standard of humanity, Scipio cannot be regarded as a person. He is a machine, which can readily fulfill all the requisite conditions for being a Calvinistic divine "instrument" except for the commitment to the Christian God. In spite of his insistent emphasis on Scipio's total dedication to the public world, Petrarch is not content to have his hero be simply a public hero. For Petrarch, Scipio's private life in his solitude is as essential to his heroic stature as his public dedication. Petrarch expresses this dual demand for Petrarchan heroism by praising this Scipionic devotion to solitude as well as to virtue in *De vita solitaria*.

It is this dual requirement for Petrarchan heroism that creates a dilemma. If Scipio is totally devoted to public life, how can he have any privacy left for his life of solitude? The Roman hero whose life is completely identified with his public role is Caesar; in this regard, he makes a perfect contrast with Scipio. Petrarch is perpetually fascinated with this contrast throughout his life. The lives of Caesar and Scipio are the two longest entries in his *De viris illustribus*. Aldo Bernardo tells us that Scipio the Younger and Caesar open Petrarch's list of men of action in the third book of *Rerum memorandarum*.[15] Bernardo also tells us that Petrarch regards Caesar and Scipio as the two greatest generals of all time.[16] Thus Caesar and Scipio have formed an almost inseparable pair in Petrarch's mind, and this surely shows his fascination with both.

In many cases Petrarch clearly states his preference for Scipio over Caesar as the ultimate model for Petrarchan heroism. In most of these cases his preference is dictated by his concern for solitude; Scipio is a hero not only for his *Africa* but also for his *De vita solitaria*. Caesar's indifference to solitude always seems to cool the enthusiasm

*Here again I would like to stress that the Boccaccian responses to Petrarchan ideas are treated as moves in the dialectical interplay of cultural themes rather than as the personal reactions of a private individual. As we have seen in the previous chapter, the Petrarchan ideals were quite familiar to Boccaccio and his contemporaries because they were simply secular versions of Christian cultural themes.

of Petrarch as the champion of interiority. Furthermore, he seems to
be distressed at Caesar's assumption of the Roman emperorship;
this side of his feeling seems to come out in his emphatic endorsement of Scipio's refusal to accept the kingship from the Spanish
people in *Epistolae seniles* 16. 5. This endorsement of Scipio's action
may be read as his disapproval of Caesar's.

Petrarch's disapproval of Caesar's action cannot, however, be
fully justified on the ground of his attitude toward solitude alone. The
career of a busy king may indeed distract from the life of contemplation, but it cannot be any more distracting than the career of a
military commander. Neither the career of a king nor that of a
general can be regarded as absolutely incompatible with the life of
contemplation. What really disturbs Petrarch is apparently his fear
that the assumption of rulership may absorb the entire person into the
office. It was one of the revered political ideals throughout the Middle
Ages that the life and will of a king or emperor must be identical
with the life and will of his kingdom or empire. In this regard, the
office of a ruler is unlike any other office and is most suitable for the
Caesarean resolution of the Petrarchan conflict between the public
and private dimensions of human existence.

The Caesarean resolution would demand complete absorption
of the individual into the state; Petrarch may be as apprehensive of
this as medieval Christians were of the mystical absorption of a soul
into the divine reality. In contrast to this resolution, Scipio stands for
the nonresolution of the Petrarchan dilemma rather than its resolution. As a man of nonresolvable conflict, however, Petrarch is much
more firmly attracted to Scipio than to Caesar. But his preference for
Scipio was far from unwavering throughout his life. Aldo Bernardo
reports that there was a period of unqualified enthusiasm for Caesar
in Petrarch's life.[17] In an earlier version of the Triumph of Glory,
Petrarch had placed Caesar as the only hero beside the goddess of
glory. In the final version, however, he places both Caesar and
Scipio as close twin companions of the goddess. This may very well
mean that Petrarch himself seriously considered the Caesarean
resolution of the Scipionic dilemma.

Although Petrarch finally refused to embrace the Caesarean resolution, it became a durable legacy to the modern world. Machiavelli's
Prince can be viewed as a program for implementing the Caesarean
resolution. Leonard Forster clearly explains how the role of Queen
Elizabeth emerged as a political transformation of Petrarch's Laura.[18] One of the most important features of this transformation is the

transference of Petrarchism from the private to the public arena. Petrarch's Laura lives in his private world; Elizabeth is the Virgin Queen married to the entire country. Hence, Elizabeth's role as a Gloriana is her adoption of the Caesarean resolution, and in this she has been followed by many other eminent figures, such as Louis XIV ("L'état, c'est moi"—"I am the state"), Frederick the Great, Napoleon, down to the totalitarian dictators of our century.

The Caesarean resolution has one unsatisfactory consequence: the identification of one sovereign will with the life of the entire state can leave no room for any other sovereign will. For example, Scipionic sovereignty in the *Africa* leaves no room for the assertion of another sovereign will under Scipio's command. Massinissa expresses this truth in his Jobean lament over Scipio's inflexible dictate on the fate of Sophonisba: "Life he [Scipio] brought / And life he took away" (*Africa*, 5. 564–65). This totalitarian tendency of the Caesarean resolution is especially incompatible with Renaissance individualism. For this reason, in the recurrent Renaissance debate on the relative greatness of Scipio and Caesar, Caesar's tyranny often shows up as the main reason for downgrading him in comparison with Scipio's propensity for the solitary existence.[19] In short, the Caesarean resolution presents an immediate threat to the Renaissance ethos in which everyone wants to have sufficient room for exercising his own sovereign freedom.* This is one of the important reasons for Scipio's immense

---

*In *Antony and Cleopatra*, Shakespeare portrays the tragic consequence of a Caesarean resolution. The imperial ambition of Octavius Caesar makes even the whole world too small for him to accommodate partnership with his fellow triumvirs, Antony and Lepidus. Octavius retains their partnership only so long as he has to rely on it to subdue the revolt of Sextus Pompeius. On vanquishing Pompeius, he swallows up Lepidus's share of the Roman Empire, which prompts Enobarbus to muse:

> Then, world, thou hast a pair of chaps, no more;
> And thrown between them all the food thou hast,
> They'll grind the one the other.
> [act 3, scene 5, lines 12–14]

At the news of Antony's suicide, Octavius himself laments the tragic, inevitable dissolution of their partnership:

> We could not stall together
> In the whole world. But yet let me lament
> With tears as sovereign as the blood of hearts
> That thou, my brother, my competitor
> In top of all design, my mate in empire,
> Friend and companion in the front of war,
> That arm of mine own body, and the heart
> Where mine his thoughts did kindle, that our stars,

popularity with noted Renaissance men, some of whom even adopted his name.

Scipio of the *Africa* really presents two possible ways of resolving the Petrarchan conflict between public and private life. The Caesarean resolution can be accomplished by stressing Scipio's public role alone and entirely dismissing his private life. An exactly opposite resolution can be reached by dismissing his public role entirely and transforming him into a totally private person. All that is required for this transformation is to endow Scipio with his own desires and concerns and let him exercise his sovereign will over them. This is the resolution that Boccacico adopts in implementing his principle of the sovereignty of humanity in the *Decameron*. This may be called the Boccaccian resolution of the Scipionic (or Petrarchan) dilemma in contrast to its Caesarean resolution. The former may be called the private and the latter the public resolution.

The public resolution can be regarded as Roman because it is based on the Roman exaltation of public duty. On the other hand, the private resolution can be regarded as Greek because it is in tune with the spirit of Greek individualism.* Boccaccio has been preparing himself for this Greek resolution all along, through his fascination with the Greek tradition, which is as intense as Petrarch's affection for the Roman tradition. Boccaccio gives many of his works Greek names, for example, the *Filocolo*, the *Teseida*, and the *Filostrato*. But his love of Greece does not come as a sharp break with Petrarch's love of Rome; the latter's love of Scipio already contains the germ of Boccaccio's philhellenism. As we saw in the previous chapter, Scipio was himself in love with Greece and was denounced for his philhellenism by his fellow Romans.

The Boccaccian resolution became possible only by virtue of the burgeoning bourgeois society of his day. The essential feature of bourgeois society is the expansion of the private domain. In feudal society, for example, most important political and social functions

Unreconciliable, should divide
Our equalness to this.

[act 5, scene 1, lines 35–48]

Crushed by the ruthless ambition of Octavius Caesar, Antony and Cleopatra come to recognize death as the only way to preserve their liberty and self-mastery (see act 4, scene 14, line 62; act 5, scene 2, line 237).

*It is very hard to determine whether the despotism of the Italian Renaissance is a public or a private resolution of the Scipionic dilemma, because of the baffling mixture of the despots' public roles and their private interests.

were exercised by the feudal lords, while only the menial functions were left to the private domain. Hence the sovereign will could be enjoyed only by kings and princes in the feudal world. In contrast to this, bourgeois society opened a vast area of significant activity for private individuals such as bankers, entrepreneurs, merchants, etc. Such a social order provided sufficient room for the simultaneous operation of many private sovereign figures, and in the meantime the political role of a king or prince could be reduced to the ancillary one of maintaining a requisite order for the exercise of private sovereign wills in the name of laissez-faire.

Many scholars and critics have called our attention to Boccaccio's bourgeois background and ethos. Vittore Branca has rightly called the *Decameron* the *chanson di geste dei paladini di mercatura*.[20] In my view, what makes the heroes and heroines of the *Decameron* the *paladini di mercatura* are their exclusively private lives. The broad canvas of the *Decameron* is not limited to the mercantile world of Renaissance Florence or Italy, but extends to the age of ancient Greece and Rome and of the feudal lords and pagan Saladins. But none of the figures ever appears in his public role in Boccaccio's masterpiece; private concern and ambition are the universal tickets for admission into Boccaccio's world. In fact, the exclusion of a Caesarean dictator is an indispensable condition for maintaining the Boccaccian arena of freedom for plural sovereign wills.

In short, bourgeois society is the indispensable matrix for accommodating the Boccaccian sovereignty of humanity and his resolution of the Petrarchan dilemma. For this reason, the Boccaccian sovereignty of humanity does not come to its full maturity until Boccaccio drops his classical settings and adopts contemporary ones. The sovereignty of Theseus in the *Teseida* is too intimately bound up with his public office and too remote from his private interest; the sovereignty of Criseida in the *Filostrato* is surely rooted in private concerns but lacks the initiative of the bourgeois entrepreneurs. Only in the *Decameron* does the sovereignty of humanity reach completeness and maturity. We shall now examine some notable sovereign figures in Boccaccio's greatest work.

The *Decameron*

The first story of the first day in the *Decameron* is spun around Ser Ciappelletto, a consummate expert at falsification and dissimulation.

A notary by profession, he takes great pleasure in drawing up fraudulent documents and in bearing false witness. He commits every conceivable personal and social sin. Even his name is a case of accidental misrepresentation and misunderstanding. His real name is Cepparello (a little stump), which has been mistaken by his French neighbors for Cappello (a chaplet or garland) and transformed into Ciappelletto.

Since he is a man of great ingenuity and cunning, he has often been employed as a business agent to handle some difficult cases for a rich merchant, Musciato Frenzesi. During one of these missions in Burgundy, he falls sick and is about to die. The two Florentine usurers in whose house he is lodging foresee and discuss the unpleasant consequences of his impending death. He is such a godless man that he is likely to die without confession. In that event, no church will receive his body. Even if he wants to confess himself before his death, he has committed so many and such horrible sins that he is not likely to be absolved. In that event, his body cannot be received into a church graveyard. Thus the two Florentine brothers will probably be forced to dump his body into a ditch, which is certain to provoke the ire of their Burgundian neighbors who are already ill-disposed toward them.

Ciappelletto happens to overhear their worried conversation, calls his hosts, and gives them his promise that he will get them out of this unpleasant difficulty. In response to his request, they fetch a venerable friar from a nearby convent to hear his confession. In the course of his confession, Ciappelletto paints his life as a sustained record of piety. This final falsification of his entire life is accomplished in such grand style that the innocent friar is convinced of his sainthood. On his death, Ciappelletto's body is eagerly welcomed into the convent church with all the devotion and veneration due a saint. His body is mobbed by the crowd seeking his favor. The fame of his sanctity spreads, and even God performs many miracles on behalf of those seeking the aid of Saint Ciappelletto.

This is the story of a sovereign will, which can execute its own designs with diabolical ingenuity and audacity. In order to convey the grand aura of Ciappelletto's sovereign character, Boccaccio repeatedly uses the word *grand* (*great*) in the early description of his personality and background. Ciappelletto is *greatly* ashamed of himself (*grandissima vergogna*) whenever his documents turn out to be anything but fraudulent. He takes the *greatest* satisfaction (*grandemente salariato*) in bearing false witness. He feels no scruples about giving false testimony while all his neighbors place a *great* trust (*grandissima fede*) in the sworn testimony. He is a *great* blasphemer. He is a *great* glutton and drunkard (*gulosissimo e bevitore grande*). Last of all, he has been well appreciated for his cunning by Musciatto, a man of power (*potenzia*) and position (*stato*). The title of *Ser* that Boccaccio gives Ciappelletto may very well be meant to convey his subtle appreciation of Ciappelleto's "greatness" as a Boccaccian hero.

Some may regard the aura of greatness around the person of Ciappelletto and his world as a device of mockery rather than of tribute, because he is not a political or military hero but a petty business agent in a bourgeois society. Obviously he is not the kind of hero whose sovereign will dictates the destiny of an empire, and his greatness cannot be taken seriously in the world of exteriority. But all the descriptions of his greatness are presented in the domain of interiority, namely, greatness in the sense of shame, in satisfaction, in trust, etc. Thus the unassuming exteriority of this petty business agent hides the abysmal sphere of his interiority. This sphere is unmistakably intimated by Panfilo's concluding remarks:

> Nor would I wish to deny that perhaps God has blessed and admitted him to His presence. For albeit he led a wicked, sinful life, it is possible that at the eleventh hour he was so sincerely repentant that God had mercy upon him and received him into His kingdom. But since this is hidden from us, I speak only with regard to the outward appearance.[21]

Panfilo's account of Ciappelletto's behavior in this story is limited to external, observable appearance not only in this instance but from beginning to end. For example, Panfilo never explains why this wicked man even thought of performing one decent act for his hosts before his death. In fact, this unexplained mystery has provoked quite a few interesting hypotheses. The most important point in this regard is not the business of determining which is the most convincing of these plausible hypotheses, but the wisdom of recognizing that Ciappelletto's ultimate motives are meant to be perpetually hidden in his inscrutable heart.

This infinite space of abysmal interiority is a common legacy from the Augustinian tradition of interiority, which Boccaccio shares with Petrarch. There is already an intimation of Boccaccian interiority in Petrarch's Scipio. Throughout the African campaign, Scipio seldom reveals anything in the domain of feeling; most of Petrarch's epic is limited to the external behavior of his hero. This is one of the reasons why Scipio looks more like a perfect robot than a real man. However, this exclusively external account cannot be taken to mean that Scipio is a hero devoid of the interior dimension. In the first place, this account is given by a champion of interiority; in the second place, Scipio is said to be a man devoted to solitude and contemplation. So Scipio may very well be a man of unfathomable interiority, whose deep thoughts and feelings are neither expressed nor revealed, and his robotlike appearance may be only a deceptive façade for this inscrutable Sphinx. This ambiguity is another manifestation of the Petrarchan dilemma between private solitude and public duty.

Boccaccio does not get caught in this dilemma and ambiguity because he conceives all his heroes and heroines as exclusively private persons. In Boccaccio's characters, the lofty Augustinian or Scipionic interiority turns into the inscrutable heart of private motives and feelings; this is not completely alien to the Augustinian tradition because Christian interiority has been understood as an area of private interest ("saving one's soul") rather than of public service. Thus, the arena for the exercise of the sovereign will is securely established in the private heart of self-interest rather than in the domain of public duty or religious piety. For this reason, Ciappelletto's cunning and audacity are first of all a matter of his heart rather than his behavior; they are the essence of his existential mode, or his way of being human. The cunning and audacity in his behavior should be construed only as external manifestations of this existential stance. His hosts express this point in their amazement:

> What manner of man is this, whom neither old age nor illness, nor fear of the death which he sees so close at hand, nor even the fear of God, before whose judgement he knows he must shortly appear, have managed to turn from his evil ways, or persuade him to die any differently from the way he has lived?[22]

Perhaps the most ingenious feature of this story is that it is presented not as a saga of human ingenuity or depravity but as a record of God's marvelous deeds. Before presenting it Panfilo says that it is going to be a story of God's infinite mercy—that is, God responds mercifully to the purity of the supplicants' motives despite their reliance on a fraudulent saint because of their ignorance. Not many people have taken Panfilo's claim at face value; instead, this story has usually been taken as a satire on credulous Christians, whose motives are not quite highly pitched. But this usual way of responding to the story may only show the bias of contemporary readers who are not well versed in the essentials of the Christian *credo*.

Some have claimed that the story of Ciappelletto is a degradation of the Christian conception of God and the ministry of his saints, but I am convinced that it does not deviate from Christian dogma in essential points. It is one of the cardinal points in the Christian creed that God can and does bring good out of evil. To increase the devotion of Christians through the instrument of a fraudulent saint is surely one fine way of creating good from evil. If God were to insulate the imposter's evil influence from the lives of the pious Christians, He would in fact be conceding to him an independent sphere of operation. Of course, that would accordingly restrict the sphere of the infinite divine will. In short, God's use of Ciappelletto's evil designs for a good purpose is eloquent testimony to the omnipotence of His will.

Some might fear that this story derogates the intercessory function of the saints. If a fraudulent saint can be used as well as a real saint, the entire ministry of Christian saints may appear to be completely dispensable. This is indeed one of the conclusions we may draw from this story, but it is in perfect accord with Christian teaching. To begin with, nobody can achieve sainthood through his own merit alone; Christian sanctity is meant not to be an achievement but a free gift from God. That is the essence of the dogma of grace, a gift rather than a reward. Panfilo affirms this cardinal point in Christian teaching by saying in his prefatory remark that God's grace does not descend upon us through any merit of our own.

The change of the homely name Cepparello (a little stump) to the glamorous one of Ciappelletto (a garland) really captures the essence of God's elevation of a lowly sinner to the exalted station of a saint; a saint is no more than a little stump for displaying one of God's beautiful garlands. To claim the indispensability of the saints' ministry would be the sacrilegious act of infringing upon the infinite domain of God's sovereignty. Like any other Christian institution, the ministry of the saints is intended to manifest God's omnipotence rather than to restrict it.

Some may be disturbed at the rather ignoble motives behind the devotion of the crowd to the false saint. In their devotion, they are all seeking personal gains and benefits through Saint Ciappelletto's favor. This self-seeking crowd may appear far from edifying or dignified, and God may not be quite pleased with gaining such a crowd's devotion. But it is virtuous people who are abhorred by the Christian God, that is to say, those who seek virtue for its own sake. The virtuous are the proud, who can stand on their virtue alone and need not rely on God's help. Hence pride is often the sin of the virtuous, which eventuates in the proud refusal to recognize the sovereignty of God's power.

Christ tells his followers to believe in him not for the sake of virtue or any other high-sounding principle but for the simple selfish purpose of saving their souls. "For I have come to call the sinners and not the righteous" (Matt. 9:13). The frank admission of selfish motive is an essential feature of Christian humility. It is this Christian humility rather than the sense of devotion to any exalted principle or cause that constitutes what Panfilo calls the "purity" of the petitioners. Christ himself teaches the humble way of seeking and receiving God's favor. "Ask, and it shall be given you; seek, and you shall find; knock, and it shall be opened to you" (Matt. 7:7). The petition of a pious Christian is meant to be simply a petition rather than a declaration of a virtuous principle, which can only contaminate the purity of the Christian heart with a sense of hypocrisy.

By elevating the lowly and the sinful to heavenly glory rather than the mighty and the virtuous, God can more emphatically display his almightly power (Rom. 9:15–18). Thus God selects a maiden of humble origin rather than a lady of manifest eminence for his Incarnation. This is the central theme of the Magnificat, the prayer of praise that Mary offers on the Annunciation (Luke 1:46–55). Of course, there are many gradations of lowly or sinful. Some are innocent while others are wicked; some are gentle while others are malicious. But these degrees make no difference in the domain of grace; God chooses from every kind of people. He has shown mercy not only to the innocent girl Mary but also to a wicked man like Paul, who is converted from a prince of persecution into a prince of the Christian faith. The *Decameron* records a conversion story similar to Paul's: Ghino di Tacco is converted from being a robber into a trusted knight of the Church (day 10, story 2). If the dispensation of grace were limited to only special grades or kinds of people, that would limit the absolutely free exercise of the divine will. If grace were given only as a just reward or desert, the dispensation of grace

would be completely bound by human merit and behavior. By
keeping grace an absolutely free gift, God manifests the sovereignty
of his will: it is bound by nothing.

Thus, on every count, this story places emphatic stress on the
sovereign will of God without deviating from Christian teachings.
Ser Ciappelletto is a dramatic example of the Boccaccian sovereign
human being, and the intriguing device of this story is to use this
sovereign human being as the medium for manifesting divine
sovereignty. In spite of all his cunning and ingenuity, Ser Ciappelletto is eventually outwitted and outmaneuvered by God. One of the
greatest blasphemers has been turned into one of the greatest bene-
factors in Christian charity. Even the possibility that he might have
been truly converted at his last hour only attests to the infinite mercy
and power of God's will, because the conversion could have come
only as a free gift from God. Hence the inscrutability of Ciappelletto's
heart is only an eloquent testimony to the inscrutability of the divine
will. It is almost inconceivable to imagine a more persuasive testimony of the sovereignty of God's will than this story.

This emphatic espousal of the sovereignty of the divine will is
simply another way of stating the dogma of predestination in the
domain of grace, which has stood as the official pronouncement of
the Church. Many medieval theologians felt the need to make some
room for the exercise of human free will and its merit, but had to do
it without infringing upon the absolute sovereignty of God's will.
For example, St. Thomas categorically affirms the necessity of grace
for salvation: man can neither avoid nor rise from sin without grace
(*Summa theologiae*, pt. 1–2, q. 109, aa. 7 and 8). He goes on to say that
even those who have already received grace cannot persevere in
doing good and in avoiding sin without receiving further continuous
divine help (pt. 1–2, q. 109, aa. 9 and 10). He tells us that God alone
is the cause of grace and that human merit can never be the cause of
it (pt. 1–2, q. 112, a. 1). He recognizes the need of preparing the
human soul for grace, but he says that the preparation is made by
God's grace, which moves the human free will (pt. 1–2, q. 112, a. 2).
He admits that the justification of the ungodly requires the movement
of free will, but he points out that this movement is simply a manifestation of the justifying grace (pt. 1–2, q. 112, a. 3). In response to
the question whether or not a man can deserve eternal life through
his own works, he replies that he can only if his meritorious works
have proceeded from the grace of the Holy Spirit; he cannot if they

have proceeded from his free will alone (pt. 1–2, q. 112, a. 3). Thus, in the celebrated debate on predestination vs. free will, all the orthodox theologians from Augustine to Aquinas have, one way or another, wound up on the side of predestination, leaving only the heterodox theologians like Pelagius on the side of free will.*

Since the acceptance of the unlimited divine will leaves little room for the exercise of the human will, it is offensive to our sense of human dignity and decency. Indeed, *offense* is an important category in Christian theology from Tertullian to Kierkegaard. But the offensiveness of Christianity can be taken on two different levels. It has chiefly been taken in the intellectual sense, since the central dogmas of Christianity, such as the Incarnation and the Trinity, violate the canon of human rationality (*quia absurdum*). The offensiveness in question can also be taken in the ethical sense, that is, the central tenets of Christian teaching presuppose a conception of man too lowly and too debasing for our sense of decency. It is for this reason that Nietzsche called the Judeo-Christian tradition a slave morality as distinguished from a master morality.

The audacity and ingenuity of Ciappelletto are not much different in kind from the audacity and ingenuity of some of Yahweh's great favorites. Let us take the case of Jacob, who does not hesitate to play a diabolical trick of deception and dissimulation on his dying father in order to steal his paternal blessing away from Esau. In spite of this, he is one of the most amply blessed persons in the Old Testament; he becomes the father of the twelve tribes. The most ingenious

---

*The doctrine of predestination is often mistaken for John Calvin's unique position, especially in opposition to the teaching of the Catholic Church. Calvin's real contribution was simply to spell out clearly and consistently the traditional dogma of the Church, which had largely been kept in the domain of Christian mystery. In this process of articulation, Calvin indeed added one extraneous element to the dogma, namely, his claim that success and prosperity in this world can be viewed as the outward indication of divine election. This claim cannot be deduced from the dogma of predestination; it only reflects the unmistakable influence of the Renaissance secular ethos on John Calvin.

On the dogma of predestination, Calvin is in fundamental agreement not only with Luther but also with Duns Scotus and William of Ockham. It is sometimes claimed that the Reformers were opposed to the Catholics of the Dominican wing but in substantial agreement with those of the Franciscan wing. This claim is usually based on the distinction of the Dominicans as intellectualists from the Franciscans as voluntarists. But this fine distinction amounts to nothing when it is brought to bear upon the doctrine of divine will, because God's will is held to be identical with his intellect in the unitary divine essence. Because of this fundamental agreement on predestination among all orthodox Christians, it took not a theologian but a humanist, Erasmus, to present a real opposition to this ancient dogma (see the Erasmus vs. Luther debate on the freedom of the will).

and the most resourceful of all is David, who climbs from his humble
origin to a throne through his resourceful ingenuity. With the cunning of a slingshot, he kills Goliath, who is intending to fight him with
a sword and a spear. He earns the affection of Jonathan, the heir
apparent to Saul's throne, so conclusively that Jonathan becomes the
most devoted agent in furthering David's ambition to inherit that
very throne. He manages to escape Saul's repeated attempts on his
life. He is by no means a man of moral scruples; he does not hesitate
to have one of his trusted lieutenants murdered in order to steal his
beautiful wife Bathsheba. Ser Ciappelletto is a Boccaccian David or
Jacob.

As God's favorites, David and Jacob can be regarded as His re-
plicas, especially because their ingenious and audacious careers
prosper with His special blessings. Because of this special relation of
the divine favor, Paul uses the episode of God's election of Jacob
over Esau to illustrate the inscrutability of the divine will (Rom.
9:8 ff.). Likewise, Panfilo uses the story of Ciappelletto for the same
purpose, because he also becomes a special instrument for manifesting God's sovereign will.

By this device, furthermore, Boccaccio may have intended to draw
our attention to the intimate connection between the Renaissance
conception of man and that of God. As we have seen in the last
chapter, Scipio of the *Africa* is the saint and hero for the Age of the
Spirit in its Petrarchan version. Boccaccio's Ciappelletto is even
more securely and more emphatically the saint and hero for the Age
of the Spirit in its secular version than Petrarch's Scipio. Hence, Ser
Ciappelletto may be regarded as the model for the Boccaccian imitation of God in power and glory just as Scipio of the *Africa* is the
model for the Petrarchan imitation of Him. If so, Ser Ciappelletto's
sovereign will would be the most favored medium for reflecting the
divine sovereign will. Conversely, the former cannot be fully understood without being placed in the context of the latter. Thus, there
is an inseparable connection between the sovereignty of the human
will and that of the divine will. Panfilo eloquently brings out this
connection by fusing the inscrutability of Ciappelletto's ultimate
motive with that of the divine will in his concluding remark.

In the second story of the first day, Neifile wants to tell another
episode that demonstrates God's loving-kindness (*benignità*). There
live in Paris two friends who are both prosperous merchants. One of
them is called Jehannot de Chevigny and the other Abraham. The

former is a Christian and the latter a Jew. Both are extremely upright
and honest. But the Christian is distressed over the fact that his good
friend is following a wrong faith and has been doing his best to convert him to Christianity, to no avail for a long while. In response to
this sustained effort, Abraham tells Jehannot one day that he is
prepared to act on his exhortation only on one condition, namely,
that he go to Rome and observe the Curia before making up his mind.

This announcement throws Jehannot into a fit of gloom because he
knows of the corruption of the papacy, which can even undermine
the faith of confirmed Christians. So he feels compelled to do everything to dissuade his friend, but the determined Abraham goes on
the trip. When he returns, he tells his Christian friend about all the
horrible things taking place in the court of Rome. But he nevertheless arrives at the incredible decision to embrace Christianity because
of the horrible sins he has witnessed in Rome. The reasons he gives
for this decision are quite remarkable:

> And as far as I can judge, it seems to me that your pontiff, and
> all of the others too, are doing their level best to reduce the
> Christian religion to nought and drive it from the face of the
> earth, whereas they are the very people who should be its
> foundation and support.
>
> But since it is evident to me that their attempts are unavailing,
> and that your religion continues to grow in popularity, and
> become more splendid and illustrious, I can only conclude that,
> being a more holy and genuine religion than any of the others,
> it deservedly has the Holy Ghost as its foundation and support.
> So whereas earlier I stood firm and unyielding against your
> entreaties and refused to turn Christian, I now tell you quite
> plainly that nothing in the world could prevent me from becom-
> ing a Christian.[23]

Like the preceding story, this one has often been interpreted as no
more than a satire on the corruption of Christianity. There is no
point in denying the satirical element, but to see no more in the story
than satire may only reflect the readers' inadequate understanding
of the religious concern in the *Decameron*. The members of the *brigata*
may not be models of Christian piety, but they clearly express their
religious concerns through their reverent references to God in telling
and responding to the stories. They set aside Fridays and Saturdays
for religious observances. Most of them still believe that eternal

punishment or bliss awaits them after death, and this belief is, of course, intensified by their awareness of the raging plague which may claim them at any moment. So religious concern is one of the few things we can never overlook without gravely distorting the world of the *Decameron*.

If we recognize the gravity of the religious concern in this story, what clearly comes through it is Abraham's sovereign will. The problem of conversion is one of the most crucial decisions Abraham has to make in this world since it will determine his eternal fate. In handling this difficult problem, Abraham shows what kind of person he really is. He is resistant to persuasion not because he is a victim of inherited custom and habit but because he has a mind of his own. He cannot accept any hearsay; he must base his decision on his own observations. He is firm but open to convincing argument and evidence. Thus his sovereign personality is amply portrayed throughout the story.

The reason Abraham gives for his conversion may sound satiric or even bizarre, but it is an adaptation of one of the seasoned arguments that has been employed by Christian apologists for a long time. Many of them have often summed up their various arguments for the validity of Christianity by finally appealing to the evidence of success: that is, the truth of Christianity can be vividly attested by its enduring success on the earth for so many centuries. (Conversely, a false religion could not have lasted so long.) Abraham finds this argument rendered even more persuasive by the behavior of the Curia, whose sole purpose appears to be to eradicate Christianity from the earth. So he concludes that the Christian God must be almighty and worthy of belief.

This argument of successful results is a language of power, which is the true language of the sovereign will. Being an astute merchant, Abraham is already familiar with the language of power and its results; he is only transferring this language from his business world to the domain of religion. Here again as in the preceding story, as Neifile claims, this human, sovereign will is being used as the reflection of the divine, omnipotent will. In fact, the personality of Abraham very much resembles that of Ciappelletto. One is determined to take great satisfaction in mocking God; the other is intent on drawing the most benefit from him. In both cases, God makes the best of them all.

Since God occupies the center of these two stories, some critics have thought that they do not belong to the *Decameron* proper, which is assumed to be a *Commedia umana*.* They feel that, at best, these two stories can be regarded only as an introduction to the *Decameron* proper in order to safeguard the integrity of Boccaccio's *Commedia umana*. This view again reflects the misunderstanding of the religious concern in the *Decameron*. In these two stories, God does not appear as the direct object of narration; he is presented only as the object of people's religious concern. This is what is meant by the concluding sentence in Panfilo's prefatory remark: "Manifestly will this appear in the tale I am about to tell; I say 'manifestly' in accordance, not with God's judgment, but with that of men."[24]

The description of God as he is in himself would require a transcendent perspective, which would indeed endanger the integrity of the literal and immanent world of the *Decameron*. On the other hand, to ignore the religious concern of the people would surely deprive the book of one essential dimension of their experience, and thereby unjustifiably impoverish the splendor of the *Commedia umana*. A full account of God as he appears in the beliefs and behavior of people is indispensable for the completeness of the world of the *Decameron*. In fact, references to God are frequently made in many other stories beside these two. In every one of these cases, God is presented as an object of human belief rather than as objective reality, to which the author of the *Decameron* clearly remains noncommittal.

The third story of the first day relates the confrontation of the sovereign will of a human being with that of another human being rather than with the divine will, as in the first and second stories. Saladin is a man of great ingenuity and resourcefulness, who has raised himself from humble origins to the sultanate of Egypt. Having encountered an urgent need for a vast sum of money, he decides to extort it from a rich Jew called Melchizedek, who in his view is too miserly to hand over such a large sum to him in response to a straightforward request. Since Saladin is reluctant to employ brutal force, he tries to trap the Jew by asking him the question: which of the three religions, Jewish, Saracen, or Christian, is the true one? Whichever answer Melchizedek may give, Saladin will gain evidence to convict him out of his own mouth and thus a sufficient pretext for extortion.

*In support of this sort of claim, Millicent Marcus says: "The story of Melchisedech and the three rings is, in a sense, the true beginning of the *Decameron*. The preceding two stories operate to clear away a narrative space which the rest of the narratives will then occupy. For the stories of Ser Ciappelletto and Abraam Guideo act to dispel any providential claims for human narrative—they serve to dissociate the word of man from the Logos" ("Wit and the Public in the Early Italian *Novella*," Ph. D. dissertation, Yale University, 1973, p. 145).

The ingenuity and resourcefulness of Melchizedek, however, are equal to those of Saladin. Melchizedek sees through to Saladin's carefully prepared trap behind his casual question and manages to avoid falling into it by his ingenious parable of the three identical rings, which eloquently illustrates the impossibility of answering Saladin's question. Saladin is so impressed with Melchizedek's adroit circumvention of his own scheme that he decides to tell the Jew of his need and to ask openly for his aid. Melchizedek responds with the same candor and openness to this, and they form an enduring friendship.

Both Saladin and Melchizedek are described as men of wisdom (*savio, savissimo*); their wisdom is their cunning and cleverness. Both of them are called men of valor (*valente, valore*); their valor is their audacity in imposing their own designs on others. Since they have the wisdom to see through each other's sovereign personalities, they themselves dread the consequence of their direct collision. In order to avoid this ugly consequence, they resort to an indirect method of feeling each other out. This indirect approach is most clearly shown in their way of speaking to each other through riddles and parables. This may be called the language of indirect discourse, perhaps the most suitable language for the confrontation of sovereign personalities.

The language of indirect discourse continues to function as an essential ingredient in the remaining stories of the first day. In every one of them, someone manages to assert his or her will, through an ingenious or cunning device, against the will of another who usually enjoys a position of a far greater power and authority than his or hers. Thus, all the stories of the first day happen to revolve around the theme of the sovereign will, although they are all told without the constraint of a set topic. This clearly shows the central concern of the *brigata*; the accidental topical unity functions as a sort of free association test for the state of their minds. Since the theme of fortune is the perennial dialectical counterpart to the theme of will and its design, the former is adopted as the topic for the stories of the second day.

What is immediately striking about these stories is the ingenuity and marvelousness that recur in the operations of fortune and form a notable parallel with the ingenuity and marvelousness of the stories of the first day. These events of fortune are, indeed, so marvelous and so ingenious as to appear to be the acts of some exceedingly resourceful intelligence; some of them are in fact attributed to Providence.

The entire *brigata* commends the fortune of Rinaldo d'Asti (2. 2) as a gift of God and his favorite saint, Julian. Landolfo Rufolo praises God for his incredible fortune (2. 4). What is even more remarkable is the intimate connection between the operation of fortune and the exercise of human ingenuity and audacity.

Some of these characters get into trouble through their own ingenuity or stupidity. Martellino brings disaster on himself through his own trickery (2. 1); Bernabò of Genoa brings catastrophe not only upon himself but on his wife as a result of his stupid bragging and betting (2. 9). In either event, the obstinate assertion of someone's will is the initial cause of the ensuing misfortune. Many are thrown into unfortunate circumstances through the evil designs of others. Andreuccio of Perugia runs into three waves of misfortune in a single night because of the willful schemes of the greedy (2. 5); Alatiel goes through nine rounds of abduction as a result of the evil schemes of the lascivious (2. 7). In some cases, human ingenuity and resourcefulness are almost as indispensable for the fortunate resolution of misfortune as the favorable operation of fortune herself. The salvation of Bernabò from his misfortune is largely due to his wife's versatility and ingenuity; the restoration of Alatiel as a virgin to her father owes much to Antigono's wise counsel.

Thus, the stories of the first two days fairly well outline the central theme of the entire *Decameron*: the sovereign human will, or rather the ingenuity and stupidity displayed by the assertion of the sovereign human will in the uncertain dominion of fortune. The interplay of the human will and fortune is not a new topic at all for Boccaccio; it is the central concern of all his writings. For example, the two galleries of frescoes in the *Amorosa visione* display this central theme. In the first two days of the *Decameron*, the theme of the human will and the power of fortune, or rather their interplay, is introduced with dialectical subtlety. The topic of the first day (the human will) emerges fortuitously, or through an accident of fortune; the topic of the second day (the power of fortune) is presented intentionally, or through an act of the human will.

In the *Decameron* the human will occupies the foreground while fortune takes her place in the background. This is clearly indicated by the devoting of the stories of the first day to the former and the stories of the second day to the latter. This point is further reinforced by the fact that the stories of third day are formally devoted to the topic of human ingenuity, but the power of fortune continues to remain as a pervasive force in the background of these stories. For example, when Masetto of Lamporecchio in the first story goes to a convent to seduce its nuns, he has no concrete plan of action beyond the general design of pretending to be mute. Even this plan is devised as a way of obtaining employment rather than as a method of seduction. Masetto develops his concrete plan of action and imposes his will on the convent by alertly responding to a series of fortuitous events.

The topics for the remainder of the *Decameron* are only some of the various facets of the central theme introduced during the first three days, that is, the manifestation of the sovereign will against the ominous background of fortune. Thus, the first three days of the *Decameron* are used to present and articulate the central theme, and the remaining seven days to further elucidate and illustrate it by highlighting some of its salient features. This three-seven division coincides with the three (men)-seven (women) composition of the *brigata*.

The Sovereign Individual in the *Decameron*

In spite of the wide range covered by its various forms, Boccaccian sovereignty is always rooted in the excessive self-centeredness of the Boccaccian individual. This individual is the prototype for the Machiavellian and the Hobbesian conception of man, which radically transformed the relation of individual and community in the West.

According to the traditional view as formulated in Aristotle's *Politics*, man should be conceived of as a member of a community, and his communal relations understood as an essential feature of his *nature*. The community is the ultimate center for the relation of man to his world. In constrast to this, the Boccaccian view clearly shifts the center of emphasis to the individual. This shift means that the individual, or rather his essential being, should be understood in its own right rather than in its relation to the community. Thus, for the first time, in the Boccaccian world man truly becomes an *individual*. The nexus between the individual and his community can no longer be considered as a feature essential to his being, but should be regarded as a link of convention or convenience that can be made or unmade at will.

While the Aristotelian view of society is organic, the Boccaccian view is atomistic. The former is a *natural* view of society; the latter is a *conventional* view. The theory of social relations, which is a matter of science in the Aristotelian view of society, becomes a problem for art and ingenuity in the Boccaccian view. As long as society is understood as an expression and extension of man's nature, a whole set of criteria governing all the social relations can be stated as a scientific theory based on the nature of man. This is the governing idea behind the medieval tradition of natural law.

As soon as society is reconceived of as an arrangement of convenience, however, every social nexus or institution ceases to be a *natural* entity and becomes an *artifice*. For this reason, the *Decameron* cannot offer any concrete rules for behavior, such as a practical rule for fulfilling love or establishing a satisfactory relationship between lovers. All it can do is to provide a few cases as examples. If one tries to draw general maxims from these examples, one has to be content with such highly abstract propositions as "Act wisely" or "Don't be stupid." In fact, one of the important functions of the Boccaccian examples is to demonstrate that there are no ready-made rules for solving our problems, and that every situation or obstacle must be confronted and resolved in its own right within the limits of our human ingenuity. This is in marked contrast with medieval ethics, whose system of virtues and imperatives is one of practical rules. In short, with the Boccaccian sovereign individual, ethics and politics are converted from the science of human nature into the art of human ingenuity.

Since every problem of human existence demands its own unique resolution, life in the Boccaccian world does indeed become a little more exciting than that in the Aristotelian world. But the price for this excitement is the enormously increased burden that is placed upon ingenuity and audacity. In short, life becomes much more taxing because there are no longer established rules for social behavior. Thus the life of the Boccaccian individual is always anxiety-ridden.

The anxiety of the individual is even further intensified by the fact that his social relations do not enjoy the durability they do in a traditional society, where they are usually as durable as natural relations of any other kind precisely because social relations are understood as natural relations. Once social relations are conceived of as artificial arrangements, they can endure only at the mercy of the wills that have conjured them up. This ephemeral character of Boccaccian society is exemplified by the social order of the *brigata* itself, which has been instituted and is destined to be soon dissolved by the act of ingenious human wills.

The most unpleasant feature of the Boccaccian individualistic society is its egocentrism. The individual is the ultimate center of human existence; his self-interest is the ultimate end for his behavior. Even the love of one person for another is ultimately for the fulfillment of the self rather than for the welfare of the other. The *Decameron* is the prototype for the Hobbesian social jungle or state of nature, in which "every man is enemy to every man" (*Leviathan*, pt. 1, chap. 13). No doubt, every man need not maintain a war against every other man all the time even in the Hobbesian world; in some cases, cooperation can be more beneficial than competition. Nonetheless, the primacy of self-interest always stands as the ultimate invariant principle of behavior in cooperation as well as in competition.

The ugly nature of naked self-interest can sometimes be covered up, and the open clash of self-seeking wills can sometimes be avoided. In fact, one of the indispensable functions of human ingenuity in the Boccaccian world is to devise the requisite means for achieving these chores of cover-up and avoidance. In spite of these efforts toward concealment and avoidance, however, the conflict of the self-seeking sovereigns is destined progressively to reveal its hideous character. As Thomas M. Greene correctly observes, the second half of the *Decameron* takes on a much harsher and crueler texture than its first half.[25] The sense of gaiety and often frivolity is gradually replaced by an increasing sense of cruelty and brutality as the *Decameron* goes on to reveal the true nature of the Boccaccian world.

Consequently, the *Decameron* brings us closer and closer to the Florentine social order, whose return to the Hobbesian state of war is described in the introduction and from which the *brigata* has briefly escaped. Distressed by this increasing domination of naked self-interest, the *brigata* resolves to devote the last day to stories of liberal or munificent deeds. Let us now briefly see how these presumably lofty deeds fare in the Boccaccian world of sovereign wills.

In the first story of the last day, Ruggieri de' Figiovanni, a valiant knight in search of a worthy lord, enters the service of the most renowned king of his day, Alphonso of Spain. In the course of his service, however, the knight becomes gravely disappointed with the grossly unjust manner in which the king rewards his courtiers. Ill-requited, Ruggieri decides to leave Alphonso's court. When he asks for the king's permission to leave, Alphonso readily grants his request and presents the knight with a most handsome mule for his journey back to Italy. On the first day of his journey, the mule's stupid behavior provokes the knight to compare the beast to the king. In the meantime, Alphonso has instructed one of his confidential servants to spy on the knight's behavior by joining him as an accidental companion and to order the knight to return to the king on the second morning of their journey.

On his return, the king asks the knight with a smile why he compared him to the mule, and the knight candidly tells him of his displeasure at not having been properly appreciated by the king. The king replies to Ruggieri that his apparent ill-treatment of him has been due not to his own stupidity but to Ruggieri's misfortune. In order to demonstrate this point, Alphonso presents Ruggieri with two chests, one of which is declared to be full of treasure while the other is filled with dirt, and asks him to choose one. When the hapless knight opens the chest of his choice, he finds it full of dirt. Thereupon Alphonso smiles and gives Ruggieri the other chest.

Thus, King Alphonso conclusively demonstrates that the target of Ruggieri's bitter complaint should have been fickle fortune rather than Alphonso's poor judgment. By this ingenious device, King Alphonso succeeds not only in correcting an erroneous view of himself held by a worthy knight but also in circumventing the unjust operation of fortune. Neither of these accomplishments can be regarded as acts of simple munificence; both can be better understood as manifestations of the king's sovereign will. He gains proper respect in the eyes of a worthy knight and adequate control over the Wheel of Fortune.

In the second story of the tenth day, the apparent liberal deed of the robber Ghino di Tacco is an outright self-seeking act. When the Abbot of Cluny falls into his hands as one of his helpless victims, he manages to earn the abbot's gratitude by curing him of a serious illness. Out of gratitude, the abbot brings about the reconciliation of Ghino with the pope; consequently, Ghino comes to trade his power and glory as a mighty robber for power and glory as a trusted son of the Church. The so-called liberality of Ghino's deed only thinly disguises the ingenuity of the self-seeking soul.

In the third story of the last day, Mithridanes tries to compete with Nathan in gaining a reputation for generosity. Despairing of ever surpassing Nathan's distinction, Mithridanes sets out to kill him and runs into a stranger who gives him all the requisite information and advice for executing his murderous plan. Utilizing this information and advice, Mithridanes comes upon the defenseless Nathan in a solitary spot, only to find that the helpful stranger is none other than Nathan himself. Poor Mithridanes is overwhelmed by this evidence of Nathan's generous heart, generous enough to give away his own life. No doubt, there cannot be many acts more generous than that of self-sacrifice—but Nathan's deed may not have been dictated by lofty motives.

As Nathan explains to Mithridanes, his entire life has been governed by the single goal of giving everything that has been asked of him. This principle of absolute generosity should be understood not as a moral but as an existential principle—that is, the principle that determines his way of being human rather than the principle of doing charitable deeds for the sake of other people. If Nathan were really concerned with the welfare of Mithridanes, he would not be willing to help him commit a crime. On the contrary, Nathan would do everything to dissuade Mithridanes from his murderous act, not for his own sake but for the sake of the other.

Throughout this episode, Nathan shows no sign of concern for Mithridanes's real welfare; his only concern appears to be his obsession to live up to his principle of generosity to the end. He knows that the request for him to give up his life indeed comes as the supreme test of his fidelity to this principle, and also that no one has ever dared to confront him with this supreme test. In a sense, he feels quite lucky to have gained this opportunity before his death; he feels equally fortunate in having to pay a relatively cheap price (i.e. relinquishing only a few of his waning years) in meeting this challenge. In fact, Nathan admits to Mithridanes that he cannot think of any better way to dispose of the few remaining years of his life than by granting Mithridanes's wish. Nathan is absorbed in the task of promoting and consolidating his indisputable position as the paragon of generosity, just as Mithridanes is obsessed with his ambition to surpass Nathan in his reputation for generosity.

The principle of self-assertion continues to be the common theme in the remaining stories of the last day, except for the last story. It would be tedious to go through every one of these stories and elucidate their thematic unity. These deeds of liberality or munificence may indeed produce some beneficial results for some people, but those beneficial results cannot render their ultimate motives any less self-seeking than any other acts of Boccaccian characters. The Boccaccian individual has only one ultimate motive: to be oneself, to assert oneself, to fulfill oneself. To be constrained by any other motive than this is the supreme sin of abdicating sovereignty of self.

Since every act of the Boccaccian sovereign self is self-serving rather than self-giving, every human relation in the Boccaccian world is bound to be self-centered. Thus, the impossibility of establishing and maintaining a truly self-giving relationship becomes one of the gravest existential problems for the sovereign self to cope with. In Sartrian terms, one individual can treat another only as an object to be manipulated and exploited instead of respecting him as a subject of his own interest and concern. The relation of one person to another ceases to be *personal* and becomes *instrumental*. In the last story of the last day, Boccaccio bravely confronts this problem of personal relationships.

If we are to look for the most perfect paradigm of the Boccaccian sovereign individual, we are most likely to find it in Gualtieri, the tyrannical husband of the patient Griselda. The dominion of his sovereign will is firmly buttressed not only by his own ingenuity and cunning but also by the social position and power he commands as the marquis of Saluzzo. Evidently knowing the difficulty of forming and maintaining a close personal relationship, he enjoys his bachelorhood for a long while and never thinks of taking a wife or having children until his subjects beg him to marry and leave them an heir and ruler after his death. They even offer to find a daughter of some eminent parents to be his bride.

Gualtieri's response to this entreaty and proposal of his subjects is typically Boccaccian. He tells them that he has been determined to stay unmarried because it is exceedingly difficult to find a suitable woman. As it turns out, by a "suitable woman" he means someone like Griselda, who can patiently put up with every obnoxious quality of his. Although he still regards the marital bond as a chain, he says, he has decided to give in to his subjects' entreaty. He insists on selecting his own bride and takes Griselda, born and raised in poverty, chiefly because he is fairly certain she will be comfortable to live with.

Having prepared the wedding feast, Gualtieri goes to Griselda's house without notice and exacts an oath of wifely obedience from her in front of her father. In the presence of all his company he strips her naked and then has her dressed in the clothes he has brought with him. Then he brings her home for the wedding. Griselda proves to be obedient enough even to please Gualtieri. His subjects praise him for having detected the lofty virtue concealed beneath her rustic village garb. They now regard him as the wisest (*il piu savio*) and the shrewdest (*il più avveduto*) man in the whole world.

But Gualtieri is not content with all this and becomes obsessed with the idea of putting Griselda through a series of cruel tests. The first of these occurs when he feigns anger at the birth of a girl as their first baby and pretends to have her killed. The second test is a repetition of the first, on the arrival of a boy, their second child. Griselda remains obedient through these two ordeals. The third test is his pretending to divorce her in order to remarry a lady of noble birth. He commands her to return to her father with the dowry she has brought him, and Griselda replies that she will go away naked because she came to him naked. But she begs Gualtieri to let her keep one shift in exchange for the virginity she has brought him but can never take back with her. He grants this request but denies his subjects' petition that she be given a dress.

In the final test, Gualtieri brings home his two children, who have been brought up elsewhere in the meantime, and tells Griselda that the girl is his bride-to-be and the boy, her brother. He asks her to help prepare the wedding feast. She manages to endure even this humiliating test with patience and grace. When he asks for her opinion of the bride, she is generous in her praise and gently asks him not to be so cruel to his new wife as he has been to her. Then and there Gualtieri decides to praise and reward Griselda for her patience and constancy by revealing the true identity of their children. At this, they all rejoice, praise Gualtieri for his wisdom, and above all highly esteem the virtue of Griselda.

This story demonstrates that only a totally selfless soul can have a loyal relationship with a Boccaccian sovereign individual. By stripping Griselda before her admission into his house and her expulsion from it, Gualtieri mercilessly exposes her utter helplessness. Griselda herself describes her relationship with Gualtieri in the language of Job: she came to him naked and will go away naked. That Job's relationship with his almighty Lord is accepted as the model for theirs is no accident, for as we have already seen, the Boccaccian sovereign individual has emerged as an imitation of almighty God in all his glory and power.

Petrarch, who regarded the *Decameron* merely as a frivolous work of his friend's youth, was immensely impressed with Griselda's story. In one of his last letters (*Epistolae seniles*, 17. 3), he took the trouble

to translate the story from its original vernacular into Latin in order
to give it the far wider and more lasting audience that he felt it
deserved. Griselda's virtue appeared to him so awesome that he dared
not recommend it as a model for any human behavior. He commends
it only as a model for serving God. In fact, J. Burke Severs says, the
Griselda story originally derives from the Patience Group of Cupid
and Psyche folk-tales, which deal with the love of a mortal for an
immortal.[26] In spite of this pagan origin, Boccaccio's Gualtieri definitely resembles the Lord of the heavenly hosts rather than the
pagan god of love. Renaissance man has often been charged with the
hubris of usurping God's place and role because of his bold attempt
to conquer nature and control fortune. Gualtieri's demand for total
devotion and obedience may very well be an example of the most
offensive and arrogant feature of this hubris.

Petrarch has every reason to experience a strong feeling toward
the Gualtieri-Griselda relationship because he is really its grandsire.
As we have seen, the Scipio-Massinissa relationship is one of absolute
sovereign and totally submissive subject, which Massinissa describes
in his version of Jobean language. If Petrarch were to serve Laura as
his truly sovereign lady, Laura would turn out to be the exact con-
verse of Griselda.* Indeed, Griselda appears to be the reverse of
everything in Criseida, whose role we have characterized as a Boccaccian adaptation of the Petrarchan ideal of the sovereign lady.
Whereas Criseida is a lady of absolute sovereignty, Griselda is a
lady of absolute obedience. While the former is accused of incon-
stancy, the latter is praised for her constancy. There is an unmistakable resemblance between their names, too, along with a subtle
phonetic contrast which may correspond to the contrast between
Griselda's servitude and Criseida's sovereignty.

The most odious characteristic of Gualtieri is not so much his
demand for absolute devotion and obedience as his inhuman way of
testing and manipulating another human being. This offensive
quality does not, of course, show up for the first time in this story;
it has been repeatedly presented in the *Decameron*. It has even in-

---

*As we saw in the previous chapter, Petrarch in his own life was obsessed with the idea
of establishing and maintaining his sovereign existence, that is, his absolute independence
of other people and fortune. It is chiefly for this reason that he left the public world and
shut himself up in seclusion. He grows quite distressed even about his love for Laura when
Augustine shows him that this love is an infringement upon his independent existence
(*Secretum*, bk. 3). The theme of Petrarchan sovereignty embodied in Scipio and Laura is
a projection of the theme of sovereignty in his own personal existence.

fected many of the stories of liberality and munificience. For example, this offensive note of manipulation defiles the tone of the supposedly loving relationship of the two devoted friends Gisippus and
Titus, each of whom tries to demonstrate, through sacrifice, his love
for the other in an exactly opposite spirit to that of Arcita and
Palamone (10. 8). In their acts of friendship, however, they treat the
poor girl Sophronia like an inanimate object, absolutely disregarding
her feelings and concerns. For another example, the same note of
manipulation and calculation pollutes Torello's hospitality toward
Saladin (10. 9). Shrewdly sensing Saladin's importance, Torello
ingeniously drives him into his carefully laid trap of hospitality and
manipulates his feelings at will. The hostility of open aggression and
contempt may indeed be less offensive than the hospitality of manipulating hosts or the liberality of calculating friends.

What is even more offensive than Gualtieri's manipulation is the
highly praised virtue of Griselda. As long as her obedience and submission affect herself alone, she may deserve some praise. But as
soon as her sacrifices involve the lives of her children, her existential
stance takes on a completely different moral tone. Confronted with
her husband's demand to murder her children for flimsy reasons, she
makes no protest against the cruel dictate, no effort to dissuade him
from the evil design, and no attempt to save her innocent children.
She may simply be intent on fulfilling the vow of total obedience she
took at the time of her marriage to him. But such blind obedience to
a patently immoral demand surely constitutes a violent offense to
our sense of decency and dignity.

Francesco de Sanctis compares Griselda's submission to her husband's cruel demand to Abraham's ready obedience to the Lord's
demand for Isaac's sacrifice.[27] For this act of obedience, Abraham
has been highly praised as the father of faith throughout the ages. It
took the sensitive heart of Kierkegaard to see through the thick layer
of traditional panegyric on Abraham and to disclose the monstrous
offense contained in the story of Isaac's sacrifice.[28] Kierkegaard
says that Abraham must have been a moral monster to accede readily to God's fiendish demand for Isaac's sacrifice. Instead of doing
what Abraham did, he claims, any decent human being would
have cursed God and died, or defiantly repudiated God's demand.
By any standard of decency and dignity, he convincingly argues,
Abraham should be derided as a coward or denounced as a monster.
Every reproach Kierkegaard levels against Abraham can be even

more justly transferred to Griselda, because the lord of her abject obedience is only a mortal.

The Griselda story gained immense popularity during the Renaissance; Petrarch's translation turned out to be only the first of many. A. C. Lee says that it was translated or adapted into almost every European language—French, English, German, Spanish, Danish, Swedish, etc.[29] The steadily increasing popularity of the Griselda story during this period may indicate that the Boccaccian sovereign self was not a fiction but a living reality. In this regard, the realism of the *Decameron* is far more stringent than that of the *Africa*, in which Petrarch tries to faithfully reconstruct the reality of Roman glory. Whereas the *Africa* expresses the realism of the dead past, the *Decameron* embodies the realism of the living present. Petrarch himself looked upon his realism of the past only as a poor substitute for that of the present; what he really wished to write was an epic of King Robert rather than of Scipio. Hence it can be said that Boccaccio truly fulfilled Petrarch's dream.

The Griselda story also gives us a suitable occasion to be clear about the naturalism of the *Decameron*, which has been stressed by Francesco de Sanctis and recently elaborated on by Aldo D. Scaglione.[30] This naturalism is rather an obvious aspect of his work, if by "nature" is meant the immanent world of corporeal reality as contrasted to the transcendent world of spiritual reality. By "nature," however, we sometimes mean spontaneous life free from all regulations and repressions. The life of a man devoted to scheming and cunning, calculation and manipulation, can be anything but a natural or spontaneous one. Hence Gualtieri is bound to be the most unnatural man in this sense; the nature of man, with the arrival of the Boccaccian individual, becomes most unnatural. As a victim of manipulation and calculation, Griselda cannot be any better off in this regard than Gualtieri. In her life of obedience, Francesco de Sanctis says, "she suffocates every natural feeling of a woman, and her own personality, and her free will."[31] The loss of spontaneity is perhaps the most grievous price the Boccaccian individual has to pay for his life of control and manipulation, at least as grievous as the loss of a wholesome or self-giving personal relationship with other people.*

*By removing all Boccaccian restraints from the Boccaccian sovereign individual, Ariosto creates the untrammeled heroes and heroines of his *Orlando Furioso*. Orlando and Angelica cannot fulfill their love for each other because such fulfillment would demand

Nominalism in the *Decameron*

To stress the sovereignty of an individual is to presuppose the uniqueness of his existence, and this uniqueness animates the spirit of nominalism that pervades the *Decameron*. No two persons are alike; no two cases are alike. Every individual presents his unique problem; every case demands its unique resolution. This spirit of nominalism is diametrically opposed to the spirit of essentialism (or realism), in which individuals are supposed to manifest their common essence or nature. The transition from the latter to the former is manifest in the movement from the exemplum to the novella, as has been carefully surveyed by Salvatore Battaglia in his essay, "Dall'esempio alla novella."[32] The function of an exemplum is not to tell a unique story of a given case, but to portray a universal or a moral contained

---

the sacrifice of their individual sovereignties. Angelica eventually comes to experience true love in caring for the helpless, wounded young foot-soldier, Medoro. This seems to show that the love of a sovereign lady cannot be realized except through the expression of her maternal instinct. The same point comes across in the love of Bradamante for Ruggiero, the adolescent hero; she pursues and rescues him out of maternal concern and possessiveness. In Ariosto's world, maternal instinct thus turns out to be the ultimate source of durable ties between individuals. To be sure, Ariosto also uses family ties, but the familial nexus in his epic appears to be the natural extension of the maternal instinct.

Ariosto is conservative and nostalgic in his revival of the maternal and familial nexus for binding together sovereign individuals, in so far as these individuals have emerged by breaking up this *natural* tie. Torquato Tasso takes the radical position of imposing the *artificial* order of impersonal organization upon the sovereign individuals of his *Gerusalemme Liberata*, but Tasso's artificial order is quite different from Boccaccio's artificial order. The latter is democratic; the former is dictatorial. These two artificial orders become the two competing models for social organization during the Renaissance, while Ariosto's natural order recedes into the realm of romance.

The problem with which these three models are concerned is quite different from Petrarch's problem in the *Africa*. The latter is the problem of realizing the absolute will of one sovereign leader in a community of nonsovereign members; the former is the problem of establishing and maintaining an order among sovereign individuals. For the sake of identification, we may call these two the Petrarchan and the Boccaccian problems. The Petrarchan problem is concerned with one sovereign will and the Boccaccian problem with many sovereign wills in one community. Thus, the Boccaccian problem is much closer to the heart of the Renaissance ethos than the Petrarchan; the former is not only much more intractable but also much more intriguing than the latter. This is one of the main reasons that make *Orlando Furioso* and *Gerusalemme Liberata* far more engaging and convincing epics for us than the *Africa*. In *Gerusalemme Liberata*, for example, Godfrey of Bouillon is given a task similar to that of Scipio in the *Africa*, that is, the task of carrying out a divine mission. But Godfrey's role as the leader of Christian warriors is distinctly in the vein of Renaissance individualism, especially in comparison with Scipio's role as the leader of the Roman expedition. In fact. Scipio's role is far more like that of Moses in Exodus than any Renaissance leader of sovereign individuals or any Roman leader of patrician citizens.

in that case. A novella, on the other hand, is simply not a medium for the portrayal of a universal maxim, nor does it stand under the canopy of a universal paradigm. On the contrary, it stands all on its own; its only function is to recount a given event in all its uniqueness.

Since Boccaccio adopts this novella form for the *Decameron*, its stories present for readers one enormous difficulty that is seldom encountered in the reading of the exempla. Since exempla are presented under the canopy of their universal maxims, they are accompanied by adequate guidelines for their interpretation. But no such guidelines are attached to the novella; every reader is compelled to formulate his own. In contrast to the objective guidelines embedded in the exempla, those for reading the novella are bound to be subjective, or rather to be derived from the readers' own perspectives. Thus one and the same story may take on different meanings for different readers.

For example, the story of Ser Ciappelletto may be interpreted either as a satire on the credulity of naïve Christians or as a pious eulogy on the mystery of the merciful divine will. The story of A-braham may be taken as a satire on the corruption of the papacy and the filthy motives of a self-seeking Jew, or as a eulogy on the loving patience of God and the piety of a godly man. The Griselda story may be read as an exaltation of her great virtue or a denunciation of her inhuman timidity. Almost every story in the *Decameron* can be given many different interpretations, although they need not always be exclusive of one another.

We have already seen the possibility of adopting different perspectives for reading one and the same story in Petrarch; there the alternative perspectives are the eternal and the temporal. The problem becomes much more acute in Boccaccio because the perspectives all belong to one and the same mundane world. Whether one praises or despises Griselda reflects one's perspective within this world. Even the question of the praiseworthiness or blameworthiness of Abraham's motive for conversion is a legitimate one to be decided by the perspectives and value scales we adopt in this world, and may not be influenced at all by the question of whether or not we believe in the other world. Likewise with the problem of God's high-handed use of the true and the false saint in the story of Ser Ciappelletto. Even if one does not believe in the Christian God, one can have different views on this problem, depending on the different perspectives and value systems one adopts. Thus, almost every story in the *Decameron* can take on an endless variety of ambiguity and complexity in interpretation.*

In the previous chapter, we saw that Petrarchan personalism provides the spirit of perspectivism in Renaissance painting. The Boccaccian perspectivism may be regarded as the literary counterpart to Renaissance pictorial perspectivism. If so, Boccaccian perspectivism stems from Petrarchan personalism. Because of this pervasive perspectivism, the judgments Boccaccio's readers try to pass on his stories often turn out to be judgments upon themselves, since these responses, wittingly or unwittingly, reveal their own prejudices and preferences, and above all their own blissful ignorance of them. This self-reflexive revelation is perhaps the main source of the Boccaccian irony in the *Decameron*.

This very possibility of conflicting interpretations can have the salutary or disastrous effect of tearing down a doctrinaire position. For example, some of those who have piously accepted Christian dogma concerning the ministry of the saints may be led to question the decency or respectability of that dogma when they confront it in its nakedness in the absolutely open world of the *Decameron*. This open world clearly presents the acceptability of other perspectives besides that of Church dogma, and thereby forces readers to question their own dogmatic perspectives. In the Boccaccian world of absolute candor and openness, one can no longer draw any comfort from the established dogmas because Boccaccio never allows them to dictate our preferences and judgments.

The multiple perspectives in the Boccaccian world inevitably lead to relativism; in other words, every judgment is relative to the perspectives that sovereign individuals adopt. Thus, Boccaccian relativism is a necessary corollary of Boccaccian nominalistic individualism. Furthermore, the Boccaccian individual cannot accept any absolute except for his absolute sovereignty, because any other absolute would infringe upon his own sovereignty. The assurance of absolute values or beliefs is a luxury and comfort available only to those individuals who acknowledge, implicitly or explicitly, their submission to objective standards or laws. But Boccaccian individuals repudiate such a submissive stance and hold themselves

*This Boccaccian perspectivism already emerges in its germinal form in the second part of the *Romance of the Rose*. For details, see the note on p. 90.

above such standards or laws. In Nietzschean language, they are beyond good and evil.

The spirit of nominalism also pervades the very organization of the *Decameron*. There are ten stories for each day and ten days altogether, and the number ten in these two cases is ultimately derived from the ten members of the *brigata*. This reminds us that the same number governs the ordering of Dante's three worlds. The division of the Paradiso into ten regions is obvious because Dante makes use of the ten Heavens of the Ptolemaic System. In my *Fragile Leaves of the Sibyl*, I have shown that, contrary to the usual assumption, Dante also makes use of the same principle of the tenfold division in his organization of the Inferno and the Purgatorio.[33] Thus the number ten as a pervasive principle of organization may be regarded as one of Dante's many legacies to Boccaccio.

There are a few interesting points of difference between Dante's and Boccaccio's use of the principle of the tenfold division. In Dante's case, the number ten is not an accidental figure, because the ten regions in each of the three worlds represent the seven natural virtues or their contraries and the three theological virtues or their contraries. This list of virtues and their contraries is complete because it enumerates all the virtues and vices required for the full realization (or perdition) of human potential, both in the natural and the supernatural spheres. That is, it is impossible to add or subtract from this list without jeopardizing its integrity. Thus, there is a reason or justification for Dante's use of the principle of the tenfold division.

As in Dante's case, the number ten in Boccaccio consists of three and seven because the *brigata* is composed of three men and seven women and because these ten people become the basis for ordering the one hundred stories of the ten days. But the number ten here signifies nothing further than the fortuitous circumstances in which three men and seven women get together and the arbitrary arrangement they make for telling ten stories ten times. Some efforts have been made to find symbolic significance for the constitution of the *brigata* or for the roles of its members.[34] The more arduous and ingenious these efforts become, the more eloquently they seem to demonstrate their own futility.

In the introduction to the *Decameron*, Boccaccio says that the coming together of the seven ladies in the venerable church of Santa Maria Novella one Tuesday morning was strictly a chance event.

Making use of this fortuitous event, the seven ladies plan an excursion and talk of the desirability of having some male company. Then and there another chance event takes place; three young men happen to appear on the scene. Pampinea thanks fortune for this unexpected gift and the ladies persuade the young men to join the adventure. Whether the title *Decameron* means "ten days" (*deca-hemera*) or "ten parts" (*deca-meros*), Boccaccio's principle of *decameronic* (ten-part) division is rooted in the contingent number of the *brigata*, and as such only indicates the perimeter of *fortuna* in which human ingenuity must find room for maneuver and operation.

The nominalistic spirit of accidental contingency also pervades Boccaccio's use of the number ten in organizing the one hundred stories of the *Decameron*. On some days (the first and the ninth) the stories are told without the constraint of a set topic, and on others the topics are set by the presiding kings or queens. Even in the latter case, the jovial Dioneo retains and exercises the privilege not to be bound by the given topic for the sake of variety and surprise. Dioneo plays the role of a nominalistic reminder that the topics and labels are no more than the products of human invention and convention.

The assignment of the stories to various topics cannot escape the nominalistic aura of arbitrary arrangement. For example, the ninth story of the second day is supposed to illustrate the power of fortune, but it could have been assigned to the third day. All that is required for this transfer would be to shift the focus of the story from the stupidity of Bernabò of Genoa to the ingenuity of his wife. Some of the stories of the fifth day (love with happy endings) could have been easily assigned to the second day (good fortune) or the third day (human ingenuity in attaining some desired end). Some of the stories for the seventh (cheating husbands) and for the eighth (cheating people in general) could have been assigned to the second day (good fortune), the third day (ingenuity), the fourth day (happy love), or the fifth day (unhappy love). There are many other possibilities for reshuffling and reassigning the stories within the given topical framework of the *Decameron*.

Many of the stories are provoked by the psychological principle of association. Filomena tells the third story of the first day because the preceding story involving a Jew reminds her of this one, also involving a Jew. Fiammetta tells the fifth story of the second day because the chest of precious stones found by Landolfo in the preceding story reminds her of the precious stones found by Andreuccio of Perugia. For the tenth story of the second day, Dioneo even abandons his prepared story and tells another one in its place, of which he is reminded by the preceding story. Free association may very well be operating in many cases where it is not expressly acknowledged as the principle of selection.

The psychological principle of free association is the epistemological counterpart to the ontological principle of resemblance in nominalism. As we may recall, according to essentialism, entities that belong to the same species share the same essence or nature, and this essential identity is designated by their names, such as "dog" or "tree." The nominalists reject this doctrine of essential identity and claim the uniqueness of the individual—that is, the nature of every individual is unique to itself and is never shared with any other. In place of essential identity, they can accept only the link of resemblance between different individuals; in other words, one thing can resemble another although the former does not share the same essence with the latter. This ontological principle is parallel to that of psychological association, where one thing reminds us of another because their resemblance to each other has established the psychological association in our minds.

Whereas the link of essential identity is fixed by the boundaries of species and their genera, the link of nominalistic resemblance knows no such boundaries. One thing can resemble another in one respect and a third thing in another respect; anything can resemble anything else in some respect. Socrates can resemble Plato as a man, his dog as an animal, a tree as a living being, a bird as a two-legged being, etc. There is absolute freedom in the logic of resemblance, and this freedom of association and resemblance permeates the *Decameron*. The first two stories of the first day resemble each other because they both deal with divine mercy. The second story in turn resembles the third story of that day because both concern a Jew. Of course, one can expect that the third story will in turn resemble the fourth story in some respect. It is this rather flexible chain of resemblance and association that binds together the one hundred stories in ten bundles, and these ten bundles in one volume.

To be sure, Boccaccio makes extensive use of the device of contrast and variety in the organization of the *Decameron*, but the relations of contrast and variety are only two of many kinds of the most universal relation, resemblance. One of the important functions of the ten members of the *brigata* is to provide a broad range of samples by telling a variety of stories every day and by providing a variety of responses to each story.* The adequate device for securing fairly representative samples is perhaps the important consideration for any nominalistic collection of finite instances from potentially infinite ones, and the *decameronic* device of using the number ten twice over may indicate Boccaccio's redoubled effort to provide this adequate device of representative collection.

The ten divisions of the *Decameron* are all presented on one horizontal plane, in contrast to the vertical scale in which the ten regions in each of Dante's three worlds are placed one upon the other. Of course, Dante's vertical scale is a scale of importance, while Boccaccio's horizontal plane is a plane of absolute equality. Every story is as important as every other story; every member of the *brigata* has the same right and duty as every other member. This absolutely egalitarian spirit is again in tune with the spirit of nominalism. If every individual is sui generis, he can be neither more nor less important than any other.

The mode of governing the *brigata* is an ingenious arrangement to accommodate the two principles of equality and sovereignty for every individual at the same time. In this regard, this Boccaccian principle of government closely resembles the principle of atomistic competition that governs the operation of the incipient capitalistic society. Whereas in feudal society the lord alone exercises sovereignty over his dominion, every entrepreneur in a free capitalistic society is

---

*As a sampling device, the numerical constitution of the *brigata* is very much like that of the Ten Commandments. In the nominalistic world, where every case is different from every other case, it is impossible to enumerate all the commandments or rules that can cover all future contingencies because their number would be potentially infinite. The only viable alternative is to single out some representative rules and establish their authority. It is perhaps in this spirit that the Pentateuch promulgates six hundred and thirteen commands or rules. The Ten Commandments can then be regarded as a further selection from these numerous rules or imperatives.

The numerical structure of the Decalogue is like that of the *brigata*; it consists of three commandments concerning the human relationship with God and seven commandments concerning interhuman relationships. In the Decalogue, man's relation with God is the central theme while his relation with his neighbors is an auxiliary one. One arbitrary (or mystical) number, three, is used to propound the central theme; another arbitrary (or mystical) number, seven, is used to express the auxiliary theme. That is, anyone whose piety is rooted in the acceptance of the central theme propounded in the first three commandments should behave in the spirit of neighborly love expressed in the last seven commandments. In the meantime, the number ten (three plus seven) gives the numerical sense of nominalistic completeness.

supposed to have the absolute right of designing and maintaining his enterprise. The feudal mode is retained in Castiglione's *Book of the Courtier*, in which the Duchess of Urbino presides over the dialogue every evening; the bourgeois mode is adopted in Boccaccio's *Decameron*, in which the presiding office devolves upon a different person every day. *The Book of the Courtier* marks the waning days of the feudal age; the *Decameron* records the emergence of the new bourgeois era.

The sovereignty of the Boccaccian individual is fully in tune with the voluntarism of the nominalists, or rather the primacy of will over intellect. The essentialists have maintained the primacy of intellect over will. According to them, the function of the intellect is to see and judge the comparative values of alternative ends (or goals) and the comparative advantages and disadvantages of the various methods of achieving them. The function of the will is to choose the ends and means that by the intellect are judged best among all possible ends and means, and to do its best to achieve those ends. This function of the will is strictly executive; that is, it is to execute what is dictated by the intellect. Thus, the primacy of intellect over will is tantamount to the subservience of the latter to the former. The nominalists' position is diametrically opposed to this. According to them, it is the will that dictates to the intellect. The intellect only executes the commands of the sovereign will.

Although the intellect in the nominalists' view is subservient to the will, the former still enjoys a far greater freedom than intellect in the essentialists' view. This greater freedom is manifested in the domain of concept-formation. According to the essentialists, the intellect must form its concepts so as to correspond to the nature of reality; the formation of concepts is especially governed by the boundaries of species and genera. But the nominalists do not recognize the objective reality of these boundaries; their concept-formation is guided solely by the principle of resemblance. Since anything can resemble anything else, the intellect has absolute freedom in forming its concept.

Concepts and their corresponding names, which for the essentialists are claimed to reflect the objective order of the specific and generic essences, are admitted to be no more than labels of convenience and convention. Whereas the formation of concepts for the essentialists is always governed by the constraint of objective order, for the nominalists it is guided solely by subjective interests, preferences, purposes, and convenience, which are all under the dominion of the will. The essentialist intellect subjects its primacy over the will to the dominion of the objective order; the nominalist intellect surrenders its absolute freedom from the objective order to the sovereignty of the subjective will.

Boccaccio the Humanist and His Anthropocentrism

When Boccaccio assumes the role of humanist and historian, he displays the sovereignty of humanity even more emphatically than he does as a poet or story-teller. As a story-teller, as we have seen, he judiciously maintains a noncommittal attitude toward the reality of supernatural beings and confines his role to reporting people's beliefs and behavior objectively. In his *Life of Dante*, however, he resolutely divests himself of this neutral stance and asserts his naturalistic position by trying to explain the alleged supernatural phenomena in terms of natural causes. Boccaccio's first target is Dante's love for Beatrice, which was claimed to be a supernatural wonder by Dante himself and has been accepted as such by his readers. Marvelous and unusual as it is, Boccaccio claims, Dante's love must have been a wonder of nature and can be attributed to natural causes:

> Now just what this affection was no one knows, but certainly it is true that Dante at an early age became a most ardent servitor of love. It may have been a harmony of temperaments or of characters, or a special influence of heaven that worked thereto, or that which we know is experienced at festivals, where because of the sweetness of the music, the happiness, and the delicacy of the dishes and wines, the minds, not only of youths but even of mature men, expand and are prone to be caught readily by whatever pleases them. [*La Vita di Dante*, chap. 3][35]

If Boccaccio is to complete the naturalistic account of Dante's love, he must eventually explain the divine reality itself within his naturalistic framework. It is to this task that he devotes chapters 9 and 10 of *La Vita di Dante*, in which he outlines his daring thesis that divine beings are only poetic fictions or fables invented or instituted by various kinds of people to account for the operation and manifestations of the powers of nature. This sort of genetic account has long been a commonplace with us, but it must have been an epoch-making idea in Boccaccio's time. In this genetic account, Boccaccio is reversing the traditional relationship between immortals and mortals. Whereas immortals had been believed to be the creators of mortals,

Boccaccio claims that the immortals are only an invention or figment of mortals' poetic imaginations.*

In his *Genealogia deorum gentilium*, Boccaccio tries to implement this genetic thesis on a massive scale by explaining the genesis of the pagan gods and goddesses. Since the stories of the immortals are only the veils of myths and fables which poets employ as the most faithful custodians of truth, to render a genetic account of these immortals is to unveil the hitherto hidden truth of pagan antiquity. Boccaccio's enterprise may be called cultural hermeneutics, in other words, the task of reconstructing a forgotten culture and interpreting its inner meaning. Duly impressed with the awesome gravity of this epoch-making project, Boccaccio compares himself to Daedalus and Prometheus:

> I leave behind the mountain snails and barren soil of Certaldo, and, raw seaman that I am, embark in my frail little craft on a stormy sea all involved with reefs, little knowing whether my voyage will be worth the trouble. For I may trace every shore and traverse every mountain grove; I may, if need be, explore dyke and den afoot, descend even to hell, or, like another Daedalus, go winging to the ether. Everywhere, to your heart's desire, I will find and gather, like fragments of a mighty wreck strewn on some vast shore, the relics of the Gentile gods. These relics, scattered through almost infinite volumes, shrunk with age, half consumed, well-nigh a blank, I will bring into such single genealogical order as I can, to gratify your wish.
>
> And yet I shudder to embark on so huge a task; why, if another Prometheus should appear, or the very one who, as poets tell, upon a time made men from clay, I hardly think they would be equal to the task, let alone me. . . . Who in our day can penetrate the hearts of the Ancients? Who can bring to light and life again minds long since removed in death? Who can elicit their meaning? A divine task that—not human!
> [*Genealogia deorum gentilium*, proemio][36]

Boccaccio conceives of his project as a cosmic voyage of recovery and interpretation, and describes it in a language reminiscent of Dante's voyage from Hell to Heaven. Boccaccio's journey is to retrace Dante's footsteps, not to portray the nature of the immortals

---

*This is largely the same thesis as that of Ludwig Feuerbach. Cf. *The Essence of Christianity*, trans. George Eliot (New York: Harper & Row, 1957).

as they appear in the three realms, but to expose the poetic truths that underlie them. Just as Dante presents his picture of one cosmos by binding together all the incidents and observations of his journey in one volume, so Boccaccio plans to assemble all the scattered relics of ancient culture into a "single genealogical order." This order would be none other than the universal history of mankind, in which the immortals will be shown as the poetic expressions of the universal truth of nature.

As we have seen in chapters 1 and 2, the universal history of mankind also plays an important role in the *Commedia*. But Dante and Boccaccio assign different places to the divine beings in their universal histories. Whereas mankind in Dante's universal history is only an allegorical medium for the manifestation of divine power and glory, the immortals in Boccaccio's universal history are just the veil of poetic fable that expresses the human conception of ultimate truth.* The relation of original and copy, archetype and ectype, is completely reversed in the transition from Dante to Boccaccio. In the *Genealogia*, to be sure, Boccaccio limits his genetic account of the immortals to the pagan divinities and does not extend it to the Christian deity. But this should be construed as an act of caution and courtesy rather than as his admission of an exception to his thesis.

In the opening paragraph of the introduction to the *Decameron*, Boccaccio also compares this masterpiece to a journey. This journey is called only a little climb, while the other one (in *Genealogia deorum gentilium*) is regarded as an immense voyage. This common metaphor of a journey may help us to discover the continuity between the *Decameron* and the *Genealogia*. While the latter may be regarded as Boccaccio's attempt to recover the relics of mankind's past, the former may be understood as his attempt to preserve its still living stories.

The *Decameron* is also a work of collection and interpretation; the *brigata* is Boccaccio's poetic agent for assembling and commenting

---

*Boccaccio's central purpose in this ambitious work is erroneously understood to be the defence of poetry. To be sure, his theory of poetry and his defense of it are indeed important, but their ultimate importance derives from Boccaccio's use of them in the substantiation of his genetic thesis. In this context, his defense of poetry gains a poignant sense of irony, for it is made as a reaction against the religious criticism of poetry—namely, that poetry in general and pagan poetry in particular are sacrilegious. This charge of sacrilege is a complaint leveled at poetry by the immortals, as it were, and such a complaint can be effectively quashed by showing that poetry has been the real mother of those immortals.

on the representative stories in Boccaccio's own world. The spirit of universalism that animates the *brigata's* collection is fully attested by the immense coverage of space and time in the *Decameron*, whose stories are drawn not only from Christendom but also from Islam, not only from Boccaccio's contemporary Europe but also from Greco-Roman antiquity, not only from the emerging world of capitalism but also from the declining world of feudalism. If so, Boccaccio really begins his ambitious study of universal history in the *Decameron* and concentrates his efforts on the recovery of the ancient pagan relics in the *Genealogia*. Hence the *Genealogia* is an extension of the *Decameron*.

Because of this continuity between the *Genealogia* and the *Decameron*, Boccaccio's contributions as a poet and as a humanist fall into one program, just as in the case of Petrarch. As we have seen in the last chapter, Petrarch's *De viris illustribus* and the *Africa* are two features of one enterprise. Boccaccio's enterprise is as much a historical one as Petrarch's, but Boccaccio's is animated by his realism and Petrarch's by his idealism. Boccaccio's is rooted in the present; Petrarch's is anchored in the past. The past is the most suitable screen for the projection of the ideal ("the past idealizes"); the present is the most effective medium for the inspection of the real ("the present realizes"). As we shall presently see, Boccaccio always tells stories of his own contemporary world even when he moves into classical settings.

Boccaccio handles the classical and Christian authorities as cavalierly as he does the immortals of the pagan world. In his defense of poetry, he wants to make use of Augustine's authority and cites Varro's threefold division of theology, which Augustine discusses in his *De civitate dei* (bk. 6, chap. 5). According to Varro, Augustine says, theology can be divided into the mythical, which the poets chiefly use; the physical, which the philosophers use; and the civil, which the common people use. Of these three categories, Augustine condemns the first and the third and approves only the second. This passage clearly places the stamp of Augustine's disapproval on the work of poets, but Boccaccio willfully changes this stamp into one of approval.

According to Augustine, as Boccaccio perversely misquotes the source, the works of great poets belong to physical theology and are beyond the reproaches and contempt deserved by mythical and civil theology (*Genealogia*, bk. 15, chap. 8). In the same irreverent way,

Boccaccio disposes of Plato's reputed criticism of poets in the *Republic*. In response to his opponents' claim that even Homer would be exiled from Plato's ideal city, Boccaccio simply says, "Whatever they say, I cannot think so, having read so much in praise of Homer"[37] (*Genealogia*, bk. 14, chap. 19). He is prepared to ignore anything that disagrees with his own conviction.

This Boccaccian freedom from authority constitutes a marked contrast with the Petrarchan fidelity to it. Boccaccio is quite conscious of this freedom and says:

> It is, therefore, my plan of interpretation first to write what I learn from the Ancients, and when they fail me, or I find them inexplicit, to set down my own opinion. This I shall do with perfect freedom of mind. [*Genealogia*, proemio][38]

He is not afraid of falling back upon his own opinions and conjectures. This Boccaccian spirit of free inquiry is one of the essential preconditions for the development of the modern scientific attitude, which begins when fidelity to authority is replaced by fidelity to reality itself. This transition can only take place when man comes of age and gains the Boccaccian willingness to stand on the authority of his own opinions and conjectures. Thus, Boccaccio contributes two essential elements toward the spirit of the modern scientific ethos: (1) the naturalistic assumption that all phenomena can be explained in terms of natural causes; and (2) the intellectual self-confidence that the human intellect can read and decipher the Book of Nature all by itself, that is, without being hindered by cumbersome authorities, divine or human.

The Boccaccian Subversion and the Scotistic Maneuver

Although Boccaccio takes an out-and-out nominalistic position in his mature works, he may be considered to cling to the old tradition of essentialism in his earlier ones. Whereas the landscape of the *Decameron* is presented in all its nakedness, or rather without the overhanging canopy of universals or paradigms, all his earlier works are placed in classical or traditional settings and are loaded with allusions to the classical legends and paradigms.* But Boccaccio's use of classical paradigms and traditional settings is quite subversive. In

---

*The gardens in which the *brigata* tell their tales may resemble the garden in the *Romance of the Rose*, but unlike that one, they do not have any allegorical canopy.

the *Teseida* he converts the traditional form of a martial epic into that of a romance for the war of love, and subverts the traditional loyalty of kinship and peership with the supremacy of love. In the *Filostrato* he subverts the ethics of fidelity with that of individual sovereignty. It is through this subversion that Boccaccio accomplishes his transvaluation of all the traditional values. Of course, this transvaluation renders it problematic for us to pass appropriate judgments on the behavior of Arcita, Palamone, Troiolo, and Criseida.

In the *Amorosa visione*, Boccaccio employs the allegorical tradition only to demolish its raison d'être by making the broad passageway wide enough to encompass everything on earth and in heaven, thereby rendering the narrow gate superfluous. Most important of all, Boccacio repudiates the medieval tradition of dream-vision by taking the dreamer out of his dream into the wakeful world and turning some essential features of his dream into reality itself.* In the *Amorous Fiammetta* he transforms Christianity into a religion of carnal love by replacing the experience of *caritas* with the ecstasy and agony of *amore*.

The *Fiammetta* is full of classical allusions. Every time Fiammetta runs into a new situation, she tries to assess it by referring it to a series of classical paradigms. Because of this obsessive habit on her part, some readers may even fear, she may never develop the capacity to have her own experience without getting it shaded or distorted by these paradigms. But she never proves herself really subservient to them; her use of them is always guided by her own judgment and decision. As soon as she decides to kill herself in book 5, she carefully goes over a long list of the classical suicides with the sole purpose of devising the most suitable way of ending her life. As decent methods of ending one's life, most of these classical paradigms fail to meet with her approval. In her view, some of them are too cruel, others are too infamous, still others are too inconvenient for the poor husband, etc. In this quite selective mood, she retains her sovereign right of decision and adapts one of the best paradigms to her unique circumstances.

But the suicide attempt fails. Instead of making another, she tries to make the best of the situation by claiming that to suffer through

*The Boccaccian subversion can be found in its germinal form in Petrarch. As we have seen in chapter 3, Petrarch's *Triumphs* clearly deviates from the norm of the dream-vision tradition by stressing the subjectivity of his final vision. We have also seen that his *Africa* is a projection of his personal *Psychomachia*, and this subjective, or personal, dimension also constitutes a radical deviation from the normal pattern of the epic tradition.

her agony is no small glory (bk. 7). She arrives at this decision without relying on any classical example, obviously because there is none available. She then cites a long list of sufferings in order to justify her acceptance of the "martyrdom." The trouble is that some of these paradigms, like the case of Dido, stand for the refusal of suffering rather than an acceptance of it; but these counterexamples in her cited list do not disturb her at all in her new glory as self-appointed martyr. The classical paradigms never bind or even influence Fiammetta's decisions and behavior; she is quite cavalier in making Machiavellian use of them.

Fiammetta's handling of classical paradigms produces another interesting result. These examples of suffering are so momentous in their scope that her own agony shrinks to the size of a puerile complaint in comparison. In spite of this glaring disparity, she claims to have sustained greater grief and misery than any other woman. She makes this quixotic claim just before reciting the endless list of her classical paradigms. Through Fiammetta's Machiavellian stance and quixotic claim vis-à-vis classical paradigms, Boccaccio converts the tragic ethos of classical tradition into the comic pathos of his bourgeois world.

In almost every one of his earlier works, Boccaccio adopts the classical tradition only to effect its internal subversion. The sovereignty of the individual is the central theme that seems to motivate and sustain all his subversive acts. Since this central theme is a unique feature of the Renaissance ethos, classical settings in Boccaccio's hands invariably take on the thematic content of his own world. In this regard, his subversive stance is very much like that of John Duns Scotus, who systematically undermines medieval essentialism while posing as its faithful champion.

Duns Scotus accepts St. Thomas's doctrine of the common nature (the essence of the species), but fuses it into his unique doctrine of *haecceitas* (individuality). St. Thomas faithfully follows Aristotle's doctrine of individuation: the common nature of a species is individuated by matter. Hence the individuality of an object is determined by the accident of matter and has nothing to do with its essential being, which is solely determined by the common nature. Duns Scotus rejects this Aristotelian-Thomistic doctrine of individuation on the ground that prime matter cannot perform this vital function of individuation because it is of itself indistinct and indeterminate (*Opus oxoniense*, bk. 2, d. 3, q. 5, n. 1). He also recognizes that neither can the common nature perform this function, because it is common to all the individuals of a given species. What is this principle of individuation, if it is not matter or form or even their combination? This is the Scotistic question.

Duns Scotus resolves this enigma by his doctrine of the primacy of individuality, that is, the principle of individuation is the *entitas individualis* itself. This is his doctrine of *haecceitas*. He holds that the very attempt to explain the individuality of an entity by appealing to a higher principle such as the principle of form or matter is misguided precisely because it *is* the irreducibly primary ontological principle. The principle of individuation should be replaced by the principle of individuality; we should accept individuality as an ultimate principle instead of trying to reduce it to some higher principle. Thus *haecceitas* is exalted as one of the highest principles in Scotism.

Equally adventuresome is Duns Scotus's account of the relation between *haecceitas* and the common nature. He claims an integral relation between the two by calling their distinction a formal one; that is, it is neither a logical (only in thought) nor a real (in fact) distinction. The common nature of every entity is so integrally fused with its *haecceitas* that every entity has not only its own unique individuality but also its own unique common nature. This admission of the double uniqueness of every individual is the Subtle Doctor's subversive maneuver for surrendering essentialism to the camp of nominalism, a surrender tendered in such subtle language that it has long remained undetected. Scotus reinforces this surrender by advocating the primacy of the will over the intellect (*Opus oxoniense*, bk. 4, d. 49, q. ex lat., nn. 10, 11, 12, 16, and 18). Thus the Scotistic conception of man looks like the original charter for the formation of the Boccaccian sovereign individual.

Duns Scotus performs his most subversive act in his theory of concept-formation, in which he maintains the univocity of analogical terms. As we have seen in chapter 2, St. Thomas proposed his doctrine of analogy in order to accommodate the Pseudo-Dionysian *anagogia* of the *similitudo dissimilium*. In the Aristotelian tradition, the function of a common name like "dog" or "tree" is to designate the likeness of different things. But the likeness (*similitudo*) in question can appear on various levels of reality; it may sometimes be contained within the boundaries of a species, sometimes within those of a genus, or it may sometimes even transcend these boundaries. The Dionysian *similitudo dissimilium* belongs to this highest level because it is the similarity of the Creator and creatures. It may be called *similitudo transcendens*—that is, the similitude that transcends all ontological boundaries.

The *similitudo transcendens* presents one serious problem to the Aristotelian doctrine of names. It has been the Aristotelian assumption that the univocal usage of a term is possible only insofar as it is used to designate the likeness, which may be called *similitudo immanens*, that is, the likeness contained within specific or generic boundaries. As soon as the usage of a term is extended beyond these boundaries, its meaning ceases to be univocal. For example, the term 'being' cannot retain a definite or definable meaning because its usage spreads over all specific and generic similitudes. But Aristotle would not say that the nonunivocal usage in question is equivocal; he tries to account for it by his doctrine of analogy. That is, the analogical usage of a term lies somewhere between univocity and equivocity.

The Dionysian *similitudo dissimilium* covers a far greater range of dissimilarity than the Aristotelian analogical terms because the chasm between the Christian God and the creature is far greater than the distance between the Aristotelian substance and its accident, or between the Prime Mover and the material substances. In his attempt to bridge this vast chasm with his doctrine of analogy, St. Thomas remains faithful to the Aristotelian spirit of moderation and the golden mean (cf. *Summa theologiae*, pt. 1, q. 13, a. 5). Since the Thomistic analogy is a doctrine of words, it can retain the air of a golden mean only so long as theologians are concerned with the problem of words and not that of concepts. With the followers of St. Thomas, however, the semantical concern of the theologians shifts from the former to the latter problem. They feel the need to translate Thomistic analogy from the language of terms (or words) into that of concepts (or ideas), because they regard the concept rather than the word as the ultimate locus of meaning.

The Thomistic virtue of moderation or the golden mean cannot be retained in this translation attempt, because a concept must always be univocal since every idea is its own one meaning. This is the crucial distinction between words and ideas. Whereas one word can refer to many ideas, one idea can refer to only one idea—namely, to itself. Translated into the language of concepts, the Thomistic doctrine of analogy of names poses the following question: does the analogical use of a word contain only one concept or more than one?

If it contains only one concept, it is univocal (one meaning). If it contains more than one concept, it is equivocal (more than one meaning). Henry of Ghent takes the latter position; Duns Scotus takes the former.

Henry of Ghent retains the Aristotelian view of the finite human intellect; that is, the formation of concepts must be contained within the definite boundaries of species and genera. As soon as our usage of a word goes beyond these finite boundaries, Henry maintains, such a usage really shifts from the employment of one concept to that of another. In diametrical opposition to this conservative position, Scotus's is a repudiation of the Aristotelian finitide of the human intellect. He holds that our intellect has the unlimited capacity to form a concept to cover any range of similitude, whether it be contained in or transcend the specific or generic boundaries. This view of the infinite human intellect whose operation cannot be constrained by the finite boundaries of species and genera is in complete agreement with Ockham's view.

David Burrell has astutely pointed out this fundamental agreement between the epistemology and semantics of Scotus and those of Ockham.[39] As Burrell explains, Ockham recognizes three levels of univocity: (1) the specific level, (2) the generic level, and (3) the transspecific and transgeneric level. Burrell carefully observes that the category of resemblance (*similitudo*) is the common principle for concept-formation on all these three levels. In short, these three levels connote only differences of degree rather than of kind. Such is also the case with Scotus: the category of similitude, whether *transcendens* or *immanens*, is the only principle that governs the formation of an infinite range of concepts.

Scotus's doctrine of univocity has usually been misunderstood in one important respect: his univocal concept is invariably assumed to capture the common essence which is the content of the Aristotelian essential definition. This is a misreading of Scotus in the Aristotelian habit. To be sure, the common or definitional essence is always the content of a univocal concept in the Aristotelian tradition. To extend this Aristotelian formula to the univocity of such transcendental concepts as 'being,' 'one,' or 'good' would be simply to forget the Aristotelian-Thomistic lesson on the impossibility of defining the common essence of these transcendental categories. Thus, many well-meaning scholars, from the eminent historian Etienne Gilson to my innocent friend David Burrell, have charged Scotus with the stupidity of forgetting, or the audacity of "ignoring both the practice of Aristotle and the warnings of Aquinas."[40] They are usually the self-appointed custodians of Thomistic orthodoxy, who look with suspicion upon almost everything that goes beyond the *Summa Theologiae* of the Angelic Doctor.

Contrary to this unreflective assumption on the part of his readers, the Subtle Doctor clearly forestalls the Aristotelian misreading that the common or definitional essence is the content of transcendental concepts:

> since nothing can be more common than being, and being cannot be predicated univocally, in common, and definitionally of everything intrinsically intelligible since it is not so predicated of ultimate differentiae nor its own attributes, it follows that nothing is the primary object of our intellect on the ground of the definitional commonness of it to everything intrinsically intelligible. [*Opus oxoniense*, bk. 1, d. 3, q. 3][41]

Here Scotus categorically denies that his univocity of 'being' is meant to express the common trait or the definitional essence of that transcendental term. Scotus goes on to explain that his univocity should be understood extensionally or denotatively rather than intensionally or connotatively:

> But it is not required that it [the univocal concept] be in each of them [the referents of the concepts] definitionally; but it is either that way, or it is univocal to them as determinable to determining, or as denominable and denominating. [*Opus oxoniense*, bk. 1, d. 3, q. 3][42]

To conceive the unity of a concept extensionally ("as determinable to determining") is precisely the nominalistic position, which is diametrically opposed to the Aristotelian intensional unity of a concept. This again confirms Burrell's claim for the fundamental agreement of Scotus and Ockham on their epistemological principles. My friend David Burrell is quite amazed to find this fundamental agreement, since it forms a striking contrast with the radical difference in their ontological preferences.[43] If one accepts the traditional view that Scotus is a faithful champion of essentialism while Ockham is a great champion of nominalism, one is bound to be baffled by the glaring discrepancy and inconsistency between Scotus's ontology and his epistemology. But as we have already seen, Scotus's so-called essentialism is an essentialism in name only, and this alone assures a perfect harmony between his essentially nominalistic epistemology and his apparently essentialistic ontology.

Peter of Aquila has suggested an appropriate label, *univocatio transcendens*, which we can effectively use in distinguishing Scotistic univocity from Aristotelian univocity, which may be called the *univocatio immanens*. Since the *univocatio transcendens* presupposes the extensional diversity of each transcendental category rather than its connotational unity (the common or definitional essence), it must be regarded as a faithful conceptual account of the Thomistic analogy of names (or terms). Timotheus A. Barth expresses this point: "What he [Scotus] really wanted to do was to provide a logically clear and epistemologically certain foundation for the *analogia entis* [of St. Thomas]."[44]

The *univocatio transcendens* is an essential feature of the Scotistic metaphysics as the science of the transcendentals. One of Scotus's singular achievements is the vast expansion of the domain of the transcendentals. The transcendentals are the most universal categories such as 'being,' 'one,' 'goodness,' and 'truth,' and most theologians of the thirteenth century claimed or used no more than half a dozen of them at best. Scotus dramatically expands the scope of these transcendentals and formalizes them into four distinct levels: (1) 'being' (*ens*) as the first of the transcendentals; (2) the properties or attributes coextensive with 'being,' for instance, 'one,' 'goodness,' and 'truth'; (3) the disjunctive attributes or transcendentals such as 'infinite' or 'finite' and 'necessary' or 'contingent'; and (4) the remaining pure or simple perfections (*perfectiones simpliciter*).[45]

The common denominator of the transcendentals on all four levels is their being simple perfections; the Scotistic expansion of the scope of the transcendentals is to make it coextensive with what St. Thomas has called the attributes of simple perfections. In chapter 2 we have seen that the names of these simple perfections are coextensive with the Dionysian divine names, and that Thomistic analogy is a semantic theory of these names or words. Since the Scotistic system of transcendentals is a systematization of the names of simple perfections, it is consequently a systematization of the Dionysian divine names. Thus, Duns Scotus's transcendentals turn out to be his categorial schema for the construction of a univocal language of the infinite.

The Scotistic Revolution and Modern Philosophy

With Duns Scotus, *univocatio transcendens* becomes the overriding task and challenge for European theology and philosophy. The ancient theology and philosophy were contained within *univocatio immanens*, because the ancient Greeks largely refused to accept the infinite in their ontology of finitude ("To be finite or definite is the very essence of being and being real"). Medieval theologians did accept the infinite, but they never dreamed of describing it except in the language of allegory or analogy until Duns Scotus's audacious proposal of *univocatio transcendens*. Since then, to devise a univocal language equally adequate for the description of both the finite and the infinite has become the central concern of European theologians and philosophers from Nicolas of Cusa and Giordano Bruno to Alfred Whitehead and Teihard de Chardin.

For this reason, modern European philosophy can never be properly understood as a mere revival of the Hellenic philosophy; it should be seen as the transformation of *univocatio immanens* (a univocal language of the finite) into *univocatio transcendens* (a univocal language of the infinite). This was a gradual but radical revolution in a language game or form of sensibility, and the medieval scholastics played the pivotal role of transition and transformation in this radical movement. Bonaventure's exemplarism, Aquinas's analogy, and Duns Scotus's metaphysics of the transcendentals are the most prominent milestones in this grand revolution.

This scholastic revolution can most clearly be shown in the medieval shift of emphasis from one set of metaphysical categories to another. In Aristotle's science of being as being, the fundamental ontological concepts are his categories (predicaments), his four causes, and his distinction between act and potency. In contrast to the prominent role of these concepts, the so-called transcendentals (*one*, *being*, *good*, etc.) are given only a tangential role. But these transcendentals begin to occupy the central position in the scholastic disputations, while the Aristotelian ontological concepts are relegated to a peripheral station. Eventually, the transcendentals come to constitute the foundation for the scholastic science of being qua being, which has a quite different orientation from Aristotle's own ontology.

Although Aristotle defines his highest science as the science of being qua being, his ontology is operationally limited to the domain of material beings. Of his four causes, all of which are fully applicable to the analysis of material substances, the material and the efficient causes are pronounced to be inapplicable to the Prime Mover. On closer analysis, however, the application of the formal and the final causes to the Prime Mover appears to be unjustifiable. Aristotle's claim that the Prime Mover is the final cause of itself in a timeless world makes no better sense than Spinoza's claim that his *causa sui* is the efficient cause of itself. His further claim that the Prime Mover as a self-thinking thought is a pure form devoid of matter stands on the dubious assumption that a timeless, incorporeal entity like the Platonic Form can act upon itself—as dubious as Descartes's claim that his ego is a pure thought completely free of all bodily attachment. Thus, even Aristotle's admittedly partial application of the four causes to the Prime Mover is quite illegitimate and unintelligible. The distinction between act and potency and the categories of predication, all of which are also primarily designed for the analysis of corporeal objects, can also be used only illegitimately in the understanding of the incorporeal, eternal entities.

In short, Aristotle's characterization of the Prime Mover as self-thinking, pure thought is produced not by the exemplary application of his ontological concepts to the most eminent being, as many Aristotle scholars have assumed, but by their own illegitimate extension from the corporeal to the incorporeal domain, whose dubious links Aristotle tries to hide beneath a set of extraneous extrapolations. This is an inevitable consequence of Aristotle's ontology. Whereas all his ontological concepts are forged on the anvil of the space-time world, his Prime Mover totally transcends the spatiotemporal perimeter, thereby completely removing the very conditions for the legitimate or intelligible application of those concepts to it.

Thus, there is an inherent tendency in Aristotle's ontology to be restricted to the domain of corporeal objects; his ontological concepts are eminently suitable for the construction of physical sciences. Perhaps Aristotle pays little attention to the transcendentals chiefly because they are of little use in the scientific investigation of corporeal substances. Probably because his science of being qua being tends to exclude the Prime Mover from its domain, Aristotle gives another definition of his highest science as the science of the highest being. He tries to establish an essential link between this science and his science of being qua being by claiming that the Prime Mover is the final cause of all material substances, so that every corporeal substance comes to have two final causes, namely, its own specific form and the Prime Mover. But Aristotle is far from convincing in explaining why the operation of the former as the final cause needs any outside help and why the presence of the absolutely self-contained Prime Mover can give that help. Thus his science of the highest being remains an extraneous addition to his science of being qua being.

Aristotle's two definitions of his highest science are customarily taken as being complementary to each other, but they turn out to be operationally exclusive of each other. Whereas his science of being qua being properly covers only the corporeal world, his science of the highest being is chiefly concerned with the incorporeal world. Thus Aristotle's two formulations of his highest science really carve out two regional ontologies in spite of the impression that they are meant to offer two complementary articulations of one universal ontology.

The medieval schoolmen are intent on devising a truly universal science of being and come to attach a greater and greater significance to the transcendentals. In contrast to the limited universality of Aristotle's ontological concepts, these transcendentals are absolutely universal. For example, the category of *one* or *being* is applicable to every entity, whether it be finite or infinite, corporeal or incorporeal, eternal or temporal. The medieval scholastics give them the name of "transcendentals" in order to highlight this absolute universality; they transcend all the boundaries of the ultimate genera, and even the ontological demarcation between finite creatures and the infinite God. Then, they gradually expand the table of these transcendentals for the construction of their own science of being qua being. Duns Scotus's metaphysics of the transcendentals is the final outcome of this gradual but sustained attempt on the part of medieval scholastics.

The salient feature of Duns Scotus's categorial system is its absorption of the finite language of Aristotle's ontology into its own infinite language. Whereas, with most scholastics, the transcendentals are conceived exclusive of or in opposition to the Aristotelian ontological concepts, the latter is converted into a division of the former in Duns Scotus's metaphysics. Thus, Aristotle's language of finite beings is fully assimilated into Duns Scotus's language of the infinite being. With this, the scholastic ontology becomes a truly universal science which can accommodate Aristotle's science of being qua being and

his science of the highest being within one univocal language—
indeed, an epochal revolution in the language of being.* This new
universal ontology can be regarded as the intellectual manifestation
of Dionysian universalism; in fact, the four levels of Duns Scotus's
transcendentals may best be seen as the intellectual crystallization of
the Dionysian ladder of ascent and descent, and also turn out to be
the precursor of Hegel's categorial ladder, stretching from the ontological abyss of pure being to the infinite plenitude of Absolute Spirit.

The formalization of the transcendentals has remained a continuing challenge for modern European philosophy well after Duns
Scotus. For example, Descartes's and Spinoza's categories of "sub-

*In the hands of Duns Scotus, for the first time, the term *metaphysics* takes on the current
meaning of "universal science" or philosophy in general. Aristotle's own *Metaphysics* was
originally a collection of his lectures of different dates, which Aristotle himself left without
a title and which was subsequently labeled *ta meta ta physica* ("after the Physics") by one
of his earliest editors (probably Andronicus of Rhodes, although it is still debated whether
he was simply recording an already established practice or his own invention). The medieval scholastics translated this phrase into a single term, *metaphysica*, by which they meant
the science dealing with what goes beyond the physical or natural order. Hence, for them,
Aristotle's *Metaphysics* culminates in his discourse on the Prime Mover in book 12, and the
term *metaphysics* becomes synonymous with theology.

There are no less than fourteen books in Aristotle's *Metaphysics*, and only one of them
is devoted to theology. Furthermore, there is little textual evidence to support the scholastic view that the doctrine of the Unmoved Mover occupies the center of this work. On the
contrary, most Aristotle scholars now believe that this doctrine must have been the young
Aristotle's adaptation of a Platonic doctrine, which ill fits with the mature Aristotle's position.

In the main bulk of his *Metaphysics*, Aristotle reflects on the sundry general problems
and principles concerning all natural substances and the so-called non-natural objects.
Probably because of this wide variety of topics and issues dealt with in the *Metaphysics*,
Aristotle may have found it hard to give the work a formal title. He may even have
thought that this untitled collection of his lectures failed to have the integrity of a unitary scientific treatise. Perhaps for the same reason his editor gave it the apparently noncommittal label *ta meta ta physica*, probably to indicate its position in the Aristotelian
corpus.

By translating this noncommittal phrase into a unitary term, the medieval schoolmen
gave it quite a different significance from its original one. Since their vocation was
theology, they were naturally eager to find a classical model for their science of the supernatural being, and thought that they had found one in Aristotle's *Metaphysics* by gladly
mistaking his doctrine of the Prime Mover for the apex of his greatest work. Thus the
medieval scholastics came to conceive of metaphysics as a unitary science dealing primarily with supernatural reality.

With Duns Scotus, metaphysics is no longer limited to the study of divinity or the supernatural order but is concerned with every level of reality. In short, it becomes not only
unitary but also universal. In this universal meaning, the term *metaphysics* has become
synonymous with philosophy in general. And it is in this sense that Kant uses the term
in his famous question, "How is metaphysics as a science possible?"

stance" are categories of the infinite substance rather than of the Aristotelian finite substance—that is, they are the transcendentals. This is why neither Descartes nor Spinoza can simply revive the old Aristotelian ontological concepts in their own language of substance ontology, but have to forge, on their own, a new set of ontological terms. To be sure, this maneuver is also clearly dictated by their allegiance to the emerging modern science. But, as we shall shortly see, this new science, in its own right, fully manifests and implements the universal spirit of scholastic ontology. The repudiation of Aristotelian science was not the consequence of, but the prerequisite condition for, the birth of modern science, a truly universal physical science.

Even Kant, who expresses his unqualified admiration for Aristotle's formal logic, does not consider the possibility of appropriating Aristotelian ontological concepts but devises his own. He calls them "transcendental" in order to accentuate their "unrestricted universality." Hegel's elaborate categorial web is only an expansion and systematization of Kant's transcendental categories to their logical limit or completeness.* Thus, all the modern categorial systems, from Descartes and Spinoza through Kant and Hegel, are no more than successive efforts to improve upon Duns Scotus's system of transcendentals, the first categorial framework for the univocal language of the infinite being.

Since all these modern categorial systems are meant to be the framework for the language of the infinite being, they cannot tolerate any sort of pluralism or dualism. For example, as Spinoza cogently demonstrates, Descartes's system of two substances is logically untenable because there can be no more than one infinite substance. Hence, Descartes's dualism eventually leads to either Leibniz's covert monism or Spinoza's overt monism. For the same reason, as Hegel shows, Kant's attempt to employ the category of noumena in limiting the application of his categories to the phenomenal world amounts to the self-contradictory procedure of reaching beyond the boundary of human reason while trying to stay within it. So his critical dualism eventually prepares for the emergence of Hegel's absolute idealism.

In spite of this innate compulsion toward the infinite, human language still remains an instrument of a finite agent—as finite as in the Hellenic days of Aristotle. Because of this incurable finitude in its

*An explanation of this point is given in T. K. Swing [Seung], *Kant's Transcendental Logic*, pp. 3–53.

agency, the ontology of the infinite being can never be presented as a finished product, as in the case of Spinoza and Hegel. Since the completion of such a self-contained infinite system as theirs would mean the accomplishment of an infinite enterprise in a finite time and medium, their pretentious claims are far more implausible and unjustifiable than Kant's modest self-restraint. So the honest practitioner of modern philosophy has to avoid not only the vice of Kantian modesty but also that of Hegelian arrogance. The only sensible thing to do is to face up to it as an interminable process, which can never be given a satisfactory closure, either at its beginning or at its end.

Spinoza's *causa sui* and Hegel's *der absolute Geist* are no more than surreptitious devices to give this interminable task the illusory appearance of a conclusive closure. They may have felt the intellectual obligation to provide such a closure chiefly because they failed to shed the habitual Aristotelian assumption that every system can and should be rounded out in a finite number of steps. In that event, they never fully understood the unique feature of their own stupendous enterprise—that is, the impossibility of its completion in human history. It took the astute Kierkegaard to see through this difficulty and to recognize the essence of modern philosophical inquiry as an endless process and task. This realization of Kierkegaard's has been fully vindicated by neo-Kantians, phenomenologists, and linguistic analysts, all of whom have been forced into the comical but pathetic posture of Kierkegaard's Don Juan, namely, to find themselves absorbed in an interminable series of analysis after analysis, while quite oblivious of its ultimate end (cf. Freud, "Analysis, Terminable or Interminable?"). Some may like to give this problematic affair the label of "open-ended" rather than of "interminable"; the change of labels may somewhat muffle but cannot alter its inexorably awesome character.

Thus, there is a perpetual tension in modern philosophy, which stems from the irreconcilable discrepancy between its infinite goal and its finite means, its infinite desire and its finite power. This discrepancy has not been introduced by the moderns, but was inherited from the medieval Dionysians. It is this irresolvable tension that has constituted the very heart of the Dionysian *anagogia*, the astounding attempt of the finite human soul to reach out toward and grasp the "unknowing darkness" of the infinite Godhead. It is again this tension that St. Bonaventure tries to resolve in his exemplarism, and St. Thomas in his analogy. Since the tension in question is, by its very nature, irresolvable, neither of them succeeds in bringing about its final resolution. Instead, they manage to disguise and mollify it in their opaque languages of allegory and analogy. Only with Duns Scotus does this tension come to be fully exposed and radically intensified, because his metaphysics of *univocatio transcendens* resolutely brings it out into the transparent arena of univocal discourse.

As it were, Duns Scotus opens Pandora's box for modern philosophy. Perhaps, it would better be called Pseudo-Dionysius's box. At any rate, with the Subtle Doctor, it has long become the fate of the moderns to live with the impossible dream, or hope, of comprehending infinite reality through finite human language. If the traditional dogma of revelation means the disclosure of divine mystery on God's own terms, the Scotistic revolution amounts to the reversal of this dogma—that is, an explication of the infinite in solely human terms. Thus, with Duns Scotus, the theocentric language of medieval Christians has been transformed into the anthropocentric language of our own age. This new anthropocentric language is by no means a revival of the language of Hellenic finitude but is really the incarnation of Dionysian infinitude. It is in this new language of the infinite that the moderns come to formulate their bold project of investing their frail humanity with the majestic aura of the Almighty. Thus, the Scotistic language of *univocation transcedens* has become the linguistic matrix for the formation of our modern ethos.

The Thematic Dialectic of the Dionysian Ethos

In chapter 2 we called Thomistic analogy the ladder for theological descent from Dionysian transcendentism to Dionysian immanentism. In this role of transition, St. Thomas manifests the same kind of tension that we have seen at the core of the Petrarchan dilemma. The ultimate question for the theology of analogy is: how much knowledge of God is derived by naming him from his creatures? St. Thomas offers no unequivocal answer to this question; in fact, he never squarely confronts it. His oblique remarks can be construed in two opposite ways: the way of negative theology and that of positive theology.

In the mood of negative theology, St. Thomas seems to claim that our analogical approach to God offers no conceptual understanding of the divine nature. For example, whereas the use of the word *wisdom* in the description of the creaturely essence involves a concept of wisdom distinct from the concepts of other perfections, the analogical use of the same term in the description of the divine essence does not involve such a distinct concept because divine wisdom is never distinct from other divine perfections (*Summa theologiae*, pt. 1, q. 13, a. 5.) There can be no conceptual understanding where no distinction is ever admitted, since conceptual understanding is an operation of distinction and discrimination. Hence the theology of analogy appears to be only a device of intimation rather than one of description; the ultimate function of analogy seems to be to demonstrate the incomprehensibility of the divine essence (*supra intellectum*; see *Summa contra gentiles*, bk. 1, chap. 14; In. 1 *Sent.* 8. 1. 1 ad 4).

In the mood of positive theology, St. Thomas seems to claim that the theology of analogy offers some conceptual understanding of God. In contrast to the proper names of singular entities which are incommunicable, he says, the name "God" is communicable by way of similitude (*Summa theologiae*, pt. 1, q. 13, a. 9). That is, the word *God* conveys some conceptual understanding because it behaves like a common name rather than a proper name. Of course, this conceptual understanding is delivered not directly but "by way of similitude," that is, in its analogical function. This function can be discharged by the analogical use of the names of simple perfections to describe the divine attributes. Thus St. Thomas seems to imply that our analogical approach to God leads to some positive understanding of his essence.

St. Thomas never clearly aligns himself with either of the two conflicting moods; like Petrarch, he is really caught between the two. The way of description (positive theology) and the way of intimation (negative theology) are the two inseparable wheels of the Thomistic analogy. In chapter 3 we saw the inherent ambiguity in Petrarch's style: his allegorical account can be read literally while his literal account can be read allegorically. We can detect a similar ambiguity in the analogical style of St. Thomas, namely the ambiguity of description and intimation.

As we saw in chapter 3, Petrarch tried to cope with his tension and dilemma by keeping himself in a perpetual cycle of ascent and descent. We can restate the Thomistic tension and dilemma with the Thomistic cycle of ascent and descent. The ladder of Thomistic analogy consists of two poles: the pole of *modus significandi* (mode of signification) of the names of simple perfections and the pole of *res significata* (object of signification) of these names (see *Summa theo-*

logiae, pt. 1, q. 13, a. 6.). In *modus significandi*, the creature is the primary analogue and the Creator the secondary analogue; in *res significata*, the Creator is the primary analogue and the creature the secondary analogue. For example, in the analogical use of the term *wisdom* we know the meaning of this word first in the domain of creaturely attributes, and then we try to extend its usage to the domain of divine attributes. On the other hand, in the realm of perfections, the divine wisdom is the ultimate exemplar, or source, from which all creaturely wisdom descends. The pole of *modus significandi* is the pole of ascent; the pole of *res significata* is the pole of descent (see *Compendium theologiae*, 27).

To make the analogical inquiry into the divine essence is to climb the pole of ascent; it begins with the language of the temporal world and tries to reach the transcendent nature of eternal being. It is very much like Petrarch's maneuver in the *Triumphs*; it runs into the same trouble as he does in the last *Triumph*. St. Thomas's trouble largely stems from the irreparable fissure which he introduces into the semantic foundation of his theology of analogy by disjoining the primary analogue of *modus significandi* from that of *res significata*. In the normal use of a word (for example, *lion*), the domain of creatures is the primary locus not only of its meaning (*modus significandi*) but also of its referent (*res significata*). It is this unity of meaning (or sense) and reference (or denotation) that assures the secure semantic foundation for our language. Even when we make extended use of an ordinary word, we can be certain of its extended meaning because we have the common basis for this extension in the unity of the primary analogue of *modus significandi* and that of *res significata*. In the case of the analogical extension of words, however, we can never have this sort of common basis and must solely rely on the pious faith that our ascent along the pole of *modus significandi* is parallel with the pole of *res significata*.

In spite of this pious faith in the semantic concordance between human language and divine attributes, the higher we climb on the ladder of analogy, the more uncertain we become of the conceptual content of analogically extended words. This uncertainty is much like the uncertainty we have noticed in Petrarch's *Triumphs*. The greater the degree of immortality that life attains in the successive Triumphs, the more uncertain one becomes about its reality and vitality. Petrarch's vision in the *Triumphs* consists in the transmutation of his vision of this world; St. Thomas's language of analogy is derived from the transmutation of the language of this world. Just as Petrarch's vision of eternity has no definite assurance of its objective reality, so St. Thomas's language of analogy has no clear assurance of its conceptual nexus with its objective referent.

In chapter 3 we have seen that Petrarch tries to overcome the uncertainty of his subjective vision by taking the way of descent in the *Africa*. St. Thomas can also take the way of descent by switching over to the pole of *res significata* and climbing down it when he reaches the top of the pole of *modus significandi*. That is to say, at the summit of analogical inquiry, he can overcome its uncertainty and inadequacy by obtaining the vision of divine essence and then coming down to the domain of the creatures. In fact, this almost happens in the illustrious career of our saint. While he is finishing up the final section (*Pars tertia*) of his *Summa theologiae*, he begins to experience his mystical vision. But he resolutely refuses to retrace his verbal way back to this world; he abruptly abandons the verbal approach altogether and becomes the silent Thomas. "Mihi videtur ut palea" ("It looks like rubbish to me") is about all he has to say about his almost finished, grand *Summa*. After the African campaign, the weary Scipio might have uttered the same exclamation about his entire earthly mission. The wise Thomas forestalls Scipionic disappointment by refusing to follow the way of descent. His refusal is, of course, a decisive mark of his fundamentally medieval sensibility, especially in contrast with Petrarch's.*

There is a radical difference between St. Thomas's heaven and that of Petrarch. The former is the heaven of Pseudo-Dionysius; the latter is the heaven of Scipio. The former is Christian; the latter is Roman. The former transcends verbal description; the latter can be fully described in human language. Scipio has no difficulty finding his way back to this world because his heavenly world is enclosed within the same verbal domain as his mundane world. St. Thomas cannot readily follow his verbal way back to this world because his mystical experience abruptly lifts him out of the verbal domain. This verbal

---

*St. Thomas's refusal to descend may be interpreted as his *incapacity* to descend, and his refusal to complete his *Summa* as a similar incapacity. This uncertainty is due to his refusal to explain his behavior after his mystical experience, and even that refusal may simply reflect his incapacity. Thus St. Thomas becomes a man of mystery after his mystical vision. If medieval man can be regarded as a man of mystery, then Renaissance man should be considered a man of ambiguity. We saw in chapter 3 that Petrarch is full of ambiguity. Mystery lies at the heart of what is believed to be indescribable and inexplicable; ambiguity appears only in the process of description and explanation.

hiatus demonstrates the discontinuity between St. Thomas's this-world and the other world, which has been reflected in the semantic fissure of his theology of analogy. In contrast to this Thomistic discontinuity, Scipio's two worlds are continuous with each other. And it is this continuity that renders his heaven attractive to Petrarch and his Renaissance ethos.

Aristotle is the Angelic Doctor's Laura; Pseudo-Dionysius is his Scipio. Just as Petrarch tries to gain a vision of eternity by transforming the earthly image of Laura, so the Angelic Doctor tries to achieve an understanding of the divine essence by transforming the natural language of Aristotle. Just as Petrarch tries to establish tangible contact with the divine world through the *somnium scipionis*, so the Angelic Doctor assures himself direct contact with the divine essence through the Dionysian mystical ecstasy. In chapter 3 we saw that the *Triumphs* of the earthly Laura is sung in the "earthly" language of the vernacular, and that the *Africa* of the heavenly Scipio is composed in the "heavenly" language of Latin. The Angelic Doctor records his experience of ascent in the language of the Aristotelian natural world, while he intimates his mystical experience in the language of heavenly silence.

With the conceptual awakening of the Angelic Doctor's followers, his theology of analogy could no longer perform the vital function of equivocation and vacillation. The semantic fissure in the Thomistic analogy that had tended to lie hidden beneath the rubric of the analogical use of names or words came to be clearly exposed, when this rubric was removed for the purpose of inspecting its underlying conceptual framework. So the ladder of Thomistic analogy falls apart and the followers of St. Thomas are forced to move either upward or downward. The conservative Henry of Ghent flies back to the heaven of negative theology; the progressive Duns Scotus resolutely rushes down to the plain of positive theology. Duns Scotus's descent is much like Boccaccio's adventure of waking from the medieval tradition of dream-vision and establishing his sovereign self on the plane of literal sense. Just as Boccaccio's plane of literal sense accommodates both mortals and immortals, Duns Scotus's plane of *univocatio transcendens* encompasses both finite and infinite beings.

By this time, we may have gathered enough evidence to establish a thematic affinity between the Bonaventure-Thomas-Scotus cycle and the Dante-Petrarch-Boccaccio cycle. The former was primarily a Parisian theological movement, while the latter was largely a

Florentine literary movement. There was a time-lag of about half a century between these two cycles, which may be accounted for by the relative backwardness of Florence in comparison with Paris. Paris was the fountainhead of Gothic culture; Florence was the flower of the Italian Renaissance. The Bonaventure-Thomas-Scotus cycle was a Gothic movement; the Dante-Petrarch-Boccaccio cycle was a Renaissance movement. In spite of these differences, these two cycles share some fascinating points of resemblance and correspondence. The central point appears to be the dialectical principle that governs the thematic development of both movements, and this dialectical principle can be expressed in the three-two-one formula.

As we have seen, the works of both Bonaventure and Dante are usually molded into a triadic structure. Bonaventure and Dante employ the third moment of this triadic structure as the device for uniting the first two moments. We have also seen that they derive this mode of synthesis from Joachim of Floris's Trinitarian figuralism and that they employ it not only on the immanent but also on the transcendent level.

As we have seen in chapters 2 and 3, the works of Aquinas and Petrarch are governed by the dyadic principle of construction, and this principle is presumably their legacy from Augustine. But there are some crucial differences between the function of the dyadic schema in Augustine's own works and its function in the works of Aquinas and Petrarch. The dyadic schema, which is largely a device of separation (for example the separation of this world from the other world) with Augustine, becomes chiefly a device of transition with Aquinas and Petrarch. For this reason, the same dyadic logic operates as a logic of renunciation and resignation in Augustine and as a logic of tension and vacillation in Aquinas and Petrarch. Hence, a true Augustinian would say that Aquinas and Petrarch are really abusing the Augustinian dyadic logic and are scandalously unfaithful to the original spirit of Augustine's teachings. This is the very essence of all the attacks that St. Thomas receives from his Augustinian critics and of all the charges that Augustine levels against Petrarch in the *Secretum*.

When Aquinas and Petrarch adopt the dyadic schema in place of the triadic one, they appear to be repudiating the Dionysian logic of continuity for the sake of the Augustinian logic of discontinuity. In the hands of Aquinas and Petrarch, however, the dyadic logic is converted from the logic of separation and renunciation into the logic of conjunction and transition, which is the abnormal logic of continuity rather than the normal logic of discontinuity. What really happens with Aquinas and Petrarch is the conversion of the Dionysian logic from its normal (triadic) form into its abnormal (dyadic) form, and this conversion is dictated by their "abnormal" state of being situated in the transition period.

It should never be assumed that Aquinas and Petrarch themselves intended to play a transitional role by adopting dyadic logic in place of triadic logic. What they really intended to achieve was to dispense with the device of mediation in the triadic logic by abolishing its third moment and to establish an immediate relation with its first two moments. For example, the *Divina Commedia* is not simply a portrayal of the other world to the exclusion of this world; it really contains both. Since this world is as much alive as the other world in the *Commedia*, Dante has been hailed as the poet of the secular world. But, in Dante's epic, this world as well as the other world is not present in its own right; the two worlds are used only as raw materials for the construction of the *Commedia*. In short, the two worlds play the role of the first two moments for the construction of the third moment in Dante's triadic schema. In the *Commedia*, these first two moments are appreciated only for their extrinsic, never for their intrinsic, value. Dissatisfied with the triadic logic for its extrinsic stance, St. Thomas and Petrarch reduce it to dyadic logic in order to establish an intrinsic or immediate relation with this and the other world.

By using dyadic logic, St. Thomas and Petrarch argue for the inherent goodness of this world as well as for that of the other. They learn from Aristotle and Laura, respectively, how to appreciate this world in its own immediacy and integrity, and even carry this momentous lesson over to their appreciation of the other world. Thus they come to insist on having even the other world in the mode of immediacy. As we have seen in chapter 3, it is this insistence that underlies the Petrarchan vision of eternity. In the theology of analogy, St. Thomas tries to find a little more direct approach to God than that of St. Bonaventure's theology of allegory. The theology of allegory is definitely an indirect approach to God because it is an attempt to see him via his reflection in the mirror of creatures. St. Thomas's analogical approach is to distill the names of simple perfections from the names of creatures and render them directly predicable of the Creator. That is clearly an attempt to construct a direct mirror of words for divine reflection in place of the indirect mirror of things.*

Even the Angelic Doctor's style of discourse clearly reveals his eagerness for immediate contact and direct confrontation. In contrast to the Seraphic Doctor's habit of hovering over and around his central theme by enumerating various conformities and correspondences whose signification is often vague or only suggestive, the Angelic Doctor's standard procedure is to pinpoint the nature of his question at the outset and bluntly state the gist of his answer, leaving the chore of clarification and elaboration for subsequent maneuvers. St. Thomas seems to retain the same sense of immediacy when he reaches the plane of mystical experience. His mystical experience appears to be much more immediate than St. Bonaventure's. Whereas the latter is eloquently expressed in human language, the former is tightly wrapped in silence. The use of language is a good sign of mediation; the absence of its use is a good sign of immediacy.

Through his efforts to establish the immediate, intrinsic relation with the natural as well as the supernatural order, St. Thomas falls into a dualistic tension similar to Petrarch's. In contrast to Petrarch's turbulent temperament, St. Thomas's rather peaceful personality may be seen as patently incongruous with such a dualistic tension. But the peaceful impression his personality makes is only the surface that covers a systematic fissure in his temperament. His temperamental split can be illustrated by the position he takes on the greatest theological controversy of his century, namely, the violent dispute between Augustinians and Latin Averroists on Aristotelianism. If St. Thomas had been a simple conservative, he would have sided with the Augustinians; if he had been a straight radical, he would have sided with the Averroists. In fact, he is criticized for being too radical by the former and for being too conservative by the latter, and the criticisms of both camps are partly true. His personality is a unique mixture of a penchant for innovation and a propensity for conservation; his virtue is also a fascinating mixture of audacity

---

*This Thomistic mirror of words should never be confused with the Augustinian mirror (or theology) of words. Whereas the Augustinian mirror is composed of the interior words of the human mind, the Thomistic mirror is composed of the names of simple perfections. Since the names of simple perfections are distilled from the names of creatures, the Thomistic mirror is composed of exterior words rather than interior words. Whereas the Augustinian mirror of interior words reflects the divine ideas in the mind of God, the Thomistic mirror of exterior words reflects the divine attributes rather than the divine ideas.

and humility. It is through an adroit use of this mixture rather than a simple sense of peace and harmony that St. Thomas activates the Aristotelian golden mean and accomplishes his resolution of the theological controversy in question.

No doubt there is a notable difference between the dualistic tension of St. Thomas and that of Petrarch. Although St. Thomas recognizes the irreducible intrinsic value of the natural order, he is absolutely certain that the value of the supernatural order far surpasses that of the natural order. Because of this certainty, he can still comfortably stay within the fold of the Church. But Petrarch appears to reverse the Thomistic scale of values and attaches greater significance to this world than to the other. This reversal is the target for Augustine's charge in the *Secretum* that Petrarch's love of Laura transfers his love of God from the position of end to that of means. It is because of this reversal that Petrarch seeks comfort within the fold of the Roman Republic rather than the Church. Roman tradition exalts this world above the other world; as we have seen in chapter 3, the Roman heaven is for the sake of the Roman earth. In short, the Petrarchan scale of values belongs to the Renaissance ethos and the Thomistic scale to the Gothic ethos.

In spite of this emphatic difference, St. Thomas and Petrarch show the common syndrome of finding themselves caught between two incommensurate attractions.* When the suspension and tension found in these two writers are removed by their successors, they take on the historical role of transition. The historical task of resolving this Thomistic and Petrarchan dilemma falls upon Duns Scotus and Boccaccio respectively. By resolutely adopting the unitary schema, they finally resolve the tension and vacillation that have been working themselves out in the dyadic framework of Aquinas and Petrarch. Scotistic metaphysics is the unitary science of the transcendentals securely resting on the plane of *univocatio transcen-*

---

*Petrarch's conflict is much more intense than that of St. Thomas, because Petrarch places the higher of the two incommensurate values on the perishable rather than the eternal world. Although St. Thomas gains a greater sense of security by assigning the higher of his two ends to eternity, he nevertheless unmistakably introduces a grave fissure into the medieval religious ethos by the very claim that there are certain things in this transitory world which can never be found in the eternal kingdom.

Furthermore, while St. Thomas can remain within the living community of his Church, Petrarch has to break away from it and seek his place in the extinct community of the Roman Republic. This spiritual dislocation also makes Petrarch's conflict far more acute than that of St. Thomas and intensifies the personalistic tone of his writings, which presents a violent contrast to the impersonal tone of St. Thomas's works.

dens; the Boccaccian sovereign self is the unitary individual firmly standing on the plane of literal sense. Unlike the Aristotelian univocal plane, the Scotistic univocal plane is meant to encompass not only immanent but also transcendent signification; unlike the literal sense of pagan antiquity, the Boccaccian literal sense is meant to include not only the carnal but also the spiritual sense.

The Scotistic-Boccaccian unitary plane finally fulfills the Thomistic-Petrarchan aspiration to establish an immediate relation with both the natural and the supernatural orders. This fulfillment shows that there is no way to establish a truly immediate relation with both orders without fusing them into one. The focal point of the Thomistic-Petrarchan dilemma has been the incompatibility of two simultaneous aspirations—that is, to retain the distinct separation of the two orders and yet to establish an immediate relation with both of them at once. The central thrust of the Scotistic-Boccaccian maneuver is to see through this incompatibility and fuse the two orders into one order of universal immediacy. The language of Scotistic *univocatio* and Boccaccian literal sense is the language of this universal immediacy. Hence, the transition from allegorical to literal language is the transition from the age of universal mediation to the age of universal immediacy.*

As the age of universal immediacy, the Scotistic-Boccaccian period

*By presenting the ethos of universal immediacy, the Scotistic-Boccaccian universal plane provides the central thematic impetus for the Protestant Reformation, which is to seek an immediate relation between man and God in place of their mediated relation through the Church. It is for the sake of immediacy that Martin Luther shifts the emphasis from sacraments to Scripture and insists on its literal (immediate) rather than its allegorical (mediated) interpretation. The story of Sir Cippelletto shows the Renaissance ethos already undergoing the drastic transformation from mediation to immediacy, because the dispensability of the ministry of the saints also implies the dispensability of the mediation of the Church, insofar as the Church is considered as a mediatory organ of human agents. Whether Calvin's conception of God is the same as or different from Duns Scotus's doctrine of absolute divine power (*potentia absoluta*) has long been a controversial topic among Reformation scholars, and most of them now appear to recognize a fundamental affinity between the Scotistic and the Calvinistic conceptions of divine will and power (see François Wendel, *Calvin*, pp. 127–29). To the best of my knowledge, no one has yet considered the affinity of the Scotists with the Reformers concerning immediacy. Along with epistemological immediacy as manifested in the *univocatio transcendens*, Duns Scotus appears to propound ontological immediacy between God and creatures. For instance, in his doctrine of the Eucharist, which is much like that of Martin Luther, he claims a little more immediate presence of the Lord than St. Thomas does. "Consubstantiation," which has been used to designate Luther's doctrine, is in fact a Scotistic expression (see above, chap. 3, p. 127 n.). Once God is conceived of as truly omnipotent and omnipresent, it seems to be impossible to admit any other mode of relation than that of immediacy between God and creatures. This point comes across forcefully in the story of Ser Ciappelletto.

has one of the essential qualifications for being regarded as the fulfillment of Joachim of Floris's prophecy on the Age of the Holy
Spirit. But there is one notable difference between Scotistic and
Boccaccian universalism. Scotistic universalism is theocentric;
Boccaccian universalism is anthropocentric. The latter burgeons
from the Renaissance ethos; the former thrives on the Gothic ethos.
In spite of this difference, these two universalisms come to cover the
same domain of discourse, because both of them are meant to be
infinite spheres whose circumferences are nowhere.*

In retrospect we may say that the Bonaventure-Aquinas-Scotus
cycle and the Dante-Petrarch-Boccaccio cycle were two rather
independent series of attempts to resolve the thematic conflict of the
emergent Dionysian ethos. In the eleventh and twelfth centuries,
the emergence of the Dionysian ethos generated the dualistic tension
of the sacred and the secular by recognizing the claims of this world
in addition to the claims of the other world. This dualistic tension is
crystallized in the dyadic logic of the Romanesque ethos, in which
such fascinating men of inner tension and conflict as Bernard of
Clairvaux and Peter Abelard were to be nurtured. This dyadic logic
operates much like that of St. Thomas and Petrarch and quite unlike
the Augustinian dyadic logic of renunciation. In its operation, Augustinian logic produces the monadic result because it is used for the

*The conception of the sovereign individual as the agent of universal immediacy is
perhaps best expressed in Pico della Mirandola's definition of man as the unique substance
of unlimited power, ranging from the earthly to the heavenly (see *On the Dignity of Man*
and *Heptaplus*). This new conception of man also underlies the Renaissance notion of the
ideal man as the prodigy of universal power and genius. 'Universal (unlimited) power'
and 'universal immediacy' are interchangeable with each other, because immediate
presence is the source of power. This titan of universal power and immediacy is the object
of Rabelaisian satire and celebration in *The Histories of Gargantua and Pantagruel*. The
Rabelaisian giants aar so immense and so copious as to encompass in their immediacy
every feature of the entire cosmos; the profane and the sacred, scatology and theology,
are equally at home in their all-encompassing presence. Even the absolute freedom that
Piconian and Rabelaisian heroes enjoy is rooted in their universal power and immediacy.
This new idea of being human becomes the living ideal for the radical wing of the Refor-
mers, the Anabaptists, who regard themselves as the children of the Age of the Holy
Spirit.

Both Pico and Rabelais offer this new ideal as their faithful articulation of Christian
faith. Pico's ideal is given as his reinterpretation of Genesis; Rabelais's ideal, as inscribed
over the gate of Thélème, is meant to be his recovery of the true meaning of the Holy
Gospel. This new ideal would surely appear to be in blatant conflict with the precepts and
practices of Christianity in their traditional formulation. But as soon as Christianity is
reconceived as it should be in the Age of the Spirit, their ideal can be appreciated as a
sincere product of Christian piety—as sincere as Erasmian Christian humanism or Joachimian Protestantism.

acceptance of the other world alone, to the exclusion of this world. Augustinian logic is the negative (or exclusive) dyadic one; Romanesque logic is the positive (or inclusive) dyadic one. The emergence of the Dionysian ethos is marked by the supersession of the Augustinian logic of renunciation and resignation by the Romanesque logic of acceptance and tension.

The Gothic ethos emerges when it resolves the Romanesque tension in its new triadic schema. We can recognize three phases in the development of the Gothic ethos: (1) the triadic (Bonaventurian) moment; (2) the dyadic (Thomistic) moment; and (3) the monadic (Scotistic) moment. The triadic moment does not begin but rather ends with St. Bonaventure; it really emerges with Joachim of Floris and the Franciscans (Rupert of Deutz is not in it yet because he is only its distant herald). The dyadic moment emerges as an attempt to overcome the dissatisfaction with the triadic resolution of the Romanesque tension; the monadic moment, in turn, appears with the recognition that the dyadic attempt is itself incomplete and inconclusive.*

Dante inherits and confronts the Romanesque dyadic tension in the tradition of *dolce stil nuovo* and adopts the Joachimian-Bonaventurian triadic schema for its resolution. Petrarch's dyadic reaction to Dante's triadic moment is the same sort of dialectical move as St. Thomas's reaction to the Bonaventurian moment. Boccaccio's monadic moment is the resolution of the Petrarchan dyadic tension in the same dialectical sense that Duns Scotus's monadic moment is the resolution of the Thomistic dyadic tension.

In both cycles of Bonaventure-Aquinas-Scotus and Dante-Petrarch-Boccaccio, the emergence of the Dionysian ethos and its dialectical development can be described in the logical schema of two-three-two-one. The initial dyadic conflict is reconciled in the triadic phase, whose synthesis is broken up in the second dyadic phase, whose tension is finally resolved in the monadic phase. The two cycles follow the same dialectical pattern of resolution because they start out with the same thematic conflict. The only important difference between the two cycles lies in their historical contexts. The Bon-

---

*In chapter 1, I have said that Bonaventurian Trinitarianism is the true expression of the Gothic ethos while Thomistic dualism is quite alien to it. That is a bit of an overstatement for the sake of emphasis, but it still remains partly true. For the Bonaventurian phase is the moment of full bloom for the Gothic ethos, while the Thomistic phase is the moment of its disintegration, and the Scotistic phase the moment of its demise.

aventure-Aquinas-Scotus cycle becomes the vehicle for the consummation of the medieval tradition; the Dante-Petrarch-Boccaccio cycle
becomes the vehicle for the initiation of the modern tradition.*

One of these two cycles nurtures the theology of allegory and then
gradually converts it into the theology of univocity; the other cycle
nurtures the literature of allegory and then gradually converts it
into the literature of literal sense. In both cases, allegorical language
produces the full bloom of Dionysian universalism, and literal language forms the rind for its final fruit. The dialectical schema of both
cycles is the move from the transcendent stage of Dionysian universalism to its immanent stage, and their common outcome is to
realize fully the original spirit of the Dionysian universal ethos. It
is this full-fledged Dionysian universalism that constitutes the essence
of the Renaissance ethos.

The Dionysian Ethos and the Faustian Tradition

It is the spirit of all-encompassing universalism that animates the
emergence of Renaissance analogy. The spirit of Renaissance analogy is to seek and find affinity and correspondence in all things
without being hindered by specific and generic boundaries. Renaissance alchemy stands on the premise that the basic metals have the
same powers as the planets to which they correspond; Renaissance
astrology operates on the premise that the virtues of the soul (microcosm) mirror the virtues of the stellar world. This rule of universal
resemblance and correspondence is an implementation of the
Scotistic and Ockhamian thesis that the category of unrestricted
resemblance is the only principle governing the formation of all our
concepts. Hence, this rule of universal similitude is the descendant of
the rule of *similitudo dissimilium* which had governed the Dionysian
anagogia.

In the Dionysian *anagogia*, the universal chain of resemblance is
established through the allegorical mediation of transcendent reality.
That is, any two finite entities resemble each other by virtue of their
resemblance to the Creator, which is brought about through their
role of allegorically reflecting the glory of the same God. In chapter
2, we saw an illustrious example of this in Bonaventure's penchant

*The Italian Renaissance can be said to begin with a repetition of the Gothic cycle, or
with the Italian attempt to seek their own resolution of the Romanesque thematic tension
instead of accepting the Gothic resolution. Because of this refusal to accept the Gothic
resolution, Italy never fully allowed the transplantation of the Gothic culture to her soil.

for universal correspondence and conformities. But Renaissance analogy dispenses with this mediation and seeks to establish the chain of the universal resemblance as the immediate relation of finite entities.

In Renaissance analogy, the universal chain of resemblance is also the universal chain of interaction; that is, the domain of resemblance is coextensive with the domain of causal interaction. Likewise, in the Dionysian *anagogia*, the universal chain of *similitudo dissimilium* represents the universal chain of mutual interaction. This conception of universal interaction is diametrically opposed to the Aristotelian view that the interaction of substances is confined within the boundaries of species and genera. Therefore, Dionysian cosmology presents an immediate threat to Aristotelian ontology, as M.-D. Chenu explains:

> Increasingly important as a challenge to the Aristotelian concept of "substance," the concept of "hierarchy" [of Pseudo-Dionysius] shattered the metaphysical scheme which locked up each nature within its own ontological perimeter. This concept entailed natures so universally and normally open to causal influence from the being above them that the action of the superior being was intimately involved in their own natural acts. This "sympathy," this *continuatio* as it was translated in Latin, was of a piece with the Plotinian idea of "participation"; it clothed reality with qualities deriving from a mysterious kinship and invested the unitary order of the universe, emanating from the One, with a religious value.[46]

The notion of sympathy is retained by all practitioners of the Renaissance occult sciences, whether or not they accept the religious significance of the One.*

The ethos of analogy in the Renaissance occult sciences contributes two fundamental features to modern science: (1) the universal scope

---

*The credit for breaking up the permanent boundaries of the Aristotelian species and genera is usually given to Charles Darwin, but his theory of evolution is only one of the ultimate consequences of the ontological and epistemological revolution initiated by the medieval Dionysians. Nominalism is a formal semantics for this revolution; Darwinian evolutionism is the extension of Joachimism to the biological sphere. The Dionysian notion of progress, from Rupert of Deutz and Joachim of Floris to Hegel and Marx, had been largely limited to the sphere of the human spirit; the real merit of Darwin's theory was to extend this limited notion of progress to the nonhuman sphere of plants and animals.

of scientific concepts, and (2) the conception of the universe as one system of causal interaction. For example, let us take the concept of the efficient cause, which has been adopted as one of the central notions of modern science. In Aristotelian cosmology, the chain of efficient causation had been tightly locked up within the specific boundaries, for example, only horses can be the efficient cause of other horses (i.e. only horses can breed horses). But modern science lifts the category of efficient causation out of the specific boundaries and applies it on the universal scale. Of course, this universal expansion of the causal principle entails that the universe is one causal system instead of being divided up into many specific channels of causation as in Aristotle's view.

Another interesting example of compartmentalization in Aristotelian cosmology is the distinction made between the sublunary and the superlunary spheres. Aristotle believes that the locomotions in these two spheres are governed by two different principles; that is, circular motion is the paradigm for the superlunary world while linear motion is the paradigm for the sublunary world. One of the fundamental steps in the development of modern science was to repudiate this sort of compartmentalization and to try to establish one principle for the locomotions in every part of the universe. For example, Galileo's principle of inertia in the terrestrial world would allow an object to travel in a circular orbit just like heavenly bodies. Because of this unitary view of the universe, modern science has been conceived essentially as one systematic whole. It is this grand ideal of cosmic unity that is celebrated in Newton's eventual reconciliation of terrestrial with celestial mechanics. In contrast to this governing ideal of modern science, the Aristotelian sciences are conceived as a group of independent disciplines. To be sure, there are different branches of modern science, but these branches are meant to be not independent enterprises but a provisional division of labor for the ultimate task of producing one unified science.

Another important difference between modern science and Aristotelian science lies in the ultimate purposes of the two. The ultimate aim of scientific inquiry in the Aristotelian view is the scientific understanding of reality, or rather the contemplation of the nature of reality; but the ultimate end of modern scientific investigation is the control and power that man gains over nature. This new scientific ethos is succinctly expressed in the Baconian aphorism, "Knowledge is power." This aphorism has become such an integral feature of our scientific sensibility that it appears to be a truism. But there are many kinds of knowledge that offer us no power and no use; for example, we can draw no benefit from the knowledge that there are stars even during the daytime or that we are all destined to die. In fact, the Stoics thought that the only use they could make of knowledge was to accept or follow reality. But the Stoic maxim would be sacrilegious or quixotic to the devotees of modern science.

The notion that control and power are the ultimate values of our knowledge is an integral feature of the Boccaccian conception of the sovereign individual, and this idea has also governed the development of the Renaissance occult sciences. The ultimate purpose of these was not to understand the occult phenomena for their own sake but to draw on and exploit the powers (virtues) of the stellar spheres or alchemic materials. In this regard, the white magic of the Renaissance was inspired by the same ideal or obsession that lured many people into its black magic. The ethos of control and power is one of the legacies that modern science inherits directly from the Renaissance occult sciences, and is most vividly manifest in the tradition of the controlled experiment. In Kantian language, it is through controlled experimentation that man compels nature to do his will instead of being a passive observer.

With his resolute will to control nature, his fellow human beings, and his own destiny, the Boccaccian man seems to fulfill all the essential conditions for being what Spengler, in his *Decline of the West*,[47] has called the Faustian man. Spengler places the emergence of this Faustian tradition in the Middle Ages; the Boccaccian tradition emerges from the Dionysian ethos of the eleventh and twelfth centuries. Spengler has characterized the Faustian individual as an agent of infinity who dares to break out of the finitude of the classical tradition; the Boccaccian individual boldly asserts his limitless sovereignty by arrogating to himself the role of the Dionysian infinite God. This arrogation is the inevitable outcome of secularizing the Age of the Spirit and imitating God in all his power and glory.

The emergence of the Faustian tradition is the transformation of the Dionysian into the Boccaccian ethos. This transformation is a transition from servitude to sovereignty, from the humble role of suffering to the impudent role of commanding, from the sense of resignation to the sense of conquest and mastery. Christopher Marlowe eloquently sums up this new mood of the Faustian sovereign individual:

O, what a world of profit and delight,
Of power, of honor, of omnipotence
Is promised to the studious artisan!
All things that move between the quiet poles
Shall be at my command. Emperors and kings
Are but obeyed in their several provinces,
Nor can they raise the wind or rend the clouds,
But his dominion that exceeds in this
Stretcheth as far as doth the mind of man.[48]

[*Doctor Faustus*, act 1, scene 1, lines 54–62]

Notes to Chapter 1

1. Princeton, 1969.
2. Hollander, *Allegory in Dante's "Commedia,"* pp. 3 ff.
3. Ibid., pp. 29 ff.
4. Ibid., pp. 8 ff.
5. Beryl Smalley, *The Study of the Bible in the Middle Ages*, pp. 2–4.
6. Ibid., p. 3.
7. Ibid.
8. Ibid., p. 5.
9. Hollander, p. 255.
10. Ibid.; E. R. Curtius, *European Literature and the Latin Middle Ages*, p. 60.
11. Cf. D. W. Robertson, "Some Medieval Literary Terminology, with Special Reference to Chrétien de Troyes," *Studies in Philology* 48 (1951): 677.
12. Auerbach, "Figura," trans. Ralph Manheim, in *Scenes from the Drama of European Literature*, p. 36.
13. Smalley, p. 7.
14. Cf. Auerbach, "Figura," pp. 28 ff.
15. Ibid., pp. 34 ff.
16. Ibid., p. 36.
17. Erich Auerbach, *Mimesis*, p. 195.
18. Hollander, pp. 76 and 258.
19. Ibid., pp. 62–63.
20. Ibid., pp. 70 ff.
21. Cf. Robertson, "Some Medieval Literary Terminology," p. 684.
22. Charles Singleton, *Dante Studies 1*, p. 9.
23. Ibid., pp. 1 ff. and 84 ff.; Hollander, pp. 40 ff.
24. Hollander, p. 86.
25. "Dante's Letter to Can Grande della Scala," trans. Paget Toynbee, in his *Dantis Alagherii Epistolae: The Letters of Dante*, pp. 199–200.
26. Translation from the Temple Classics.
27. Cf. Robertson, p. 680.
28. *Translations of the Latin Works of Dante Alighieri*, p. 348; Singleton, p. 14.
29. Toynbee, trans., p. 199.
30. Singleton, p. 15.
31. Ibid., pp. 14 ff.; Hollander, p. 18.
32. Smalley, p. 28.
33. Auerbach, "Figura," p. 41.
34. Ibid., p. 42.
35. Ibid., p. 55.
36. Cf. Smalley, p. 28.
37. Trans. Dominican Fathers, in *The Summa of St. Thomas Aquinas*.

38. Toynbee, trans., p. 199.
39. Singleton, p. 91.
40. Auerbach, "Figura," p. 71.
41. Singleton, p. 91.
42. Cf. Auerbach, "Figura," p. 75.
43. Ibid.
44. Cf. Auerbach, *Mimesis*, p. 195.
45. Robson, "Dante's Use in the *Divina Commedia* of the Medieval Allegories on Ovid," in *Centenary Essays on Dante*, Members of the Oxford Dante Society, pp. 1–38.
46. T. K. Swing [Seung], *The Fragile Leaves of the Sibyl*, pp. 124 and 130.
47. Ibid., p. 390.
48. Ibid., pp. 39 ff.
49. Trans. John D. Sinclair, *Dante's Inferno*, p. 27.
50. Hollander, p. 261.
51. Cf. Singleton, p. 57.
52. Trans. T. G. Bergin, in *The Divine Comedy*.
53. Kenelm Foster, O.P., "A Propos of a New Book on Dante," *Blackfriars* 43, no. 509 (November 1962): 480.
54. Swing, pp. 168, 190, 217, 240, 263, 289, and 312.
55. Ibid., pp. 359, 372, 407.
56. Cf. Hollander, app. 4, pp. 308 ff.
57. Ibid., pp. 233 ff.
58. Ibid., p. 251.
59. Cf. ibid., p. 259.
60. Ibid., pp. 81 ff. and 220 ff.
61. Ibid., p. 57.
62. Ibid., p. 261.
63. Ibid.
64. Ibid.
65. Foster, "New Book on Dante," p. 483.
66. Swing, p. 12.
67. Trans. Raymond Bernard Blakney, in *Meister Eckhart*, p. 148.

Notes to Chapter 2

1. Translated in David Thompson, ed., *Petrarch*, p. 27.
2. Ibid., p. 29.
3. Ibid., pp. 30–31.
4. Ibid., p. 32.
5. *Confessions*, bk. 10, chap. 8, p. 15, translated in ibid., p. 34.
6. Cf. F. Copleston, *History of Philosophy*, 2 : 92.
7. Cf. Glenn R. Morrow, trans., Proclus, *A Commentary on the First Book of Euclid's Elements*, p. xxiv.
8. Cf. E. R. Dodds, trans., Proclus, *The Elements of Theology*, 2d ed.

9. Ibid., p. ix.
10. Morrow, trans., Proclus, *A Commentary on the First Book of Euclid's Elements*, pp. 3–14.
11. Ibid., p. 16.
12. Cf. Copleston, 2 : 60.
13. M.-D. Chenu, O.P., *Nature, Man and Society in the Twelfth Century*, pp. 80–81.
14. Joseph Pieper, *Scholasticism*, p. 50.
15. Étienne Gilson, *History of Christian Philosophy in the Middle Ages*, p. 128.
16. Chenu, p. 6, n. 5.
17. Ibid., p. 23.
18. Ibid., p. 25.
19. Ibid., pp. 65 ff.
20. Ibid., pp. 49–50.
21. Ernst Robert Curtius, *European Literature and the Latin Middle Ages*, p. 119.
22. Chenu, p. 54, n. 7.
23. Trans. D. W. Robertson, Jr., in Saint Augustine, *On Christian Doctrine*, p. 10.
24. Chenu, p. 25.
25. Ibid., pp. 177 ff.
26. Ibid., pp. 184–85.
27. Ibid., p. 190.
28. Pieper, *Scholasticism*, p. 55.
29. Ibid., p. 48.
30. Ibid., p. 53.
31. Trans. José de Vinck in *The Works of Bonaventure*, 1 : 57–58.
32. Ratzinger, *The Theology of History in St. Bonaventure*, p. 8.
33. Ibid., p. 31.
34. Ibid., p. 92.
35. Chenu, *Nature, Man and Society*, pp. 124 ff.
36. Ibid., p. 135.
37. Ibid., p. 117.
38. Ratzinger, p. 78.
39. Ibid., p. 78.
40. Pieper, p. 46.
41. M.-D. Chenu, *The Scope of the Summa of St. Thomas*, p. 11.
42. Ibid., pp. 9–10.
43. Ibid., pp. 16–17.
44. Ratzinger, pp. 141 ff.
45. J. F. Quinn, *The Historical Constitution of St. Bonaventure's Philosophy*, p. 494.
46. Efrem Bettoni, *Saint Bonaventure*, p. 50.
47. E. Gilson, *The Philosophy of St. Bonaventure*, p. 185.
48. Trans. Battista Mondin, in *The Principle of Analogy in Protestant and Catholic Theology*, p. 33.
49. Chenu, *Nature, Man and Society*, pp. 82–83.
50. James S. Preus, *From Shadow to Promise*, p. 12, n. 11.
51. Robert Hollander, *Allegory in Dante's "Commedia,"* p. 16, n.
52. Thomas G. Bergin, *Dante*, p. 57.

53. Translation in the Temple Classics edition, p. 99.
54. Bergin, *Dante*, p. 107.
55. E. Gilson, *Dante the Philosopher*, p. 126.
56. C. S. Lewis, *The Allegory of Love*, pp. 44 ff.
57. Dante Alighieri, *On World-Government*, p. xi.
58. A. P. d'Entrèves, *Dante as a Political Thinker*, p. 49.
59. Swing, *Fragile Leaves of the Sibyl*, pp. 87, 91 ff., 97–98, 101, 105, and 121.
60. Translated in Thompson, *Petrarch*, p. 34.
61. T. G. Bergin, *Petrarch*, p. 47.
62. Trans. José de Vinck, in *The Works of Bonaventure*, 1 : 5–6.
63. Trans. Morris Bishop in Thomas G. Bergin, ed., *Petrarch: Selected Sonnets, Odes and Letters*, pp. 60 ff.

Notes to Chapter 3

1. Translation in David Thompson, ed., *Petrarch*, p. 61.
2. William H. Draper, trans., *Petrarch's Secret*, pp. 44, 53, 78, 93, 103, 120, 132, 138, 140, 152, and 188–89.
3. T. G. Bergin, *Petrarch*, p. 143.
4. Trans. Hans Nachod, in Ernst Cassirer et al., eds., *The Renaissance Philosophy of Man*, p. 57.
5. Morris Bishop, *Petrarch and his World*, p. 351.
6. Draper, *Petrarch's Secret*, pp. 43, 45, 89, 110, 118, 133, 139, 142, and 147.
7. Francesco de Sanctis, *History of Italian Literature*, 1 : 280.
8. R. R. Bolgar, *The Classical Heritage and its Beneficiaries*, p. 147.
9. Draper, p. 176.
10. Bishop, *Petrarch and his World*, p. 213.
11. Ibid., pp. 213–14.
12. Theodore E. Mommsen, *Medieval and Renaissance Studies*, p. 182.
13. Bergin, *Petrarch*, pp. 121–22.
14. Norman O. Brown, *Love's Body*, p. 192.
15. S. Kierkegaard, *Philosophical Fragments*, p. 16.
16. S. Kierkegaard, *The Sickness unto Death*, pp. 17 ff.
17. Ibid., p. 109.
18. Bergin, *Petrarch*, p. 178.
19. Ibid., p. 170.
20. Trans. T. G. Bergin, in "Petrarch's *Bucolicum Carmen I: Parthenias*," included in Julius A. Molinaro, ed., *Petrarch to Pirandello*, p. 7.
21. Ibid.
22. Ibid., p. 13.
23. Ibid., p. 9.
24. Ibid., p. 11.
25. Ibid., p. 3.

26. Aldo Bernardo, "Dramatic Dialogue in the Prose Letters of Petrarch," *Symposium* 5 (1951): 302–16; "Dramatic Dialogue and Monologue in Petrarch's Works," *Symposium* 7 (1953): 92–119.
27. Bernardo, "Dramatic Dialogue and Monologue in Petrarch's Works," p. 92.
28. Robert M. Durling, *The Figure of the Poet in Renaissance Epic*, pp. 67 ff.
29. Ibid., p. 73.
30. Trans. Anna Maria Armi, in her *Petrarch: Sonnets and Songs*, p. 245.
31. Ibid., p. 249.
32. Durling, p. 73.
33. Leonard Forster, *The Icy Fire: Five Studies in European Petrarchism.*
34. Trans. Morris Bishop, in his *Petrarch and his World*, p. 154.
35. Forster, p. 5.
36. Princeton, 1966.
37. Cf. Cleanth Brooks, *The Well-Wrought Urn*, p. 223.
38. Ibid., p. 224.
39. Trans. Ernest H. Wilkins, *The Triumphs of Petrarch*, p. 112.
40. Ibid., p. 108.
41. Bergin, *Petrarch*, pp. 161 ff.
42. Armi, *Petrarch*, p. 179.
43. Wilkins, *Triumphs of Petrarch*, p. 64.
44. Cf. de Sanctis, p. 276.
45. Bergin, *Petrarch*, p. 166.
46. Ibid., pp. 101 ff.
47. C. S. Lewis, *The Discarded Image*, p. 68.
48. Aldo Bernardo, *Petrarch, Scipio and the "Africa,"* p. 126.
49. Giuseppe Toffanin, *History of Humanism*, p. 113.
50. Trans. James H. M. Campbell in his *"Petrarch's Africa"* (M.A. thesis, Yale University, 1933), p. 62.
51. Ibid., p. 61.
52. Bernardo, *Petrarch, Scipio and the "Africa,"* p. 100.
53. Campbell, "Petrarch's *Africa*," p. 103.
54. Bergin, *Petrarch*, p. 103.
55. Ibid., p. 113.
56. Cf. Bernardo, *Petrarch, Scipio and the "Africa,"* p. 196.
57. Ibid., p. 96.
58. H. H. Scullard, *Scipio Africanus*, p. 237.
59. Cf. ibid., p. 234.
60. Bernardo, *Petrarch, Scipio and the "Africa,"* p. 13.

Notes to Chapter 4

1. De Sanctis, *History of Italian Literature*, 1:313.
2. Aldo Bernardo, *Petrarch, Scipio and the "Africa,"* pp. 49 ff.
3. Ernest H. Wilkins, *A History of Italian Literature*, p. 105.

4. De Sanctis, p. 308.

5. Wilkins, p. 104.

6. Nathaniel E. Griffin and Arthur B. Myrick, trans., *The "Filostrato" of Giovanni Boccaccio*, p. 29.

7. Ibid., p. 65.

8. Ibid., p. 26, n. 1.

9. Ibid., p. 35, n. 4.

10. Ibid., p. 361.

11. Robert P. apRoberts, "Love in the *Filostrato*," *The Chaucer Review* 7(1972): 7.

12. Griffin and Myrick, p. 425.

13. Sanford B. Meech, *Design in Chaucer's "Troilus,"* p. 12.

14. Griffin and Myrick, p. 425.

15. Bernardo, *Petrarch, Scipio and the "Africa,"* p. 100.

16. Ibid., p. 75.

17. Ibid., p. 66.

18. Forster, *The Icy Fire*, pp. 122 ff.

19. Bernardo, *Petrarch, Scipio and the "Africa,"* p. 178.

20. Vittore Branca, *Boccaccio medievale*, p. 92.

21. Trans. G. H. McWilliam, in Giovanni Boccaccio, *The Decameron*, p. 81.

22. Ibid., p. 79.

23. Ibid., pp. 85–86.

24. Trans. Richard Aldington, in *The Decameron of Giovanni Boccaccio*, p. 14.

25. Thomas M. Greene, "Forms of Accommodation in the *Decameron*," *Italica* 45 (1968): 307.

26. J. Burke Severs, *The Literary Relationships of Chaucer's Clerkes Tale*, p. 4.

27. De Sanctis, *History of Italian Literature*, p. 337.

28. S. Kierkegaard, *Fear and Trembling*.

29. A. C. Lee, *The Decameron: Its Sources and Analogues*, pp. 348 ff.

30. De Sanctis, p. 340; Aldo D. Scaglione, *Nature and Love in the Late Middle Ages*, pp. 48–49.

31. De Sanctis, p. 337.

32. *Filologia Romanza*, vol. 7 (1960), and included in *Giovanni Boccaccio e la Riforma della Narrativa*, pp. 1–81.

33. Swing, *Fragile Leaves of the Sibyl*, pp. 29 ff.

34. E.g. Joan Ferrante, "The Frame Characters of the *Decameron*: A Progression of Virtues," *Romance Philology* 19 (1965): 212–26; Angelo Lipari, "Donne e Muse," *Italica* 15 (1938): 132–41, and more fully in his "The Structure and Real Significance of the *Decameron*," in *Essays in Honor of Albert Feuillerat*, Yale Romanic Studies, 22, pp. 43–83.

35. Trans. James Robinson Smith in *The Earliest Lives of Dante*, p. 19.

36. Trans. Charles G. Osgood in *Boccaccio on Poetry*, pp. 10–11.

37. Ibid., p. 89.

38. Ibid., p. 12.

39. David Burrell, *Analogy and Philosophical Language*, pp. 186 ff.

40. Ibid., p. 180.

41. Trans. James J. Walsh, in Arthur Hyman and James Walsh, eds., *Philosophy in the Middle Ages*, p. 576.

42. Ibid., p. 577.
43. Burrell, pp. 185–86.
44. Timotheus A. Barth, "Being, Univocity, and Analogy according to Duns Scotus," in John K. Ryan and Bernardine M. Bonansea, eds., *John Duns Scotus, 1265–1965*, p. 261.
45. Allan B. Wolter, *The Transcendentals and their Function in the Metaphysics of Duns Scotus*, pp. 10–11.
46. Chenu, *Nature, Man, and Society*, p. 83.
47. Oswald Spengler, *The Decline of the West*, vols. 1 and 2.
48. Quoted from Irving Ribner, ed., *Christopher Marlowe's "Doctor Faustus"* (New York, 1966), p. 6.

Bibliography

Aldington, Richard, trans. *The Decameron of Giovanni Boccaccio*. New York: Doubleday, 1930.

apRoberts, Robert P. "Love in the *Filostrato*." *The Chaucer Review* 7 (1972): 1–26.

Armi, Anna Maria, trans. *Petrarch: Sonnets and Songs*. New York: Pantheon, 1946.

Auerbach, Erich. "Figura." In his *Scenes from the Drama of European Literature*. Translated by Ralph Manheim. New York: World Publishing Company, 1959.

———. *Mimesis: The Representation of Reality in Western Literature*. Translated by Willard R. Trask. Princeton, 1953.

Barth, Timotheus A. "Being, Univocity, and Analogy according to Duns Scotus." In John K. Ryan and Bernardine M. Bonansea, eds., *Studies in Philosophy and the History of Philosophy*, vol. 3 (*John Duns Scotus, 1265–1965*). Washington, D.C.: Catholic University of America, 1965.

Battaglia, Salvatore. "Dall'esempio alla novella." *Filologia Romanza* 7 (1960). Also included in his *Giovanni Boccaccio e la Riforma della Narrativa*, pp. 1–81. Naples: Liguori.

Bergin, Thomas G. *Dante*. New York: Orion, 1965.

———. *Petrarch*. New York: Twayne, 1970.

Bergin, Thomas, G., trans. and ed. Dante Alighieri, *The Divine Comedy*. New York: Appleton, 1955.

———. "Petrarch's *Bucolicum Carmen I: Parthenias*." In Julius A. Molinaro, ed. *Petrarch to Pirandello*, pp. 3–18. Toronto: University of Toronto, 1973.

———. *Petrarch: Selected Sonnets, Odes and Letters*. New York: Appleton, 1966.

Bernardo, Aldo. "Dramatic Dialogue in the Prose Letters of Petrarch." *Symposium* 5 (1951): 302–16.

———. "Dramatic Dialogue and Monologue in Petrarch's Works." *Symposium* 7 (1953): 92–119.

———. *Petrarch, Scipio and the "Africa."* Baltimore: Johns Hopkins, 1962.

Bettoni, Efrem. *Saint Bonaventure*. Translated by Angelus Gabatese. Notre Dame, Ind., 1964.

Bishop, Morris. *Petrarch and his World*. Bloomington: Indiana University, 1963.

Blakney, Raymond Bernard, trans. *Meister Eckhart*. New York: Harper and Row, 1941.

Bolgar, R. R. *The Classical Heritage and its Beneficiaries*. Cambridge, 1958.

Branca, Vittore. *Boccaccio medievale*. Florence, 1956.

Brooks, Cleanth. *The Well-Wrought Urn: Studies in the Structure of Poetry*. New York: Harcourt, 1947.

Brown, Norman O. *Love's Body*. New York: Random House, 1966.

Burrell, David. *Analogy and Philosophical Language*. New Haven: Yale, 1973.

Campbell, James H. M., trans. "Petrarch's *Africa*." Master's thesis, Yale University, 1933.

Chenu, M.-D. *Nature, Man and Society in the Twelfth Century: Essays on New Theological Perspectives in the Latin West*. Translated by Jerome Taylor and Lester K. Little. Chicago: University of Chicago, 1968.

————. *The Scope of the Summa of St. Thomas*. The Monist Reader—1958. Translated by Robert E. Brennan and Albert M. Landry. Washington, D.C.: Monist, 1958.

Chierici, Joseph. *Il grifo dantesco (unità fantastica e concettuale della Divina Commedia)*. Rome: Instituto Grafico Tiberino di S. De Luca, 1967.

Colie, Rosalie L. *Paradoxia Epidemica: The Renaissance Tradition of Paradox*. Princeton, 1966.

Copleston, Frederick. *A History of Philosophy*. Vol. 2: *Medieval Philosophy* (Augustine to Scotus). Westminster, Md.: Newman, 1960.

Curtius, Ernst Robert. *European Literature and the Latin Middle Ages*. Translated by Willard R. Trask. New York: Bollingen, 1953.

d'Entrèves, A. P. *Dante as a Political Thinker*. Oxford, 1952.

de Sanctis, Francesco. *History of Italian Literature*, vol. 1. Translated by Joan Redfern. New York: Harcourt, 1931.

de Vinck, José, trans. *The Works of Bonaventure*. 5 vols. Paterson, N.J.: St. Anthony Guild, 1960–70.

Dodds, E. R., trans. Proclus, *The Elements of Theology*, 2d ed. Oxford, 1963.

Dominican Fathers, trans. *The Summa of St. Thomas Aquinas*, vol. 1. New York: Benziger Bros., 1946.

Draper, William H. *Petrarch's Secret or The Soul's Conflict with Passion*. London: Chatto and Windus, 1911.

Durling, Robert M. *The Figure of the Poet in Renaissance Epic*. Cambridge, Mass.: Harvard, 1965.

Ferrante, Joan. "The Frame Characters of the *Decameron*: A Progression of Virtues." *Romance Philology* 19 (1965): 212–26.

Forster, Leonard. *The Icy Fire: Five Studies in European Petrarchism*. Cambridge, 1969.

Foster, Kenelm, O.P. "A Propos of a New Book on Dante." *Blackfriars* 43, no. 509 (November 1962): 477–83.

Gilson, Étienne. *Dante the Philosopher*. Translated by David Moore. New York: Sheed and Ward, 1949.

———. *History of Christian Philosophy in the Middle Ages*. New York: Random House, 1955.

———. *The Philosophy of St. Bonaventure*. Translated by Dom Illtyd Trethowan. Paterson, N.J.: St. Anthony Guild, 1965.

Greene, Thomas M. "Forms of Accommodation in the *Decameron*," *Italica* 45 (1968): 297–313.

Griffin, Nathaniel E., and Myrick, Arthur B., trans. *The 'Filostrato' of Giovanni Boccaccio*. Philadelphia: University of Pennsylvania, 1929.

Heidegger, Martin. *Being and Time*. Translated by John Macquarie and Edward Robinson. New York: Harper and Row, 1962.

Hollander, Robert. *Allegory in Dante's "Commedia."* Princeton, 1969.

Kaske, R. E. "Dante's *DXV*." In John Freccero, ed. *Dante*, pp. 122–40. Englewood Cliffs, N.J.: Prentice-Hall, 1965.

Kierkegaard, S. *Fear and Trembling*. Translated by Walter Lowrie. Princeton, 1941.

———. *Philosophical Fragments or A Fragment of Philosophy*. Translated by David F. Swenson and Howard V. Hong. Princeton, 1962.

———. *The Sickness unto Death*. Translated by Walter Lowrie. Princeton, 1941.

Lee, A. C. *The Decameron: Its Sources and Analogues*. New York: Haskell House, 1966.

Lewis, C. S. *The Allegory of Love: A Study in Medieval Tradition*. Oxford, 1936.

———. *The Discarded Image: An Introduction to Medieval and Renaissance Literature*. Cambridge, 1964.

Lipari, Angelo. "Donne e Muse." *Italica* 15 (1938): 132–41.

———. "The Structure and Real Significance of the *Decameron*." In *Essays in Honor of Albert Feuillerat*. Yale Romanic Studies, vol. 22, pp. 43–83. New Haven: Yale, 1943.

Lynch, William F. *Christ and Apollo*. New York: Sheed and Ward, 1960.

McInerny, Ralph M. "Metaphor and Analogy." *Sciences Ecclésiastiques* 16 (1964): 273–89. Also in James F. Ross, ed. *Inquiries into Medieval Philosophy*, pp. 75–96. Westport, Conn.: Greenwood, 1971.

McLuhan, Marshall. *The Gutenberg Galaxy*. Toronto: University of Toronto, 1962.

McWilliam, G. H., trans. Boccaccio, *The Decameron*. Baltimore: Penguin Books, 1972.

Marcus, Millicent. "Wit and the Public in the Early Italian *Novella*." Ph.D. dissertation, Yale University, 1973.

Meech, Sanford B. *Design in Chaucer's "Troilus."* Syracuse, N.Y.: Syracuse University, 1959.

Mommsen, Theodore E. *Medieval and Renaissance Studies.* Edited by Eugene F. Rice, Jr. Ithaca: Cornell, 1959.

Mondin, Battista. *The Principle of Analogy in Protestant and Catholic Theology.* 2d rev. ed. The Hague: Martinus Nijhoff, 1968.

Morrow, Glenn R., trans. Proclus, *A Commentary on the First Book of Euclid's Elements.* Princeton, 1970.

Nachod, Hans, trans. Petrarch, "On his own Ignorance and That of Many Others." In Ernst Cassirer et al., eds. *The Renaissance Philosophy of Man*, pp. 47–133. Chicago: University of Chicago, 1948.

Osgood, Charles G., trans. *Boccaccio on Poetry: Being the Preface and the Fourteenth and Fifteenth Books of Boccaccio's "Genealogia deorum gentilium."* New York: Library of Liberal Arts, 1956.

Pieper, Joseph. *Scholasticism: Personalities and Problems of Medieval Philosophy.* New York: Pantheon, 1960.

Preus, James S. *From Shadow to Promise: Old Testament Interpretation from Augustine to the Young Luther.* Cambridge, Mass.: Harvard, 1969.

Quinn, J. F. *The Historical Constitution of St. Bonaventure's Philosophy.* Toronto: Pontifical Institute, 1973.

Ratzinger, Joseph. *The Theology of History in St. Bonaventure.* Translated by Zachary Hayes. Chicago: Franciscan Herald, 1971.

Robertson, D. W., Jr. "Some Medieval Literary Terminology, with Special Reference to Chrétien de Troyes." *Studies in Philology* 48 (1951): 669–92.

Robertson, D. W., Jr., trans. Saint Augustine, *On Christian Doctrine.* New York: Library of Liberal Arts, 1958.

Robson, C. A. "Dante's Use in the *Divina Commedia* of the Medieval Allegories on Ovid." In *Centenary Essays on Dante* by Members of the Oxford Dante Society, pp. 1–38. Oxford, 1965.

Scaglione, Aldo D. *Nature and Love in the Late Middle Ages.* Berkeley: University of California, 1963.

Schneider, Herbert W., trans. Dante Alighieri, *On World Government or De Monarchia.* New York: Library of Liberal Arts, 1949.

Scullard, H. H. *Scipio Africanus: Soldier and Politician.* Ithaca: Cornell, 1970.

Severs, J. Burke. *The Literary Relationships of Chaucer's "Clerkes Tale."* New Haven: Yale, 1942.

Sinclair, John D., trans. *Dante's Inferno.* Oxford, 1939 and 1961.

Singleton, Charles. *Dante Studies 1: Commedia: Elements of Structure.* Cambridge, Mass.: Harvard, 1954.

Smalley, Beryl. *The Study of the Bible in the Middle Ages.* Oxford, 1932.

Smith, James Robinson, trans. *The Earliest Lives of Dante.* New York: Henry Holt, 1901.

Spengler, Oswald. *The Decline of the West.* 2 vols. Translated by Charles F. Atkinson. New York: Alfred A. Knopf, 1926 and 1928.

Swing [Seung], T. K. *The Fragile Leaves of the Sibyl: Dante's Master Plan.* Westminster, Md.: Newman, 1962.

———. *Kant's Transcendental Logic.* New Haven: Yale University Press, 1969.

The Temple Classics trans. *The Convivio of Dante Alighieri.* London: J. M. Dent, 1912.

Thompson, David, ed. *Petrarch: An Anthology of Petrarch's Letters and of Selections from his Other Works.* New York: Harper and Row, 1971.

Toffanin, Giuseppe. *History of Humanism.* Translated by Elio Gianturco. New York: Las Americas, 1954.

Toynbee, Paget, trans. *Dantis Alagherii Epistolae: The Letters of Dante.* Oxford, 1920.

Van Steenberghen, Fernand. *Aristotle in the West: The Origin of Latin Aristotelianism.* Translated by Leonard Johnston. 2d ed. Louvain: Nauwelaerts, 1970.

Walsh, James J., trans. and select. Duns Scotus, *The Oxford Commentary on the Four Books of the Sentences.* In Arthur Hyman and James J. Walsh, eds. *Philosophy in the Middle Ages: The Christian, Islamic and Jewish Traditions,* pp. 560–604. New York: Harper and Row, 1967.

Wendel, François. *Calvin: The Origins and Development of his Religious Thought.* Translated by Philip Mairet. New York: Harper and Row, 1963.

Wilkins, Ernest Hatch. *A History of Italian Literature.* Cambridge, Mass.: Harvard, 1954.

Wilkins, Ernest Hatch, trans. *The Triumphs of Petrarch.* Chicago: University of Chicago, 1962.

Wittgenstein, Ludwig. *Philosophical Investigations.* Translated by G. E. M. Anscombe. New York: Macmillan, 1953.

———. *Lectures on Aesthetics, Psychology and Religious Belief.* Edited by Cyril Barrett. Berkeley and Los Angeles: University of California, 1972.

Wolter, Allan B. *The Transcendentals and their Function in the Metaphysics of Duns Scotus.* St. Bonaventure, N.Y.: Franciscan Institute, 1946.

Index

Africa, 122, 123, 132, 136, 170*n*, 173, 228: and Scipio's Dream, 141–43; view of cupidity and ambition in, 144–45, 149, 155; Machiavellian tactics of its characters, 145, 147, 149; Petrarch's personalism in, 145, 155–56; fortune vs. providence debate in, 149–51; conception of virtue in, 150; theme of fame and glory, 152–53; resolution of Petrarch's conflict in, 156–61; relation to the *Triumphs*, 161–64; conflict between public and private spheres, 192; imitation of God in, 201; Petrarch's descent from the divine to the human plane, 246, 247. *See also* Scipio Africanus Major, Publius Cornelius

Alan of Lille, 77, 80: on allegory, 7; *Anticlaudianus de antirufino*, 60; *De planctu naturae*, 60, 90, 94; Dionysian sensibility of, 60–62; *Regulae caelestis iuris*, 61; view of universal revelation, 74

Albert the Great, 68, 69: as character in the *Commedia*, 102

Allegory: Dante's distinction between allegory of poets and allegory of theologians, 3, 13, 16, 18, 21, 26, 49; Pauline, 22; Philonian, 22; relation to analogy, 33, 77–89; of things, 73, 78–80, 81, 89–94, 96–97; of words, 73, 78–80, 91–94. *See also* Figuralism; Fourfold allegory; Personification allegory

Anabaptists, 253*n*

Anagogia, Dionysian, 81, 91–92, 105, 106, 109, 232, 242, 255–56

Anagogy or anagogical sense. *See* Fourfold allegory

Analogy. *See* Theology of analogy

Anselm of Canterbury, Saint, 67, 75, 76: *Proslogion*, 67

apRoberts, Robert, 185–86

Aquinas, St. Thomas. *See* Thomas Aquinas, Saint

Ariosto, Ludovico Giovanni: *Orlando Furioso*, 216*n*

Aristotelians and Aristotelianism, 68–69, 114

Aristotle, 129, 235, 241: his introduction to the Latin West, 76; Aristotelian essence, 85–86; *Politics*, 207–08; doctrine of individuation, 233; ontology of, 237–39; *Metaphysics*, 240*n*; and St. Thomas, 247, 249; his sciences compared to modern science, 256–58

Auerbach, Erich: figural realism of the *Commedia*, 3, 11, 27–31, 45, 48; on Origen's Platonism, 9; on Tertullian, 9–10; on Augustine's figuralism, 22; on fourfold allegory, 23; literal fundamentalism of, 27–31, 47, 93; *Mimesis*, 32*n*; on Beatrice, 37. *See also* Auerbach-Singleton school

Auerbach-Singleton school: interpretation of the *Commedia*, xv, 13–21 passim, 45; distortion of medieval allegory, xvii–xviii; on Dante's use of fourfold allegory, 15, 26; on the literal sense of fourfold allegory, 16–17, 20–21; Beatrice as a Christ-figure, 37, 46. *See also* Auerbach, Erich; Singleton, Charles

Augustine of Hippo, Saint, xvii, 10, 26, 31, 67, 71*n*, 75, 114, 120: *De utilitate credendi*, 22*n*, 93; figuralism of, 22, 40; and Biblical exegesis, 28, 92–93, 124; *De doctrina christiana* (*On Christian Doctrine*), 28, 62, 93; denigration of women, 31, 60, 169, 170; *De civitate dei* (*City of God*), 40, 53, 62, 63, 71, 104, 228; *De trinitate* (*On the Trinity*), 40, 42, 47, 70, 72, 79*n*, 101, 104, 168; influence on Dante, 40–41, 62–66; metaphor of the mirror, 42, 70–71; *Confessions*, 52, 53, 94, 101, 104; *De magistro*, 53; and the Pelagians, 53; Christian interiority of, 53–54, 57, 113; and Manicheanism, 54; on history of mankind, 62–63; essentialism of, 68; theology of words, 72–74, 250*n*; on divine ideas, 79*n*; influence on Bonaventure, 81;

DATE DUE